God revealed

Other books by Graham Cooke

God revealed

Your Image of Him Changes Everything

being with God series

Graham Cooke

Chosen
Grand Rapids, Michigan

© 2003, 2005 by Graham Cooke

Published by Chosen Books
A division of Baker Publishing Group
P.O. Box 6287, Grand Rapids, MI 49516-6287
www.chosenbooks.com

Originally published under the title *The Nature of God* by Sovereign
World Limited of Tonbridge, Kent, England

Printed in the United States of America

Library of Congress Cataloging-in-Publication Data is on file
at the Library of Congress, Washington, D.C.

ISBN 0-8007-9384-6

There is only one Person I can dedicate this book to—the Holy Spirit. I am constantly amazed at His wisdom, revelation and power in my life. I love His dedication to, and His passion for, the Lord Jesus Christ. The way He reveals the Son to me has changed my life. His physical, emotional, mental and spiritual representation of the Father to me has continuously made me more excited and in awe of the great love of God for me.

contents

acknowledgments

Heather; Ben with Sioux, Seth and Yvonne; and of course, Sophie: What a great, wacky family we are ... I love it!

Carole Shiers, my personal assistant and faithful ministry partner for many, many years: Thank you.

To the respective churches in Southampton (UK) and Vacaville (USA) that I call home: Thank you, especially to my leaders, Billy and Caroline Kennedy (UK) and David and Deborah Crone (USA), for including us and being our friends.

To Tim and Darlene Dickerson who graciously provide a home, support and, above all, true, loving friendship that withholds nothing: What a great blessing our relationship is for me and my family.

Finally, to Jordan Bateman, thank you for helping me enormously with the journal project, and great thanks to Tim Pettingale, my publisher and friend, whose passion for books and the written word is only outdone by his love for Jesus.

introduction

I strongly believe that a major shift is coming in the
Western Church. We are entering a time when the
Church will stop explaining who God is and begin
proclaiming His nature, His acts and His glory.

God doesn't need to be explained—He needs to be
lauded. He needs to be proclaimed and worshiped. He
needs people who are going to shout out who He really
is and what He's really like. His Good News is the best
news of all. In a world consumed by heartache, sin, pain
and bad news, Christians can offer the Good News of
who God really is.

Many people—Christian and non-Christian alike—
have a wrong view of God. They see Him in a number of
ways, none of which properly reflects the majesty of His
presence. It's important that we capture the image that
God wants to sow into our hearts. What we think about
God is the single most important part of our spiritual
journey. Our image of God will drive every single area
of our life and declare how we show up in the world. Do
we live a life of faith, boldness and conviction? If we
don't, we need to examine our perception of God.

People who are doubtful about what God wants to do

need to strongly upgrade their image of Him. God wants us to be confident in Him, and in His love for us.

I wonder how many of us have lost—or maybe never had—that intimate knowledge of God as our Father. He must be the most important thing in our world. We're shaped, emotionally and spiritually, by the image of God we carry in our hearts and minds. He loves us. He enjoys us. He is deeply personal with us, as well as being the almighty God of the entire universe.

God is paradoxical—He is faithful to me even when I am not faithful to Him. His love and faithfulness must win our hearts to a deeper level in Him.

Graham Cooke
March 2003

God revealed

Whenever we move into a new spiritual dimension of our calling and our ministry, we must take the time to upgrade our relationship with God. Our calling comes at different levels at different times; it is a progressive journey of discovery. When God takes us into the next phase of our calling, our relationship with Him must also change.

Throughout our lives, we will enter into many different phases and experiences. It might be a marriage or the birth of a child, a significant work promotion, a new responsibility, a new ministry or any other type of change. In seasons like these, we must take the time to upgrade our peace and rest in the Lord. If we enter a new situation without fully immersing ourselves in the stillness of God, we will live on our adrenaline and not out of our spirit. This power boost may seem sufficient at the moment, but for every adrenaline high, there is also an adrenaline low. We cannot sustain that needed adrenaline rush over the long term. Eventually, our energy will wither

> "The law of the LORD is perfect, converting the soul."
> Psalm 19:7

away, and the new season will overwhelm us. We must learn to live in a place of rest in the Spirit.

Every experience of God, even resting in Him, should enable us to see Him in a different light. Therefore, we need to constantly reevaluate our relationship with Him and take a deeper look at our walk with Him. We must critically examine our current picture of God and determine whether it is strong enough for the next stage of our life and calling. If it's not, the stress that we will experience will put pressure on us to quit or scale down our involvement in the new seasons of our lives. That same battle fatigue causes us to shrink back from the challenges facing us. Exhausted, we will talk ourselves out of taking the risks necessary to advance the Kingdom of God. God has given us the ability to live under His wing—we must recognize that we exist within the safety of His love and grace, and not on our own.

I cannot emphasize this enough—every time we are led into a new phase of our journey, we must take time to upgrade our image of God. We can travel confidently into any new experience, no matter how challenging or difficult, in our relationship with Him. God wants to build up your confidence right now, taking it to a whole new dimension.

When we enter a new season, it is important to ask ourselves relevant questions regarding its likely impact on all of our relationships and current responsibilities. Present levels of stress will need to be adjusted in the light of the deeper peace and rest that will be required on the next leg of the journey.

It is much easier to cope with change if it takes place gradually over time rather than as a large, overwhelming transformation that requires immediate extensive attention. Two questions, found in Acts 2:12 and 37, should be asked on a consistent basis:

- ► What does this mean?
- ► What must we do?

How will these adjustments affect our relationship with God and one another? How will this new season deepen our love, joy and peace in the Holy Spirit?

We need to gain a fresh and more powerful image of the nature of God. We need to practice our peace and our patience so that we can break through, in harmony with others, into a new dimension of the Spirit.

Moses gets upgraded

Moses' relationship with God is a strong example of how a person's view of the Lord can be upgraded during specific seasons of life. In Exodus 3, Moses is toiling in the wilderness, far from the glory of God and completely removed from his former life as a prince in Egypt. He wasn't even tending his own flock of sheep— he was working for his father-in-law! Still, God had a plan for Moses' life, and a desire to see this lonely shepherd upgrade his image of who God wanted to be for him. This desire brought Moses to the burning bush, where God could speak to him about his future, Israel's deliverance and His own nature. "I AM WHO I AM," God said in Exodus 3:14, completely shifting Moses' view of God. This perception changed Moses' life, turning the stuttering murderer into Israel's deliverer. It was a powerful calling on his life, but it had to be accompanied by an upgrade in his relationship with God.

> "You prepare a table before me in the presence of my enemies; You anoint my head with oil; my cup runs over."
>
> Psalm 23:5

After fulfilling that call and leading Israel out of Egypt, Moses' friendship with God was again upgraded as his calling further increased:

> Then the LORD said to Moses, "Depart and go up from here, you and the people whom you have brought out of the land of Egypt, to the land of which I swore to Abraham, Isaac, and Jacob, saying, 'To your descendants I will give it.' And I will send My Angel before you, and I will drive out the Canaanite and the Amorite and the Hittite and the Perizzite and the Hivite and the Jebusite. Go up to a land flowing with milk and honey; for I will not go up in your midst, lest I consume you on the way, for you are a stiff-necked people."
>
> And when the people heard this bad news, they mourned, and no one put on his ornaments. For the LORD had said to Moses, "Say to the children of Israel, 'You are a stiff-necked people. I could come up into your midst in one moment and consume you. Now therefore,

take off your ornaments, that I may know what to do to you.'" So the children of Israel stripped themselves of their ornaments by Mount Horeb.

Exodus 33:1-6

Moses' call had changed. In Exodus 3, it was primarily about bringing Israel out of bondage and oppression—Moses was a deliverer. Now, in Exodus 33, it wasn't about bringing people out; it was about taking people in. His call was now to bring Israel into its land of promise. He had to be consumed with inheritance, not deliverance. And whenever a call changes, your relationship with God must change first.

> "Fear not, for I am with you; be not dismayed, for I am your God. I will strengthen you, yes, I will help you, I will uphold you with My righteous right hand."
>
> Isaiah 41:10

If there was one man who could have been content with where his relationship with God was at, it was Moses. In Exodus 33:7-11, we are given a taste of how strong that bond was:

Moses took his tent and pitched it outside the camp, far from the camp, and called it the tabernacle of meeting. And it came to pass that everyone who sought the LORD went out to the tabernacle of meeting which was outside the camp. So it was, whenever Moses went out to the tabernacle, that all the people rose, and each man stood at his tent door and watched Moses until he had gone into the tabernacle. And it came to pass, when Moses entered the tabernacle, that the pillar of cloud descended and stood at the door of the tabernacle, and the LORD talked with Moses. All the people saw the pillar of cloud standing at the tabernacle door, and all the people rose and worshiped, each man in his tent door. So the LORD spoke to Moses face to face, as a man speaks to his friend. And he would return to the camp, but his servant Joshua the son of Nun, a young man, did not depart from the tabernacle.

"Joshua the son of Nun, a young man, did not depart from the tabernacle." I'm pretty sure I wouldn't either! All of Israel would watch as their leader went to the meeting place and the cloud came down upon the tent. It was an awesome sight, and a strong testimony to Moses' relationship with God: "So the LORD spoke to Moses face to face, as a man speaks to his friend." Despite all of the favor Moses had had, it was time for another upgrade in his relationship with God. He needed an even deeper relationship because the call on his life had been changed so dramatically—the burning bush and tent of meeting were no longer enough. In preparation for the stress and pressure of the "next big thing," Moses had to have his relationship with the Lord upgraded. And Moses wanted that upgrade badly.

God took Moses and put him in a specific place of longing and desire for the one thing God really wanted to give him. In heaven, there was a conversation over Moses' life between the Father, the Son and the Holy Spirit. "Look at Moses," the Trinity said. "He's at a new place in his life. What is it I want to do for him? Well, I

want to show him who I really am. I want to upgrade his
picture of Me. What I'll do is get him to ask Me a
question, so he can get a picture of Me that will sustain
him through everything he is going to have to go
through. I want to show him My glory, My supremacy
and My sovereignty."

That day in the Tent of Meeting, God maneuvered
Moses into a corner where the prophet realized he had
favor from the Lord to ask anything. God wasn't saying
no to Moses at this point, so he decided to push
everything as far as he could. Eventually, Moses asked
the question for which God had been waiting: "Please,
show me Your glory," Moses asked in Exodus 33:18.
Those five words were exactly what God wanted to
hear. It's as if He said, "What a great idea! Let's do
that!" We can read the rest of the account in Exodus
33:19–23:

> But He said, "You cannot see My face; for no man shall
> see Me, and live." And the LORD said, "Here is a place by
> Me, and you shall stand on the rock. So it shall be, while
> My glory passes by, that I will put you in the cleft of the
> rock, and will cover you with My hand while I pass by.
> Then I will take away My hand, and you shall see My
> back; but My face shall not be seen."

"I want you to be with Me," the Lord basically told
Moses, "but My glory would incinerate you. Instead, I'll
protect you in the cleft of this rock, and you will be able

to see My back." God arranged the entire scenario to put Moses right where He wanted him, all because God hungered to show him something he had never seen before. And then God walked past him. I can't even imagine this; it's beyond our ability to fathom. Moses not only got to see the back of almighty God, he got to hear Him proclaim truth about Himself, as we read in Exodus 34:6–7:

"Therefore the LORD will wait, that He may be gracious to you; and therefore He will be exalted, that He may have mercy on you. For the LORD is a God of justice; blessed are all those who wait for Him."
Isaiah 30:18

> "The LORD, the LORD God, merciful and gracious, longsuffering, and abounding in goodness and truth, keeping mercy for thousands, forgiving iniquity and transgression and sin, by no means clearing the guilty, visiting the iniquity of the fathers upon the children and the children's children to the third and the fourth generation."

Whenever the Lord talks about Himself, take serious note of what He is saying.

mission impossible?

God has not called us to do what seems possible, reasonable or normally attainable; He has called us to do the impossible. He wants us to stretch beyond our ability, our faith and our capacity to reason. He wants us to do more than we could ever imagine or dream. If you are reading this and think that your call is attainable, it's time for an upgrade! Christians are not supposed to be doing what is possible. We're supposed to be doing what is impossible and outrageous. To accomplish our calling, we must put our hand in the hand of God, learning to be completely dependent on the Holy Spirit for everything.

We have not truly learned to be dependent on the Holy Spirit in every facet of our lives—we continually try to make our own way. One of the common charismatic prayers I have come to dislike is, *Holy Spirit, come.* For me, the prayer is not, *Holy Spirit, come,* but, *Lord, take not Your Holy Spirit from me.* The Holy Spirit is ever-present, so our whole approach should be to create a life in which He is free to work.

Do what You want to do, and let us know what that is, must become our prayer. In our relationship with God, we must not do anything that will upset our delicate balance with Him. Our task is to preserve our relationship with Him, not have to seek one because we have not walked with Him properly.

When the Lord tells us to seek Him, it is for one of two reasons. First, we may have backslidden or become indolent in our walk and must recover the ground of our relationship with Him. Second, we may be coming into a new season and must take the time to develop a deeper expression of God in our hearts. In this context, He seeks us first to establish His desire in us. Our job is to make Him welcome and do the things that will keep the Holy Spirit with us.

That balance hinges on our obedience. "You are My friends if you do whatever I command you," Jesus said in John 15:14.

> "God is with the generation of the righteous."
> Psalm 14:5

A relationship with God depends on our obedience to Him. If we heed His commands, we will abide in His love. Obedience is a key to the presence of God—learning to simply rest and stay in God is a spiritual discipline.

new revelation

Many of us are coming into a new thing right now, with a new call or new responsibilities or a new role. What does it mean for you this year? What does it mean for your relationship with God?

In this upgrade, God wants to declare something else to you about Himself. You see, God always wants to be something significant for us. The question shouldn't be, "Why is this happening to me?" The "why" question is never answered on earth. It is the wrong question. It should be, "What is it that God wants to be for me now that He couldn't be at any other time, in any other way?" What is it about your current situation that is designed to bring you into a deeper relationship with God? Every circumstance in our life is about that—difficulty and blessing. If you're being severely challenged right now, God wants to be something for you. If you're walking in incredible favor and

Forgiven

My beloved one,
How can you be depressed by your own sinfulness when the
    wonders and joys of My mercy are freely available?
Dear one, why be nailed by the enemy when the keys of My
    unfettered grace can open every prison in your life?

Why be subject to the relentless condemnation of the evil one
    when the love of the One who is Almighty is yours to delight in?
Do you not know that the enemy is defeated?
Do you not appreciate that you are endlessly forgiven?

I am going to peel away this part of your life and expose the grace
    that is freely available. I am not obsessed by sin—I have dealt
    with it by judging Christ.
I am obsessed by you loving My grace, and experiencing the joy of
    My life within your heart.

You have always been forgiven. You must learn to forgive yourself.
Become as gracious as your God. Do not nail other people (even if
    you legitimately can), but be endlessly forgiving. They who are
    forgiven much also love much.

Enjoy forgiveness; revel in it! I am not disillusioned with you, for I
    never had any illusions about you.
I have always understood who you are and the struggles you face.
Why would I not love you, since I am Love itself?

Live as one not condemned, but released.
Then take the key of My grace and unlock the prison door of as
    many captives as you can find.
Forgiveness grows when it is employed.

transformation, He's showing you His nature in that, as well.

God wants to declare what He is becoming to you. Like Moses, you have fresh favor to ask Him to go deeper. God is the sneakiest Person on the planet. You cannot have a desire for Him that is unmatched by His desire for you. In fact, if you really want to know where you are with God, check out what is in your own heart. What are you "sighing about" right now? During those times you sit in the presence of God and your heart sighs for Him, what is it you are sighing for? Understand that your sigh originated in His heart. It is His longing for you, reaching out to you!

> "However, when He, the Spirit of truth, has come, He will guide you into all truth; for He will not speak on His own authority, but whatever He hears He will speak; and He will tell you things to come."
> John 16:13

When you understand what it is your spirit is sighing for, you will understand exactly what He wants to do. You cannot have a desire or longing for God that He did not put there. Your heart for Him is simply a reflection of His heart for you; God has us longing for the things He most wants to give us.

a purposeful God

When God showed Moses His glory, it was not a spontaneous act. God was being purposeful with His servant; He had this planned for quite a while. It was part of His step-by-step plan to reveal Himself to Moses.

What is the nature of your current request of God? In your relationship with Him, what are you asking for? What is the Holy Spirit doing in your life right now? What is He provoking in you? For what are you longing? You must think through and meditate on these questions, because God's plan for the next phase of your call is already in action. He has been purposeful with you from the very beginning.

a call to leadership

This purposefulness is especially difficult for church leaders to grasp, but it is absolutely vital to the health of the Kingdom that leaders take hold of it. When Moses went to meet with the Lord, all of Israel could see it. They knew he had a deep relationship with God, and this inspired them.

I love to see leaders on their faces worshiping in a meeting. I believe, having been in thousands of churches and meetings over my life, that the quality of a church's worship is directly dependent on the observable quality of the relationship the church's leaders have with God. If they are on their faces before Him, the rest of the church is, too. If they are sitting in the front row of the church, flipping through their Bibles and acting bored, it is impossible to expect the rest of the house to be engaged with God. If anyone is going to be lost in

> "Give to the Lord the glory due His name; bring an offering, and come before Him. Oh, worship the Lord in the beauty of holiness!"
> 1 Chronicles 16:29

worship, it has to be leadership. We must see our leaders worshiping God.

I truly believe that there is no place for burnout in the Church. People who burn out in ministry haven't properly upgraded their relationship with God. If you don't take care of your relationship with God, your ministry actually becomes a focal point, and you fall into idolatry. What you think about most is what you love the most. If you are consumed with your ministry, your leadership, your church, your role or whatever else, and you are not consumed by who God is for you, then you're headed into idolatry, and burnout looms around the corner. Therefore, God must be foremost in our hearts.

intimacy and favor

When God is cemented as the priority of our hearts, we see our relationship with Him deepen in ways we never thought possible. There is a place in the Holy Spirit set aside for every one of us where we can make the enemy tired, depressed, weary, confused and exasperated. It's a place where our relationship with God has a profound effect on the enemy and the people among which we live. What we think about God can shatter the hold of darkness on our friends and family. Our intimacy with God should be our most intimidating weapon against the enemy. We have all seen people trying to operate in authority when they just don't have it—it's painful to

see. As well-trained charismatic Christians, we think
getting louder is how we should try to take authority.
But our authority comes out of who we are in Christ,
and our capacity to intimidate the enemy comes out of
our intimacy with God.

The Lord's favor is available to every single one of us.
It's favor to understand God, to go to a deeper level in
Him and to upgrade our vision and
image of who God is for us. It's part of
coming into the next phase of
accomplishing the impossible. It's a
necessary revelation of who God is. It's
amazing how God works. When you
move into a deeper place with Him, the

> "The LORD is my strength and
> song, and He has become my
> salvation; He is my God, and I
> will praise Him; my father's
> God, and I will exalt Him."
> Exodus 15:2

stress that flows out of your life and ministry actually
cements and establishes your upgraded relationship
with Him.

The antidote to stress and crisis is upgrading our
fellowship with God. I know there are different things
on my agenda this year related to my call, and I know
that makes me vulnerable. I'm going to have to wade
through some stuff about myself, fight my feelings of
inadequacy and battle insecurity. I'm confident where I
am right now, but when God increases the call in my
life, I know I have to go back to working through all of
those issues again. I have to translate my weaknesses
into joyful vulnerability. I must upgrade my relationship
with Him, becoming more intimate than ever before.

What distinguishes a true believer, someone who is

walking in the Spirit as opposed to living out of their soul—mind, will and emotions—is the favor that ties into our intimacy with God. In Exodus 33:15-16, Moses made it clear what he needed from the Lord during the next season of his life:

> "If Your Presence does not go with us, do not bring us up from here. For how then will it be known that Your people and I have found grace in Your sight, except You go with us? So we shall be separate, Your people and I, from all the people who are upon the face of the earth."

Favor comes from having the presence of God traveling with us. We know we carry that favor when He lives among us. We are people of His presence; we must learn how to abide in it. We must learn how to rest, dwell and remain in God's arms.

our attention span

Learning to be still is difficult in a world dedicated to grabbing our attention. I remember years ago when my wife and children asked me to get a dog. I didn't need to be prophetic to know this was going to end in trouble for me. But when the whole family aligns against you, it's impossible to resist, so against my better judgment, we got this beast. It was just a fur ball, and to be honest, you couldn't tell which end was which.

Naturally, there had been promises made beforehand: "Don't worry, Dad, I'll feed it, I'll walk it, I'll look after

it." Those commitments lasted about three and a half
weeks. Eventually, this thing became an
evil influence in our house. It pounced
everywhere. We were living in the
country then, and there were horseback-
riding stables down the road. Our dog
would squeeze under the fence, jump on
a horse's back and ride it around the
field! I think the stupid animal was a cross between a
stuntman and Superman.

> "I, even I, am He who comforts you. Who are you that you should be afraid of a man who will die, and of the son of a man who will be made like grass?"
> Isaiah 51:12

Anyway, I resolved to teach this beast to sit, even if it
killed me. It took me two full months—the animal just
wouldn't take me seriously. It had the attention span
of a gnat. "Sit!" "Sit!" "Sit!" "Sit!" I would say.
Eventually, wonder of wonders, it sat. And then, after a
few more sessions, it sat and stayed for me. I considered
it a miracle on the level of Moses' parting of the Red
Sea.

A few months later, I was on a tour of Malaysia and
the Philippines. The spiritual warfare was incredible; I
remember being at one place where we had to walk
through hundreds of Muslim people who were throwing
things and spitting at us. Everyone in the conference
was nervous, as windows were being broken and all
sorts of other things were happening.

In my spirit, I heard God telling me to "sit and stay."
Where had I heard that before? In this warfare situation,
I was supposed to learn about peace and rest. The Lord
told me that He wasn't going to take care of things out

there until I took care of things in my own heart. What was happening out there was designed to teach me to be at peace and at rest in the room. God had given me a place in Christ where He wanted me to sit and stay; that whole tour of Asia was one battle after another, teaching me how to abide, rest and remain in God.

being established in Christ

The Holy Spirit has come to establish us in Christ. Conversely, the enemy has come to take us out of who we are in Christ. The Holy Spirit wants to establish our standing. The enemy wants to bring us into the state of seeing ourselves as powerless, helpless and buried under pressure; but we must see ourselves as who we are in Jesus. The Holy Spirit is working to establish us in Christ, and we must learn how to abide there. We must not be moved.

Our goal, then, is to cooperate with the Holy Spirit and stay with Him in this process. We can then learn how to live in peace, and how to remain in God. The term "Prince of Peace" is more than a title—it is part of God's nature that He wants to implant in us.

If we cannot learn that lesson, we will not survive on the battlefield. Breakthroughs don't come without a fight. There is a call to battle on every one of our lives. What precedes the fight is increasing our skill in battle by learning the ability to see God as our refuge and fortress. He is our high tower, our righteous One; in Him, we are safe. We must learn to live in a place where God is supreme.

Eventually, we learn to trust in the nature of God. I believe that God still wants to protect us in the cleft of a rock, and allow His goodness to pass before us. He wants us to see His lovingkindness in our lives. In my own relationship with God, I have found Him to be a paradox—two apparently conflicting ideas contained in the same

> "Do not be afraid, Abram. I am your shield, your exceedingly great reward."
> Genesis 15:1

truth. He is the kindest and happiest Person I have ever met; a gentle Father, always smiling, always gracious, always good and always restful. In His presence, there is joy and peace. At the same time, He is the most powerful Being in the universe—He is both the Prince of Peace (Isaiah 9:6) and a Man of War (Exodus 15:3).

We only need a refuge when we come under attack; we must learn where that safe place is and go there when we're in trouble. This isn't rocket science or quantum physics; it is common sense. God is our secret place, so hidden that the enemy can't even get into the neighborhood.

God is generous, consistent, unchangeable, eternal, everlasting and always the same. He never gets disillusioned with us; He never had any illusions about us in the first place. He knew exactly what He was taking on with us, and we can't surprise Him. He knows everything about us—He's seen the worst of us. In fact, the very moment we were at our worst was the day we realized He had chosen us and was calling us back to Him.

Before Moses proclaimed God's name in Exodus 33–34, he talked about God's compassion. God loves being compassionate. He knows that He is the most compassionate Person in the universe. He loves being gracious and slow to anger. He is merciful, forgiving, truthful and faithful.

> "Remember, O Lord, Your tender mercies and Your lovingkindnesses, for they are from of old."
> Psalm 25:6

God revealed His nature to Moses and then maneuvered the prophet to ask Him the one question He was longing to answer. God wanted Moses to be serious about Him; He wanted to share why Moses should love Him. God is wrapped up in being who He is—He knows what He loves about Himself. He loves being gracious and compassionate, and He loves extending mercy. He loves pouring out grace. "Moses," He said, "this is all yours. This is the list of My qualities that I will reveal to you over the coming months and years." What God shares about Himself is meant for us to experience.

be Thou my vision

What is your vision of God? How you see Him is how you see yourself. It determines how you view your life, your church, even the events that are going on in the Body of Christ. If you fail to see Jesus as your Prince of Peace, that may be why you cannot find any rest.

Seeing Him as your personal Prince of Peace means you're not allowed to worry anymore; peace and worry simply can't coexist. The way we live is profoundly shaped by our image of God.

Are you a sinner who struggles with the love of God, or are you a lover of God who occasionally struggles with sin? How do you see yourself? The more you have the wrong picture of God, the more religious and legalistic you may become. Modern Pharisees are people who do not know who God is for them. They don't understand the nature of God. They don't live in His compassion or mercy. They live by a rulebook, and they lose sight of what He is really like, much like the Pharisees in Jesus' time. They couldn't recognize who Jesus was, or His revelation of the Father. "If you have seen Me, you have seen the Father," Jesus tried to explain. "The Father and I are one and the same." Even when He performed signs and wonders, a historic way of recognizing God, they couldn't figure it out.

We must see God as our provider, or we will always be anxious about our needs being met. Every time we are in need, it should be an adventure because we are not intimidated; instead, we should be fascinated about what God might do. We must believe He is our provider and become intrigued by how He might meet our needs.

> "Behold, He who keeps Israel shall neither slumber nor sleep."
> Psalm 121:4

Is He the God who gives us His own life and character? If we're in conflict, we must view the fruit of the Holy Spirit as His provision for the integrity of our lifestyle. There is a whole bundle of God's nature upon which we can draw when we are in conflict.

an active God

God is not passive in our circumstances, but active on our behalf. We cannot be resigned to our situations— we must be constantly looking for the power of God to break through. Many of us have just learned to put up with things; the Western world is completely passive to the things of God. We put up with all kinds of nonsense in our culture, our society, our communities and our families. When our backs are against the wall, we should fight with everything in us. Instead, when our backs are against the wall, we wither. We must not become resigned to the situations around us; we must constantly look for the power of God to break through for us.

> "So shall they fear the name of the Lord from the west, and His glory from the rising of the sun; when the enemy comes in like a flood, the Spirit of the Lord will lift up a standard against him."
> Isaiah 59:19

What is your perception of God when you pray? Is He inclining His ear toward you, or do you feel as though you have to persuade Him, or trick Him, into listening? If your image of God is that He is interested and delighted in you, your whole prayer life and approach to Him will be changed. You'll love prayer! For many Christians, prayer is a chore, something we have to do in order to get our weekly allowance from God. Our view of Him is so skewed that we cannot come to Him properly. When distortions creep into our picture of God, the negative effects are felt in every part of our life. Those issues ripple through our relationships, values, ethics, integrity, love, joy and peace. They affect our righteousness and purity.

We need to reflect wisely upon our image of the Lord's nature. What is it that God wants to be to you in this current season of your life? That is the question for which we must have an answer. We must know what it is the Holy Spirit wants to upgrade in our lives. Every test, every conflict we face in the months following the upgrade will test us on those breakthroughs. God is not punishing us when things go wrong; troubles don't arise because He can't protect us. God will not reject us, even if we're not perfect. When we do well, God approves of us. When we do poorly, God accepts us. He is compassionate either way. The love of God is never less than 100 percent; He just doesn't know how to be otherwise. He is unchanging and consistent. He takes joy in the fact that He is the Lord and that He never changes. He is the same yesterday, today and forever; we can be confident of who He is for us.

God's kindness

I have tried to prove the previous paragraph wrong. There have been times in my walk with the Lord when I have been downright deliberately disobedient and God has still blessed me. I remember one particular occasion when I just couldn't stand it anymore—His blessing was making me angry.

"Why are You doing this?" I demanded. "I'm being rebellious, and You keep blessing me! What's wrong with You?"

When I got quiet, He answered me. *This is what I'm like—live with it,* He said. *I'm not going to change; I'm always going to be like this. I like being like this, so live with it.* His grace broke the power of sin in me.

Can our hearts be won by God's grace and kindness? It's an interesting question, isn't it? Too often, we close ourselves off from the goodness of God because we're so depressed about our own performance as a Christian. Where does this negativity originate?

> "But He is unique, and who can make Him change? And whatever His soul desires, that He does."
> Job 23:13

One day, I was walking down my church's corridor when I saw someone coming toward me. I asked him how things were going, expecting the usual Christian cliché: "Oh, fine." But I got nothing of the sort.

"I'm really depressed," he said glumly. *Why me?* I immediately thought. *Why did I ask this on a day when I have to get somewhere?* Yet the first thing out of my mouth stunned both of us.

"How do you know?" I asked. "Who gave you that information?" We weren't talking about clinical depression, but rather someone who was simply down.

"What do you mean?" he replied.

"Who told you that you are depressed?"

"I don't follow," he said, perplexed.

"Well," I forged ahead, "was it your wife who told you?"

"No."

"Was it one of the elders?"

"No."

"Where did you get the information, then?" I asked.

"I don't know," he answered.

"Well, don't you feel the tiniest bit dumb then—saying you're depressed and not knowing who gave you that diagnosis?"

"Until now, no," he said.

Some of us have minds like a vacuum cleaner—we suck up any old rubbish. The enemy can come and say, "Feel depressed," and we fall into depression. We should probably check these things out before we jump into them. We must always check the source of our information—from where does it come? If the enemy is trying to sell us something, what might God be saying instead? It's easy to listen to the wrong person and end up broken. Maybe what needs to be broken and reshaped is our image of who God wants to be for us. God loves us for who we are right now—the good, the bad and the ugly. And He also loves us for who we are going to be.

Let's track those negative thoughts down and take them captive, as Paul told us to do. Slap the handcuffs on them. We need to come to a place where we say, "I'm not going to think that way." Holding our thoughts captive is an important part of upgrading our image of God. We learn to say no to the old image we once had, and yes to the image that's unfolding. We can cooperate with the establishment of that new image in our hearts and lives.

> "Indeed, the darkness shall not hide from You, but the night shines as the day; the darkness and the light are both alike to You."
> Psalm 139:12

Ask the Lord to give you a scripture that reflects the nature of God for you during this season. We can build a strong relationship on a biblical foundation. With Abraham, God said He was his shield. With David, God said He was his refuge, fortress and hiding place. We, too, can have a vivid picture of who God wants to be for us.

my snapshot of God

My own picture of God is that He is the kindest Person I have ever met. Almost fourteen years ago, God began to give me a revelation of His kindness.

I believe God wants to show each one of us the panorama of His nature. He wants to show you everything. But there is one aspect of His character that He will want to be yours in particular. This is your doorway into His presence. I love the compassion, mercy, integrity and grace of God—but my access point to Him is always His kindness.

God has been relentlessly kind to me these past fourteen years—day in, day out, month in, month out,

year in, year out. Every day, the kindness of God has
been in my face; I can't get away from it. I can't
remember a day in years when there
hasn't been some word of God, some act
of kindness, to help me. His kindness is
relentless—I love that description. I've
come to such a place of dependence on
the kindness of God that I have an
expectation for it every day. Something
kind is going to happen to me. I wake up
and I wonder what the kindness will be today. It is my
image of who He is. That kindness He has shown me
makes me want to be kind and generous to others. It
carries forward. What is Jesus like to me? This is the
Christ whom I have personally encountered:

> "But let him who glories glory
> in this, that he understands
> and knows Me, that I am the
> LORD, exercising
> lovingkindness, judgment, and
> righteousness in the earth. For
> in these I delight."
> Jeremiah 9:24

- ▶ He has an immense, immeasurable and eternal
  compassion. His compassion is always greater than
  my sin.
- ▶ He is scandalously forgiving. His mercy burns as it
  destroys shame.
- ▶ He has unbounded patience, unending goodness.
- ▶ His love is so compelling ... it heals us. It strips
  away all our pretense and restores us to
  happiness.
- ▶ His grace is the empowering Presence within that
  enables us to feel good about ourselves.
- ▶ His mercy is His total favor given gladly to the
  undeserving heart.

- He is the kindest Person I have ever known. His goodness is so outrageous and shocking ... it is actually disreputable to the religious-minded person.
- He is the happiest Person I know; He has the sunniest disposition.
- He is enthusiastically fervent in His pursuit of us.
- He is amazingly humble and gentle, but He is also a powerful warrior king who loves to fight and who laughs at His enemies.
- He has a fabulous servant spirit, needing no title, status or position, but joyfully sets an example of simple, heartwarming slavery.
- His love is enthralling. It captivates and commands us to be the same.
- His love is designed to overwhelm all things, especially fear, shame and low self-esteem.
- He loves being trusted. He is delighted and astonished when we use our faith.
- He will *never* keep a record of our sins or failings.
- He has mercy that can never be properly understood or articulated ... just experienced! The only way we can explain mercy is by being merciful ourselves!
- Jesus the Redeemer gives us value in the eyes of the Father.
- He sees and speaks to our potential. He both protects us and releases us to fulfill all that He wants us to see and know about ourselves.

the disciples' view of God

In Matthew 16:13–20, we learn much about how the disciples perceived Jesus. Let's look at the story:

> When Jesus came into the region of Caesarea Philippi, He asked His disciples, saying, "Who do men say that I, the Son of Man, am?"
>
> So they said, "Some say John the Baptist, some Elijah, and others Jeremiah or one of the prophets."
>
> He said to them, "But who do you say that I am?"
>
> Simon Peter answered and said, "You are the Christ, the Son of the living God."
>
> Jesus answered and said to him, "Blessed are you, Simon Bar-Jonah, for flesh and blood has not revealed this to you, but My Father who is in heaven. And I also say to you that you are Peter, and on this rock I will build My church, and the gates of Hades shall not prevail against it. And I will give you the keys of the kingdom of heaven, and whatever you bind on earth will be bound in heaven, and whatever you loose on earth will be loosed in heaven."
>
> Then He commanded His disciples that they should tell no one that He was Jesus the Christ.

At least four distorted images of God were expressed by the disciples—the men who knew Jesus best—in this passage: "You're John the Baptist," "Elijah," "Jeremiah," "one of the prophets." The one man who put it all together, who upgraded his image of God, was Simon Peter. The instant he did, God announced His call

on Peter's life: "On this rock, I will build My church."
Peter's perception of God changed, and it would carry
him through the trials and tribulations
of the next season of his life.

"He shall receive blessing
from the LORD, and
righteousness from the God
of his salvation."
Psalm 24:5

"Who do you say that I am?" This
question strikes at the very heart of our
relationship with God. "Who do you say
that I am?" Who is God for you? Have
you confessed and proclaimed who God is? Have you
declared His role in your life?

God doesn't have identity crises—and He doesn't want
you to have them, either. His nature must shape who we
are. "Who do you say that I am?" It's time for us to
answer that question. Having the right picture of God
will lead us into blessing, destiny and breakthrough.

It did for Peter. "You are the Christ, the Son of the
living God," he said. Jesus probably grinned and winked
at him—He loved that answer, as His response indicated.
Peter's answer pushed him to a new dimension of faith
and calling; it gave him a new focus for his ministry.
And Jesus prophesied that the entire Church would be
built on Peter's revelation that Jesus is the Son of God.
God builds the Church upon the image we have of Him.
That view is the very bedrock of our authority.

it all starts with God

I have always been touched by the simple truth that
John expressed in 1 John 4:19: "We love Him because

Conquering Fear

My dear one, you are not in the grip of fear but in the hands of
Love itself.
Fear of man, fear of the unknown, fear of making mistakes, fear of
looking foolish, of trying new things, fear of not being loved, or
being good enough.

Fear makes you tense, dark, unable to see things the way I see
them.
Let Me touch your heart with My perfect, all-embracing love and
so drive out all your fears.

This next season is about your journey into the heart of My love for
you.
I need you to turn your back on fear and face up to My love. We
are not battling fear—we are embracing the love that is always
present in every circumstance.

For every fear that has gripped you, My love will overwhelm your
heart as you learn to stand before Me as a much-loved child.

Beloved, it is My desire that you thoroughly enjoy this season of
freedom from fear to fully embrace My love.
You will know what it is to stand and live in the perfect love of the
Father's heart.

ENJOY THIS! I intend to enjoy you becoming more loving and more
intimate with My grace.
The breaking of fear will give you a whole new lease on life.
I'm looking forward to love, every day with you.

He first loved us." Everything starts and ends in God. Our role is to be the best middle possible. God works in a cycle: He gives us something, it touches us, and we return it to God. He loved us, that love touched us, and now we return that love to Him.

Paul understood this idea, too, as we see in Romans 11:35–36: "Or who has first given to Him and it shall be repaid to him? For of Him and through Him and to Him are all things, to whom be glory forever." It's such a simple truth, and yet it confounds many Christians. When God asks us to be something, He gives us the physical, spiritual and emotional tools and gifts to do it. He is to us what He wants us to be to the world. When God asks us to love someone, it's because He intends to love us. Whatever God wants from us, He will give us first.

The various apostles tried every possible language trick to communicate this revelation to the early Church. "Every good gift and every perfect gift is from above, and comes down from the Father of lights, with whom there is no variation or shadow of turning," wrote James (James 1:17). Things come from God, and we return them to Him. The disciples, having spent time with Jesus, understood this principle. Only God can love God fully; we have to partner with His Spirit in order to love Him completely.

When God asked us to "love the LORD your God with all your heart, with all your soul, with all your mind, and with all your strength" (Mark 12:30), He was actually promising that He will love us with all of His heart, all of His soul, all of His mind and all of His strength. This is life in the Spirit: The very thing He wants from us, He gives us first.

Upgrading our view of God becomes a wonderful opportunity as we move into a new season. The principle of love and being loved is that it originates in the heart of God for you. His love always begins the process of our loving others. Jesus promised as much in John 17:20–26:

> I do not pray for these alone, but also for those who will believe in Me through their word; that they all may be one, as You, Father, are in Me, and I in You; that they also may be one in Us, that the world may believe that You sent Me. And the glory which You gave Me I have given them, that they may be one just as We are one: I in them, and You in Me; that they may be made perfect in one, and that the world may know that You have sent Me, and have loved them as You have loved Me.
>
> Father, I desire that they also whom You gave Me may be with Me where I am, that they may behold My glory which You have given Me; for You loved Me before the foundation of the world. O righteous Father! The world has not known You, but I have known You; and these have known that You sent Me. And I have declared to them Your name, and will declare it, that the love with which You loved Me may be in them, and I in them.

It is critical for us to understand that God wants to love us in exactly the same way that He loves Jesus.

Nothing less than that is good enough for the Father.
When we discover the gift God is giving us, we step into
the next phase of our lives and callings. We return His
love through our worship, praise, adoration, service,
lifestyle, choices, speech, prayer and a thousand other
ways. We glorify God because He has given us
everything.

don't miss the gift

Every day, in every circumstance, there is a gift from
God present in our lives. Often the more desperate the
circumstances, the greater the gift being offered. But we
can easily miss it if we don't look for it.

God has put each of us into the one place where we
are always favorable to Him—in Christ. Being in Christ
is the only place where our prayers will be answered.
It's the only place where we can be assured of receiving
revelation. It's the only place where we can find every
promise God has put on our lives. He has put us into
Christ. We can never earn God's love; it's a perfect gift.
But because the Father loves the Son, and because both
dwell within us, we cannot avoid being loved by God.

It doesn't matter if our day is good, bad or ugly: We
are loved by Him. That's why we came to God in the
first place. We were sinners, but He loved us. We are
destined to experience that same love as saints. Hour
after hour, day after day, year after year, His love comes
down to us, touches us, and we return it to Him. Our job

is to receive that love and give it away as quickly as possible, knowing that it is going to come back to us deeper, bigger, wider and stronger.

Imagine how easy ministry would be if we understood that our number one priority should be to allow the love of God to touch us. Every single day, our response to God's love should be to let Him lavish it upon us. We are to let Him speak to us, breathe on us and smile over us. Our mission is to do the things that make Him happy. Christianity isn't difficult; it's not rocket science. It is about living under the love of God and doing whatever pleases Him.

called to love ourselves

God's nature allows us to feel good about ourselves. Thanks to His grace, we can feel great about who we are, who we were and who we will become. God loves where we are going—and we should, too. It seems so foreign to our Christian culture, and yet it is a fundamental truth: We can love ourselves because God finds us incredibly lovable. If we are to "do what we see the Father doing," as Jesus said, we must love ourselves!

I love where I've been, where I am and where I am going. I love what has changed in me and what I am becoming. I love the fact that I am going to change even more. By the grace of God, I'm not what I was; in the future, that same grace will transform me again. I look forward to being different.

This isn't narcissism; it's doing what we see the Father doing. It's God's nature to love us. I am incredibly lovable because I am loved incredibly. Same with you! You and I deserve to be loved by God because of Jesus' sacrifice for us. "Child," Jesus says, "I've paid the price for you to be loved. Now you can have everything you want and deserve, because you're in Me, and I am in you. I deserve everything, and I make My home in you." Anything less than this truth is just incorrect evangelical "claptrap," meant to hold us down in the name of false humility. It's nonsense. How can someone be in Christ and not deserve the blessings that come with that grace? How can you be in Christ and be unworthy? You can't!

We must allow the love of God to work on our inadequacies, insecurities and fears. Love was made to conquer inadequacy. But in the light of the love of God in which we live, inadequacy doesn't matter. God can do anything and everything. He takes our inabilities and transforms them into actions. He deliberately chooses weak, foolish people whom the rest of the world ignores. God uses the imperfect perfectly.

> "Then the LORD will drive out all these nations from before you, and you will dispossess greater and mightier nations than yourselves."
> Deuteronomy 11:23

I have often thought that I would never hire God to run a company's personnel department. He'd be a disaster! A good business would never recruit someone who is going to be a failure. When we recruit, we want the best. God, on the other hand, chooses the worst and says, "I'm going to do something magnificent through you. And it's all on Me." When He accomplishes that miracle, all we can do is stand back and echo Paul's words in Philippians 4:13: "I can do all things through Christ who strengthens me."

A deep sense of freedom comes with understanding the fact that we don't have to do anything to be loved by God. He loves us simply because it is His nature to love us. God is love. And as we become more like Him, it becomes our nature to love others.

called to love others

The love of God continually inspires me to love others. The general rule of life in the Spirit is that whatever we need, we must first give away. For example, when we need money, we ought to give to someone worse off than us. If we need healing, we should find someone sicker than us and pray for their restoration. Likewise, if we want to experience more of the loving nature of God, we should go love someone else.

We must practice and become brilliant at receiving the love of God. Jesus loves us—now we can love others. This is the true nature of Kingdom ministry: We receive the love of God and spread it to everyone we meet. When we receive the Holy Spirit, He helps us process the love that God has for us. The Spirit enables us to work

His love through, understand it, comprehend it and become rooted in it.

God's love for us never changes, because He never changes. The Holy Spirit, like a baker kneading dough, pushed God's love into our being, softening the hardest parts of our hearts. We love because we are beloved. As we grow in this love, we begin to love the seemingly unlovable people around us.

God brings difficult people into our lives for a reason. He wants us to learn how to love them so that we will discover how wonderful God is. These hard-to-love people are what I call "grace-growers." They are in our lives to teach us how to operate in God's love. It's the Father's way of pushing us quickly into a deeper, wider expression of His love. Naturally, we protest the very suggestion that we love the unlovable: "I can't love this person," we tell God. *I know,* He winks back at us, *but I can.* When God brings a difficult person into our lives, He is putting us in a moment of divine acceleration. He's sending us deeper into His nature.

To get there, we must feel inadequate. Every biblical hero of the faith felt inadequate until God's love overwhelmed them. Moses, Abraham, Joseph, Mary, Esther, Gideon, Paul, Peter: all of them. Love and inadequacy always walk together. By taking the easy route and avoiding difficult people, we actually avoid a miracle in our own lives. We must embrace the grace-growers in our lives in order to embrace the miracle of God's love that comes with them.

love and insecurity

God's love doesn't just work on our inadequacies; it works on our insecurities, as well. When I speak with young Christians about living in the nature of God, my advice to them is always very simple: Never try to deserve God's love—just receive it gladly. We deserve His love because of the Christ within us, and we need to learn to just accept that fact.

When we come alive to the love of God, depending on it for everything in our lives, the Holy Spirit turns all of our inadequacies and insecurities into joyful vulnerability. That may not seem like an important step, but it is a huge leap in the things of the Spirit. People hooked on the love of God can stand before Him with all of their flaws and imperfections and see what Christ sees. We can stand before Him and say, "I can't do this, Lord—but I know You can. I'm not equal to this task— but You are."

I know for a fact that God didn't choose me because I'm brilliant. He chose me because I'm a doofus. For thirty years, I've been the Mr. Bean of the prophetic world. If there are library rooms in heaven with DVD recordings of all of our ministry moments, then mine are no doubt filed in the comedy section. I'm nothing without the love of God.

God's love doesn't make us incredible; He's just being incredible in us and through us. When the anointing comes, we are brilliant, and when it lifts, we go back to being Homer Simpsons. D'oh! But our inadequacies and insecurities—our inner Homer Simpsons—should make us very vulnerable to the love of God.

God will never turn away from someone because of who they are in the flesh. When we were lost in sin, God went looking for us. He knows everything about us. He has no illusions when it comes to us. Nothing is hidden from Him—not our best days, not our worst days. He loved us when we were full of evil. But God doesn't love us more now than He did then; He loves us exactly the same whether we are a saint or a sinner. What has changed is our ability to receive that love.

I feel the love of God more now than I did ten years ago, but it's not Him who has changed—it's me. He doesn't love me any more now than He did then, but I have increased my capacity to receive that love. He has always loved me fully, every day.

In God's realm of infinite possibility and grace, the very thing that we think will disqualify us is the doorway through which the Father delivers His heart and affection for us. He chose us because we are weak and foolish. His power is perfected in that weakness, because God's grace is always enough. The apostle Paul understood this, as we see in 2 Corinthians 12:9:

> "And in Your majesty ride prosperously because of truth, humility, and righteousness; and Your right hand shall teach You awesome things."
> Psalm 45:4

"And He said to me, 'My grace is sufficient for you, for My strength is made perfect in weakness.' Therefore most gladly I will rather boast in my infirmities, that the power of Christ may rest upon me." What did Paul say when God explained that His grace was sufficient? "Woo hoo!" Paul suddenly realized that his weakness and sin had never been a problem for God. The Father dealt with all of that at Calvary. God isn't obsessed with sin—He is obsessed with life, joy and seeing His children be the best they can be. He is obsessive when it comes to loving us fully and completely. He is completely fixated on seeing us go as high, as far and as deep in Him as we want.

So, what did Paul do when he received this truth in his spirit? He boasted about the things in which he was weak, because he knew God was about to unleash something incredible in his life in those same areas. Anything that he had ever let disqualify him, or that had made him cringe about himself, became things to brag about. *It's not about me*, Paul thought, *it's about who God is.*

It should come as an enormous relief to all of us that God's power can rest on anything. He chose weak people because He likes His power to rest on weak people. It's as simple as that.

a continuous flow

God's love never ceases. It is a continuous flow from His being to ours. While we can take ourselves out of that flow of love, we can never stop it. It's like Niagara Falls: We can be there, on the Maid of the Mist, and get caught up in the spray—or we can take ourselves out of it. Either way, the water still flows. We cannot stop the flow of the love of God toward our lives.

Maturing Christians make the choice to stay in the flow of God's love. They would rather die than step out from under it. "He made us accepted in the Beloved," as Ephesians 1:6 phrases it.

That love in us changes us, because love kills fear. God's love grabs our fear by the throat and destroys it. "There is no fear in love; but perfect love casts out fear, because fear involves torment. But he who fears has not been made perfect in love," promises 1 John 4:18. It is impossible for us to be punished by God for our sin, because He has already punished Christ. But it is entirely possible for us to be loved outrageously by Him.

What a sacrifice the cross was! Jesus was separated from the Father so that we could always be present with Him. When we don't allow ourselves to be present before God, we actually insult the cross of Christ. We call Jesus' supreme sacrifice worthless. Christ was pushed away from everything He loved so that we could each be drawn closer to the heart of God. To not take that step toward Him is to spit on our Savior's sacrifice.

We do not have to do anything to earn God's love, as we see in Romans 8:31-39:

> What then shall we say to these things? If God is for us, who can be against us? He who did not spare His own Son, but delivered Him up for us all, how shall He not

with Him also freely give us all things? Who shall bring a charge against God's elect? It is God who justifies. Who is he who condemns? It is Christ who died, and furthermore is also risen, who is even at the right hand of God, who also makes intercession for us. Who shall separate us from the love of Christ? Shall tribulation, or distress, or persecution, or famine, or nakedness, or peril, or sword? As it is written:

> "For Your sake we are killed all day long;
> We are accounted as sheep for the slaughter."

Yet in all these things we are more than conquerors through Him who loved us. For I am persuaded that neither death nor life, nor angels nor principalities nor powers, nor things present nor things to come, nor height nor depth, nor any other created thing, shall be able to separate us from the love of God which is in Christ Jesus our Lord.

"If God is for us, who can be against us?" What a powerful statement! The truth is that God is for us. He is one hundred percent behind you as an individual. He is one hundred percent behind me. It doesn't matter what we think or where we are in our lives: God is for us, and no one can stand against us. When we're down or being attacked, God is for us. Nothing out there can overcome that kind of support, if we know how to stay within the perfect love of God. No enemy can chase us into the Holy of Holies of God's presence. Nothing can get at us as long as we live in Christ.

A difference exists between our state and our standing. Our *state* is how we see ourselves. If we allow the enemy to lure us out of our safe place in Christ, we will see ourselves as weak, powerless, ineffective and worthless. But our *standing* is about who we are in Christ. When we learn to live in Christ, we take on His attributes. That's why I can write things like, "I'm brilliant." I know I'm brilliant because I stand in Christ and He's brilliant. There is something stupendous about being in Christ.

None of us put ourselves there—He put us there. However, it is our responsibility to learn how to stay and live in Christ. All things are possible when we live in His love. The only way the enemy can get us is to trick us into living in our state—in how weak and ineffective we are—rather than in our standing with God. If the enemy can make us panic when we should be at peace, he has got us out in the open where he can attack. If he makes us anxious when we ought to be trusting, we're fair game. If we're worrying when we should be at peace, we're up for grabs.

The Holy Spirit works to keep us firmly grounded in the love of Christ. He helps us choose to stay and dwell in God's love. "I am the vine, you are the branches. He who abides in Me, and I in him, bears much fruit; for without Me you can do nothing," Jesus said (John 15:9). We have to cooperate with the Holy Spirit in this; we have to choose to be loved outrageously by God.

God is in us to win us. Nothing works against His power. The only time we can be attacked is when we allow the enemy to trick us to come out of the fortress of God's love.

In Christ, a gift is always available

When we live in Christ, there is always a gift available to us. When the Holy Spirit convicts us of sin, it's because He has the antidote in His hand. Conviction will never come without a gift, because "every good gift and every perfect gift is from above, and comes down from the Father of lights, with whom there is no variation or shadow of turning" (James 1:17). The Holy Spirit will not convict us unless He has something with which to replace our sin; otherwise we would withdraw and end up in enemy territory.

Conviction is a friend, but condemnation is an enemy. The Holy Spirit uses conviction to bring us to repentance. The enemy accuses and abuses us to lead us into condemnation. The enemy knows, after generations of battling Christians, that condemnation paralyzes human beings. But conviction is a friend because it leads us to the cross of Christ. It leads us to confession. The Holy Spirit

"Great is the Lord, and greatly to be praised; and His greatness is unsearchable." Psalm 145:3

pushes us back to Jesus—we feel bad about our sin, and the Spirit gives us a gift to replace it.

Many of us have gifts stored up around the house of

God that we have never seen, opened or used. God is a giver. He loves to give. My best advice to you is to put yourself in a place to receive those gifts.

Receiving more gifts from God is a relatively simple matter. All we need to do is give away whatever He gives us. "Freely you have received, freely give," Jesus counseled (Matthew 10:8). Christians should be the most generous people on earth because we operate under the principle of giving. The whole point of God putting us into Christ is so that He can lavish us with good gifts. Because of Jesus, it is impossible for God not to give. His generosity in your life could save your entire community: That's how much He wants to give you. God gives us more than we could ever handle for the specific purpose of giving it away to everyone we meet.

No one in a city could escape the generosity of God if a church really woke up and saw what was available to them in Christ. We could be a massive contribution to thousands–or millions–of people. Sometimes I think that darkness is triumphing in the world only because the Church is asleep in the light. We don't realize the abundance God has given us, or the quality of life He has called us to lead.

God gives intentionally

God has a plan of the things He wants to lavish on us, as we can see in Matthew 7:7–18:

Ask, and it will be given to you; seek, and you will find; knock, and it will be opened to you. For everyone who asks receives, and he who seeks finds, and to him who knocks it will be opened. Or what man is there among you who, if his son asks for bread, will give him a stone? Or if he asks for a fish, will he give him a serpent? If you then, being evil, know how to give good gifts to your children, how much more will your Father who is in heaven give good things to those who ask Him! Therefore, whatever you want men to do to you, do also to them, for this is the Law and the Prophets.

Enter by the narrow gate; for wide is the gate and broad is the way that leads to destruction, and there are many who go in by it. Because narrow is the gate and difficult is the way which leads to life, and there are few who find it.

Beware of false prophets, who come to you in sheep's clothing, but inwardly they are ravenous wolves. You will know them by their fruits. Do men gather grapes from thornbushes or figs from thistles? Even so, every good tree bears good fruit, but a bad tree bears bad fruit. A good tree cannot bear bad fruit, nor can a bad tree bear good fruit.

This passage is all about God's intentionality to give. His answer is always yes to us, as we see in Luke 11:9–13:

So I say to you, ask, and it will be given to you; seek, and you will find; knock, and it will be opened to you. For everyone who asks receives, and he who seeks finds, and to him who knocks it will be opened. If a son asks

for bread from any father among you, will he give him a
stone? Or if he asks for a fish, will he give him a serpent
instead of a fish? Or if he asks for an egg, will he offer
him a scorpion? If you then, being evil, know how to
give good gifts to your children, how much more will
your heavenly Father give the Holy Spirit to those who
ask Him!

Jesus lives to captivate our hearts. We must stop
running away from Him and let ourselves be caught by
the love of God: "Keep yourselves in the love of God,
looking for the mercy of our Lord Jesus Christ unto
eternal life" (Jude 21). Salvation is a gift from God to be
totally enjoyed in weakness. Nothing can stop God from
loving us.

In John 4, Jesus met a Samaritan woman who felt
unworthy of even speaking to Him. But Jesus responded
to her by offering a gift: "If you knew the gift of God,
and who it is who says to you, 'Give Me a drink,' you
would have asked Him, and He would have given you
living water" (John 4:10). He offered her a Kingdom
life. What a perfect response to her unworthiness!

To succeed in the Spirit, we need to learn the full
dimension of the gift-based Christ. We explore that
uncharted territory every day of our lives, thanks to the
power and guidance of the Holy Spirit. This is not
supposed to be difficult. I don't know how God could
have made it any easier for us. We have to know the gift
of Jesus within us and explore the benefits of His living
in us.

Jesus knows how to pray for us. He is inside us, with
the help of the Holy Spirit, coaching us to dream beyond
all logic and reason.

the dream giver

God enables us to dream so that we can partner with
Him in a way that is currently beyond us. His dream
opens us up to the impossible.

I remember having a dream five or six times in a
two-week period. In it, I saw a number of orphans
whom no one wanted. They were in a tacky old
warehouse with all of the windows blown in. They
huddled in a corner with no food, no water and no beds
in which to sleep. No one cared about them; they were
despised and rejected. In my dream, I saw them leave
that place and enter a beautiful mansion. These children
grew up to be champions in the country that had
rejected them. It gripped me.

After a few days, I prayed and asked God what the
dream was about.

Graham, He said, *I want you to partner with someone
to turn orphans into champions.*

I did some research and found a group called the
Caminul Felix Orphanage, and learned that their
vision was to turn orphans into champions. They ran
two incredible homes for orphans. I started to give
them money and support them. They are wonderful;
the older children help the younger ones. Some of

the children have grown up and become champions. There is a different spirit upon them. They all speak more than one language and are familiar with technology. They are brilliant, gifted, wise and loving Christians.

I had another dream on back-to-back nights. In the dream, I went and bought a cow, wrote an address in Nigeria on the cow, put a stamp on it and mailed it there. Yes, I mail cows in my dreams. After I woke up, I scoured the Internet and found an organization called "Send a Cow." Cows are sent to the poor in developing nations and become almost mobile factories. They give milk, fertilize the ground and produce meat. They change entire villages. I've been buying cows through that charity ever since. One woman, from the proceeds of her cow, built a school for forty children.

Another dream I had on several occasions was about rescuing girls from slavery. In my dream, I would drive a large van into big cities and pull slave girls into it. When I researched my dream, I found an organization in India that goes into the villages of Nepal and buys children who would otherwise be sold into slavery. The families think the girls are better off going to a wealthy home, but the first thing that happens to them is a brutal, awful gang rape. Then the girls are sold into a life of prostitution.

I joined a group of people and helped form a charity called Bishram Griha. Together, we rescue girls from the streets of Bombay. They are unwanted and unloved, but we take them in and give them a life. We train them, pray for them, cry with them, bless them and help them any way we can.

I once dreamed of having a house in France where people could go, pray and be trained in the ministry. I found others with a similar interest and now we have a base in Normandy.

I once had a dream about evangelists in India. Evangelists there are terribly poor because they are reaching out to a people that won't give them anything. In my dream, God told me to provide for these evangelists. I saw them and their families struggling on a road.

> "For now we see in a mirror, dimly, but then face to face. Now I know in part, but then I shall know just as I also am known."
> 1 Corinthians 13:12

When I prayed about it, I felt God tell me to buy a herd of goats and send it to them. I found an organization that could help me, and we did just that. Goats are a sign of wealth in India, so these families can flourish while the evangelist travels and preaches the Gospel.

God gives us dreams so that we can move beyond our current logic. If a dream of God touches us, we'll move toward that new thing. God loves us so much that He wants to give us more than we could ever expect to receive. But He will never give us anything just for ourselves—we are called to give it away, too. We must always keep our eyes open for someone to whom we can give.

God gives more than finances

In our Western culture, we almost always conclude that God's gifts are financial. This is not the case! While God does bless us in that way, He gives us hundreds of other gifts, as well. When we ask, we receive.

If you ever feel as though you need wisdom, ask God for it. He gives wisdom away liberally. That's what I do: I sit in the presence of God and ask Him to talk to me. I try to focus on meditation for at least four months a year. I love asking God questions; in my experience, He is always eager to talk.

I also know that if God doesn't talk initially, He always will eventually. Sometimes He wants us to wait on Him. But waiting in the presence of God is a pleasure in itself. I remember one occasion when I woke up at 5 A.M. and heard God say, *I'm going to talk to you today, so wait on Me.* I waited on Him from 5 A.M. until 11:45 P.M.—when He finally spoke. I had a wonderful time with God that day.

God is generous with wisdom because He wants us to know His plans.

inherit for others

None of us inherit a gift or blessing from God just for ourselves; we inherit for our entire community. "The earth is the LORD's, and all its fullness, the world and those who dwell therein," sang David in Psalm 24:1.

Wherever you live, the people around you belong to
God. In fact, the Lord has positioned you where you are
so that He can pour His blessing through you. He wants
to release resources, blessing and prosperity through
you to your friends and neighbors. His motive is simple:
He wants to save everyone around you.

When we live in the place God has set aside for us, we
are a revival. When we receive His gifts, we revive
everything around us. When a revived person walks
through the desert, they leave water in their footsteps.

I'm tired of visiting churches where Christians sit
around like the invalid who had been sitting at the pool
of Bethesda for 38 years, just waiting for
something to happen (John 5). Guess
what? It's already happened—Jesus has
already died for us, and He's not going
to do it again! He has set aside a place
for each of us into which we must enter.
We are the opened windows of heaven.

> "I have declared to them Your name, and will declare it, that the love with which You loved Me may be in them, and I in them."
> John 17:26

We are the revival for which we have prayed. God wants
to give each of us more than we can cope with and
enough for our whole community.

Christians have lazily expected God's move to be
something big and magical. The truth is that God's
move will just keep coming and coming and coming. It
will keep flowing. Every time a revived person gets next
to someone else, they will have something to give them.
But if we don't see our lives as a contribution, God will
not be able to give us anything.

My job on earth is to give out whatever God gives me. The faster I can give it away, the better it is for me. I am called to be ridiculously generous—and so is every Christian on earth. Our lives are to be an adventure. Nothing about us should be boring or mundane. We're on the edge of something incredible.

we condemn ourselves

When we fail to believe that God can do these things, we condemn ourselves to a lower plane of existence. When Satan accuses Christians who don't fully know who they are in Christ, those Christians will always end up believing the lie and condemning themselves: "I'm no good," they will say.

We are the ones who condemn, but the answer to that self-condemnation is Christ. Jesus has paid the price and raised us up to sit at the Father's right hand. He intercedes for us. God is free to give to me because of Christ. The Father is satisfied because of the blood of Jesus. We are justified in Christ.

God loves us by choice. He wasn't stuck with us; He chose us. The One who knows us best, loves us best. His heart for us resonates throughout Scripture. "For no matter how many promises God has made, they are 'Yes' in Christ. And so through him the 'Amen' is spoken by us to the glory of God," Paul taught in 2 Corinthians 1:20. We don't just conquer the enemy; we conquer everything in the region that God has given us.

A church is a company of people who rise up in a community and occupy it on behalf of God. When we live in that kind of authority, we have final say on what comes into our vicinity. We get to say what goes on. We get to overwhelm the crime rate—not the police. We get to keep drugs out of the area because of our prayers. We see sex shops closed because of our love for Christ and people. We get to work with the poor—not the government. We get to see people released from bondage. The land and the people are our inheritance. They have been given to us, by God, to be prospered into the Kingdom.

When we worry about our own needs being met, we're shortchanging the power of the Gospel. Our only concern must be, through the love and provision of Christ, to meet the needs of the community around us. God is out to smash Christianity's preoccupation with itself and its own needs. We are to be preoccupied by the needs of the community and realize that we are the windows God has opened through which He will pour the resources of heaven. We must stop living as if God is one step away from bankruptcy.

We condemn ourselves when we fail to overcome our agitation, anxiety, panic, fear, worry, dread, timidity, dismay and trepidation. The love of God casts all of that out. We cannot be anxious and trust God at the same time. The two are incompatible; they cannot exist in the same place at the same time.

We cannot be fearful and have the love of God. We

havc to choose one or the other. Life in the Spirit is all about making choices. We are called to explore the depths of God's love for us. We must mature past the question, "Does God love me?" Of course, He loves us; it is immature to constantly demand that reassurance. Instead, we need to believe who we are, and that God has outrageously provided for us.

an undiscovered territory

God has given each of us an undiscovered territory in our lives, and it's our pleasure to adventure with Him in exploring it. If someone gave you a ten-mile parcel of land a thousand miles away from your home, would you go look at it? Of course! It's human nature to want to see what is there, to see what the possibilities are. Is there a mountain on the land? Or a river running through it? Could it be developed? We ought to have that same curiosity about the spiritual territory in our lives that God is revealing to us.

God's love is too large to fathom—but it's an incredible adventure to try. It's deep enough to cover everything, high enough to conquer everything, wide enough to encompass everything and long enough to last forever. His love for us is beyond what we can comprehend.

We must ask ourselves what it means to be rooted in that kind of love. Acceptance of God's love means living a life of grace, not performance. It means loving others like He does—unconditionally and unwaveringly. God can expect the best from us because He knows that He can succeed in us. He knows we want our lives to conform to His nature.

what God is looking for

Throughout the Bible and the history of the world, God has been up front about what He wants. God is looking for a Bride whom He can love forever. He wants a Church that He can love outrageously. His dream girl is a warrior bride. When she joins Him forever, she will wear a beautiful, spotless gown—with combat boots underneath.

That's the kind of Church for which God is looking—people who reflect His nature as a Warrior and as the Prince of Peace. People who understand that He is both God the Righteous Judge, and God the Lover of our Souls. We are called to be a bride that can't be messed with: We know who we are, to whom we belong, and that we are radically loved. We are loved with a passion so intense that it broke hell into pieces.

This is our call and destiny, and the nature of God toward us.

conclusion

Confidence in God comes when we understand two things: who He is, and who we are. I don't mind the spiritual warfare that surrounds my life because I have such a clear understanding and love for the kindness of God. I actually enjoy the struggle, because I know He wants to be kind to me. Everything I face is just a tool for God to use to show me more of His kind nature. The right image of God opens heaven to us. Hell itself cannot overcome a man or woman who carries the right image of God in their spirit.

When God sent Moses to Egypt to duel with Pharaoh, He gave specific instructions: "Thus says the LORD: 'Israel is My son, My firstborn. So I say to you, let My son go that he may serve Me. But if you refuse to let him go, indeed I will kill your son, your firstborn'" (Exodus 4:22–23). But while Moses worked with Pharaoh, God went behind the scenes and hardened the king's heart, whispering to him, "Don't listen to him." One could forgive Moses for thinking: *Please, stop helping me, Lord!*

God hardened Pharaoh's heart because He had an agenda. God wanted to show His power to Israel's enemies. He wanted to teach His people about faithfulness, covenant and perseverance. He had to— the journey to the Promised Land was going to be a grueling one, and the Israelites had to learn to trust God completely.

I cannot overstate the confidence that comes from knowing who God wants to be for us. Just as Jesus prophesied that His Church would be built on Peter's revelation of the Son of God, so every single church on earth today is built on its people's perception of who God is for them. Churches must have a corporate image of what God wants for their community. Too many churches don't know what their identity is in Christ, but they desperately need that authority.

Our expectation of God increases when we have the right image of God in our heart. Where are you, right now, in your journey with God? Do you need a breakthrough this year into a different level of relationship with Him? Maybe you are coming into a new level of authority, ministry or anointing. Take time to upgrade your relationship with God. Perhaps you're disillusioned right now. Maybe you feel burned out or cynical. Your recovery is only available through Christ, and through who Christ wants to be to you. That is your starting point; humans don't have a right to be hurt—we have a right to be healed.

> "Behold, I will bring it health and healing; I will heal them and reveal to them the abundance of peace and truth."
> Jeremiah 33:6

What is it that God wants to be to you this year? What adventure are you going to have with Him? What is it that God wants to show you? What is He longing in His heart to show you? God has a desire for you, and you alone. He knows what He wants to be for you, and He wants to reveal it to you. He wants to lead you through experience after experience as you learn His nature. He wants you to find His truth in joy and difficulty, in pleasure and pain. God will establish who He wants to be for you.

We don't need to worry about how this revelation will come; we just need to cooperate with Him fully. It's all we can offer Him, and it's all that He wants. "Who do you say that I am?"

a meditative journey

God does not live in a box; He has no predetermined flight plan, no processes set in stone, as to how He upgrades His relationships with His children. His love for us is completely unique and individual. However, we have learned from the Bible that there are things to which God is attracted; things of which He loves to be a part. With that in mind, we offer these ten steps as a guide to help you upgrade your perspective of God for the next season of your life.

1. Thanksgiving
We enter His gates with thanksgiving ... for what are you thankful? What has God given you? What gifts has He lavished upon you? Take some time and offer Him a heartfelt psalm of thanksgiving, focusing on the blessings He has given you.

   If your current circumstances are difficult or hard, for what can you be thankful in terms of God's heart toward you? That He said He would never leave nor forsake you is worthy of thanks alone.

2. Worship

Adore God. Magnify His name. Tell Him of His wondrous deeds. Praise Him for His great majesty. If thanksgiving opens His gates, then worship opens His heart. Don't rush ... just worship Him, in spirit and in truth.

To *magnify* has two meanings: First, to see something bigger than it is in actual size, and second, to see something as big as it really is. We tend to magnify our problems and not the Lord. See Him as big as He is.

3. Stillness

It is in stillness and peace that God begins to speak. Remember, His voice wasn't in the whirlwind or the thunder; it was in the still and quiet. Be still and know that He is God. Rest there. Live there. Connect with the Almighty there. Still the clamoring in your thoughts. We all have a background conversation in our minds that either feeds our fears or lifts our spirits. Stillness promotes a God-consciousness.

4. See Him as your Prince of Peace.

Embrace God as your Prince of Peace; draw on His restful nature to sustain you. As troubles rise in your heart, ask the Prince of Peace to soothe you. He is your refuge, your strong tower. If it helps, picture a strong tower, ruled by God. Live in it.

5. See Him as your Man of War.
God is also your protector; paradoxically, He is gentle as a Lamb, and fierce as a Lion. He is your shield, your sword, your strength. Let Him fight your battles for you … don't take matters into your own hands. Allow Him to be fully God in your life—the provider of peace, and the protector of your life.

6. Examine your new season.
Tell God what you are facing. Share your fears, your dreams. Hide nothing—He knows and sees all anyway. Listen as He whispers to you.

Expect the Lord to give you "a spirit of wisdom and revelation in the knowledge of Him" (Ephesians 1:17).

7. What does He want to teach you?
Begin to ask God questions. What does He want to teach you in this next season of life that He could only teach you this way? What lessons are there for you to learn? Through what must you travel on this next leg of your journey together? What pitfalls does He want you to avoid? On what will you be tested? What glory does He want to bestow on you?

It is important at least that you write your questions down and develop an expectation that God will answer them. The revelation that comes will lead you into a new experience of Him.

8. What does He want to be for you?
Now ask Him what He wants to be for you. Knowing where you are headed, He has a plan to reveal something new and fresh about Himself to you. What is it? What is God like? What does He have for you? Take your time ... patience may be one of things He wants to show you.

He will give you a vision of all that He wants to be for you. Your circumstances will then be filled with promise. You will perceive every problem as an opportunity to experience all that God longs to be for you.

9. Ask Him for those things.
Remembering everything the two of you have shared over the past several minutes, ask Him for all of it. Ask Him to be more real to you than ever. Be specific—you may want to craft a written prayer emphasizing God's desires for you. Ask for everything that heaven holds for you.

Write a reply to God detailing what your response will be to each situation that is under adjustment.

10. Abide in Him.
Just be. Don't rush out. Don't be panicked. Just be with Him. In the Garden of Eden, God and Adam would sit and talk with one another. Neither had anywhere else they'd rather be. Live in God. Abide in Him. Love Him. Minister to Him. Just be.

your picture of God

Answer as many questions as you need to!

▶ What is your current picture of God? Write it down in four to six sentences or phrases.

▶ How long have you had this image? Is it time for an upgrade?

▶ Is your image biblical? Can you put Scripture(s) alongside it? Do so!

▶ What do you need to change?

▶ What do you need God to be to you in this current season?

▶ Sit quietly, relax and ask the Holy Spirit to give you a vision of God for this next season. Keep persevering until the whole picture emerges *and* your faith begins to rise and worship flows.

▶ What Scripture can support this image?

▶ What is the Spirit saying to you through this picture and this word?

▶ How can you become this image of God to the people around you? What must change in you?

▶ Now keep this picture alive through praise and worship!

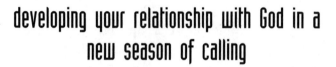

developing your relationship with God in a new season of calling

Answer the following questions as you meditate on what it is God wants to show you during the next season of your life.

1. Into what are you moving? A new season, calling, revelation, response, role or something else?

   . . . .
   . . . .
   . . . .

2. What could this situation show you about God that couldn't happen through another means?

   . . . .
   . . . .
   . . . .

3. Right now, what is it that the Lord wants to do *in you* that will enable you to occupy this new place for Him in the Spirit?

   . . . .
   . . . .
   . . . .

4. What is it that the Lord wants to be *through you* for the people around you?

   . . . .
   . . . .
   . . . .

5. Given that our spiritual maturity arises out of our knowledge of the ways of God, what are the likely situations/people, both positive and negative, that God may use to develop your answers to Questions 3 and 4 above?

   . . . .
   . . . .
   . . . .

6. At the end of this season, how do you think your upgraded relationship with God will impact your effectiveness in ministry?

   . . . .
   . . . .
   . . . .

an inheritance word for this season

In the context of our relationship with God, there are times when He asks us a direct question that connects His desire for us with our longings for Him.

He spoke to Solomon, "Ask what you wish me to do for you" (1 Kings 3:5). With Ahaz, His approach was similar, though more poetic: "Ask a sign for yourself from the LORD your God; make it deep as Sheol or high as heaven" (Isaiah 7:11).

Jesus asked the question, "What do you want Me to do for you?" (Matthew 20:32). Although the background of this situation was healing, we do understand in Christ that all the interventions of God are relational in context. Jesus was fully aware of the Father's real pleasure in giving us the Kingdom (Luke 12:32).

"Every good gift comes down from the Father of lights," wrote James (James 1:17) ... so be wise in what you ask for (4:3)!

When asking God to upgrade your image of Him, it is important to ask for an inheritance word. These are pieces of the Bible that He brings to your attention and asks you to meditate on for long periods of time. As a son or daughter of the Almighty, you have an inheritance, and God wants you to know what it is. Jesus Himself, after spending forty days and forty nights being tested in the wilderness (see Luke 4), returned to civilization and went straight to a synagogue. He opened the Scriptures to Isaiah 61 and proclaimed it as His inheritance. "Today, this word is fulfilled in your hearing," He said.

I love receiving inheritance words, as they reveal to me what it is God wants to be for me in the next season of my life. He will often wrap the upgraded view we need to have of Him into a poignant piece of Scripture. Our job is to seek those verses out and get everything we can out of them. Then we must apply them to our lives during the new season.

God will give you an inheritance word, if He hasn't done so already. The word will set you up to discover what you're going to experience during the next stage of your journey of faith. It may be two or three passages of the Bible, but He will put it in your heart, and it is your inheritance. Ask for it. When you receive a passage, don't read anything else for a while. Read it and re-read it. Memorize it, if you can. Take it apart, piece by piece. Study it. Look it up in Bible commentaries. Research the original language. Ask God to illuminate His truth in it. *Every ounce of revelation is yours to experience.* This passage is part of the conversation in heaven about you, so use it for all it is worth. Then write a crafted prayer about it, asking for the things that have been laid out as promises in your inheritance word.

[See my book *Crafted Prayer* for more on crafted prayer and inheritance words.]

assignment

Lectio Divina

Lectio Divina (Latin for "divine reading") is an ancient
way of reading the Bible—allowing a quiet and
contemplative way of coming to God's Word. *Lectio
Divina* opens the pulse of the Scriptures, helping readers
dig far deeper into the Word than normally happens in a
quick glance-over.

In this exercise, we will look at a portion of Scripture
and use a modified *Lectio Divina* technique to engage
with it. This technique can be used on any passage of
Scripture; I highly recommend using it for key Bible
passages that the Lord has highlighted for you, and for
anything you think might be an "inheritance word"
for your life.

> Then the LORD said to Moses, "Depart and go up from
> here, you and the people whom you have brought out of
> the land of Egypt, to the land of which I swore to
> Abraham, Isaac, and Jacob, saying, 'To your
> descendants I will give it.' And I will send My Angel
> before you, and I will drive out the Canaanite and the

Amorite and the Hittite and the Perizzite and the Hivite and the Jebusite. Go up to a land flowing with milk and honey; for I will not go up in your midst, lest I consume you on the way, for you are a stiff-necked people."

And when the people heard this bad news, they mourned, and no one put on his ornaments. For the LORD had said to Moses, "Say to the children of Israel, 'You are a stiff-necked people. I could come up into your midst in one moment and consume you. Now therefore, take off your ornaments, that I may know what to do to you.'" So the children of Israel stripped themselves of their ornaments by Mount Horeb.

Moses took his tent and pitched it outside the camp, far from the camp, and called it the tabernacle of meeting. And it came to pass that everyone who sought the LORD went out to the tabernacle of meeting which was outside the camp. So it was, whenever Moses went out to the tabernacle, that all the people rose, and each man stood at his tent door and watched Moses until he had gone into the tabernacle. And it came to pass, when Moses entered the tabernacle, that the pillar of cloud descended and stood at the door of the tabernacle, and the LORD talked with Moses. All the people saw the pillar of cloud standing at the tabernacle door, and all the people rose and worshiped, each man in his tent door. So the LORD spoke to Moses face to face, as a man speaks to his friend. And he would return to the camp, but his servant Joshua the son of Nun, a young man, did not depart from the tabernacle.

Then Moses said to the LORD, "See, You say to me, 'Bring up this people.' But You have not let me know whom You will send with me. Yet You have said, 'I know you by name, and you have also found grace in My sight.' Now therefore, I pray, if I have found grace in Your sight, show me now Your way, that I may know You and that I may find grace in Your sight. And consider that this nation is Your people."

And He said, "My Presence will go with you, and I will give you rest."

Then he said to Him, "If Your Presence does not go with us, do not bring us up from here. For how then will it be known that Your people and I have found grace in Your sight, except You go with us? So we shall be separate, Your people and I, from all the people who are upon the face of the earth."

So the LORD said to Moses, "I will also do this thing that you have spoken; for you have found grace in My sight, and I know you by name."

And he said, "Please, show me Your glory."

Then He said, "I will make all My goodness pass before you, and I will proclaim the name of the LORD before you. I will be gracious to whom I will be gracious, and I will have compassion on whom I will have compassion." But He said, "You cannot see My face; for no man shall see Me, and live." And the LORD said, "Here is a place by Me, and you shall stand on the rock. So it shall be, while My glory passes by, that I will put you in the cleft of the rock, and will cover you with My hand while I pass by. Then I will take away My hand, and you shall see My back; but My face shall not be seen."

And the LORD said to Moses, "Cut two tablets of stone like the first ones, and I will write on these tablets the words that were on the first tablets which you broke. So be ready in the morning, and come up in the morning to Mount Sinai, and present yourself to Me there on the top of the mountain. And no man shall come up with you, and let no man be seen throughout all the mountain; let neither flocks nor herds feed before that mountain."

So he cut two tablets of stone like the first ones. Then Moses rose early in the morning and went up Mount Sinai, as the LORD had commanded him; and he took in his hand the two tablets of stone.

Now the LORD descended in the cloud and stood with him there, and proclaimed the name of the LORD. And the LORD passed before him and proclaimed, "The LORD, the LORD God, merciful and gracious, longsuffering, and abounding in goodness and truth, keeping mercy for thousands, forgiving iniquity and transgression and sin, by no means clearing the guilty, visiting the iniquity of the fathers upon the children and the children's children to the third and the fourth generation."

So Moses made haste and bowed his head toward the earth, and worshiped. Then he said, "If now I have found grace in Your sight, O Lord, let my Lord, I pray, go among us, even though we are a stiff-necked people; and pardon our iniquity and our sin, and take us as Your inheritance."

1. Find a place of stillness before God. Embrace His peace. Calm your body, breathe slowly ... clear your mind of the distractions of life. Ask God to

reveal His rest to you. Whisper the word
"Stillness." This can take some time, but once
you're in that place of rest, enjoy it. Worship God
out of it.

2. Read the passage twice, slowly.

   a. Allow its words to become familiar to you, and
      sink into your spirit. Picture the scene—become
      part of it. Listen for pieces that catch your
      attention.

   b. Following the reading, meditate upon what you
      have heard. What stands out? Write it down.

      . . . .
      . . . .
      . . . .
      . . . .

   c. If a word or phrase from the passage seems
      highlighted to you, write it down.

      . . . .
      . . . .
      . . . .

3. Read the passage twice, again.

   a. Like waves crashing onto a shore, let the words
      of the Scripture crash onto your spirit. What are
      you discerning? What are you hearing? What
      are you feeling? Write it down.

      . . . .
      . . . .
      . . . .
      . . . .

b. What is the theme of this passage? Write it
down.

. . . .
. . . .
. . . .
. . . .

c. Does this passage rekindle any memories or
experiences? Write them down.

. . . .
. . . .
. . . .
. . . .
. . . .

d. What is the Holy Spirit saying to you? Write it
down.

. . . .
. . . .
. . . .
. . . .

4. Read the passage two final times.
    a. Meditate on it.
    b. Is there something God wants you to do with
    this passage? Is there something to which He is
    calling you? Write it down.

. . . .
. . . .
. . . .
. . . .
. . . .

c. Pray silently. Tell God the thoughts this Scripture is bringing to your mind. Ask Him for His thoughts. Write down your conversation— as if you and God were sitting in a coffee shop, two old and dear friends, sharing.

. . . .
. . . .
. . . .
. . . .
. . . .
. . . .
. . . .

5. Pray and thank God for what He has shared with you. Come back to the passage a few more times over the coming weeks.

This is one of the most classic songs about the love of God that I have ever heard. Written by my friend Joe King, it never fails to move me.

I Will Always Love You [1]

I loved you long before you met Me
And then you gave your life to Me
But should one day you turn and walk away
I will always love you; I will always love you,
I will always love you; yes, I will, I always will.

My love will never cease towards you
But should I have a change of heart
It is because My heart has ceased to beat
I will always love you; I will always love you,
I will always love you; yes, I will, I always will.

When all around you seems in darkness
When you have plumbed right to the depths
No pit is so deep I'm not deeper still
I will always love you; I will always love you,
I will always love you; yes, I will, I always will.

And when the day has almost ended
When evening comes and walls you in
When there is no one else to comfort you
I will always love you; I will always love you,
I will always love you; yes, I will, I always will.

---

[1]   *I Will Always Love You* from the album *Next To You* available through www.joekinguk.com. Used with permission.

Here are My arms for you to cling to
Here are My wounds where you can hide
Here are the tears that I have cried for you
I will always love you; I will always love you,
I will always love you; yes, I will, I always will.

My love is constant as the sunrise
As changeless as the stars of night
My child, as sure as the returning tide
I will always love you; I will always love you,
I will always love you; yes, I will, I always will.

Joe King contact details:
   joekinguk@aol.com
   www.joeking.com

FAQs
(frequently asked questions)

Q. *Who is Graham Cooke and how can I find more information about him?*

A. Graham Cooke is a speaker and author who splits his time between Southampton, England, and Vacaville, California. He has been involved in prophetic ministry since 1974. He founded and directed the School of Prophecy, which has received international acclaim for its advanced series of in-depth training programs. Graham is a member of Community Church in Southampton (UK). He is married to Heather, and they have three children: Ben, Seth and Sophie. You can learn more about Graham at:

www.grahamcooke.com

or by writing him at:

P.O. Box 91
Southampton
England SO15 57E

Q. *How can I become a prayer partner with Graham?*

A. Check his website, www.grahamcooke.com, for all of the information you need.

Q. *Has Graham written any other books?*

A. Graham has written several other books: *A Divine Confrontation: Birth Pangs of the New Church* (Destiny Image), *Developing Your Prophetic Gifting* (Chosen), *Crafted Prayer* (Chosen), *Drawing Close* (Chosen), *The Language of Love* (Chosen), *The Secret of a Powerful Inner Life* (Chosen) and *When the Lights Go Out* (Chosen). All are available at most Christian bookstores or at www.grahamcooke.com.

about the author

Graham Cooke is married to Heather, and they have three adult children: Ben, Seth and Sophie. Graham and Heather divide their time between Southampton, England, and Vacaville, California.

Graham is a member of Community Church in Southampton (UK), responsible for the prophetic and training program, and working with team leader Billy Kennedy. In California, he is part of the pastoral leadership team, working with senior pastor David Crone. He has responsibility for Insight, a training program within the church and for the region.

Graham is a popular conference speaker and is well known for his training programs on the prophetic, spiritual warfare, intimacy with God, leadership and spirituality. He functions as a consultant, specifically helping churches make the transition from one dimension of calling to a higher level of vision and ministry. He has a passion to build prototype churches that can fully reach our postmodern society.

A strong part of Graham's ministry is in producing finances and resources to help the poor, supporting many projects around the world. He also financially supports and helps to underwrite church planting, leadership development, evangelism and health and rescue projects in the third world. If you wish to become a financial partner for the sake of missions, please contact Graham's office, where his personal assistant, Carole Shiers, will be able to assist you.

Graham has many prayer partners who play a significant part in his ministry. For more information, check his website.

Contact details for Graham Cooke:

▶ **United States:**
Vaca Valley Christian Life Center
6391 Leisure Town Road
Vacaville, CA 95687

email: fti.admin@vvclc.org

▶ **United Kingdom:**
Sword of Fire Ministries
P.O. Box 1, Southampton SO16 7WJ

email: admin@swordfire.org.uk

▶ **Canada:**
Jenny Bateman
Friends at Langley Vineyard
5708 Glover Road, Langley, BC V3A 4H8

email: jenn@shopvineyard.com

▶ Website: http://www.grahamcooke.com

Electrifying the East Coast Route

Electrifying the East Coast Route

The making of Britain's first 140 mph railway

Peter Semmens
MA CChem FRSC MBCS MCIT FRSA

PSL
Patrick Stephens Limited

Front endpaper *No 91 008 speeds northwards with a Leeds train in the summer of 1990.* (Peter Kelly)

Title page *Class '91' No 91 011* Terence Cuneo *with Mark IV stock near Offord.* (BR)

Rear endpaper *No 91 003 leaves York with a BR staff charter train on 23 September 1989.* (Neville Stead)

First published in 1991

British Library Cataloguing in Publication Data

Semmens, P. W. B. (Peter William Brett) *1927 –*
    Electrifying the east coast route: the making of
    Britain's first 140 mph railway.
    1. Great Britain. Railroads
    I Title
    385.0941

    ISBN 0-85059-929-6

Patrick Stephens is a member of the Haynes Publishing Group P.L.C., Sparkford, Nr Yeovil, Somerset BA22 7JJ.

Printed in Great Britain

10 9 8 7 6 5 4 3 2 1

CONTENTS

FOREWORD

A couple of years ago I contributed the Foreword to Peter Semmens's book *Speed on the East Coast Main Line*. In the time that has followed, the 'InterCity 225' electrification scheme for the East Coast Route has progressed, and we are now poised to begin our fastest ever Anglo-Scottish services with the new trains. This will mark the end of the biggest single project on British Rail since the days of the Modernisation Plan, which has been completed within budget.

As well as describing the way in which the present project has been carried out, Peter Semmens has given readers the historical background to previous electrification schemes involving the route. But the economic case for such a project to be authorized had to be made by InterCity. We are a commercial operation, relying entirely on our customers to earn our living. We thus constantly need to improve those aspects of rail travel they consider are important, encouraging them to choose our trains rather then the competing road or air services. Speed is one of the most vital factors, and the improved journey times, which have already been achieved on the electrified West Yorkshire services, will now benefit those travelling between London, the North East and Scotland. In addition to faster speeds, the new 'InterCity 225' trains provide many new features designed to make the time pass more pleasantly for those aboard. Although our new trains will initially be running at the same top speeds as the diesels they replaced, they incorporate the most powerful locomotives ever to run in this country. Their 225-km/h (140 mph) capability is shared by the coaches, and in due course we hope to introduce general 225 km/h running.

I am glad that this great step forward in the story of InterCity is being marked by a book which gives an insight into the work put in by so many of the people in the railway industry to bring this project to a successful conclusion.

JOHN PRIDEAUX
Managing Director, InterCity

ACKNOWLEDGEMENTS

When writing any book on such an important and extensive subject as a £420m railway electrification scheme, an enormous amount of assistance is needed from those carrying out the job. My grateful thanks are due to all of them, and the help of the following must be acknowledged specially:

Dr John Prideaux, Managing Director, InterCity, for kindly writing the Foreword.

Don Heath, Project Manager for the East Coast Electrification, and now British Rail's Director, Projects, for his numerous insights into the complexities of the project.

All the staff of the Public Affairs Departments of the Eastern and Scottish Regions, under their current managers, Bert Porter and John Boyle. Their respective Press Officers, Brian Ward and George Reynolds, have kept me informed about progress, and Alan Moorby at York has helped me choose from the excellent official illustrations which have been taken by the BR photographers, showing the work being carried out.

Mr Noel Broadbent, British Rail's Electrification Engineer; Mr Malcolm Stuart, Deputy Electrification Planning Engineer; Mr Roger Pope, BR's Signal Engineer (Projects) based at York, for kindly checking the references to signalling and telecommunications in the text; Mr Laurie Holland, InterCity Marketing Manager for the East Coast Route, and Mr Stuart Baker, InterCity Route Manager (Yorkshire Services) for providing the advance information on the new electric services, as described in Chapter 11; Mr Michael Scott, Publicity Manager, GEC Alsthom; Mr Peter Kelly, the Editor of *The Railway Magazine*, for permission to reproduce some of the material used in my monthly 'Locomotive Practice & Performance' articles; The Public Relations Department of National Power, for information on the electric supply industry in South Yorkshire and Humberside; and Phil Atkins and John Edgington from the Library at the National Railway Museum, York.

The names of those who have supplied logs of runs or photographs are acknowledged where they appear in the text. I am also grateful to the Railway Performance Society for permission to quote from the 'Fastest Times' data

compiled by their members. All photographs that are not otherwise acknowledged are by the author or from his collection.

Very special thanks are due to my neighbour in the village, Mr Alan
Goldfinch, who was the Eastern Region's Chief Mechanical & Electrical
Engineer at the time that the electrification was authorized. He was then the
potential 'user' of the new technology, but, in the course of BR's engineering
reorganization, he subsequently became responsible for the whole of the
Board's Electrification & Plant, so was subsequently to oversee the installation of much of the fixed equipment. He has kindly read my text and made
many useful comments, for which I am most grateful.

Except for a few direct quotes, all the opinions expressed in the book are
my own.

INTRODUCTION

The start of electric services from King's Cross to Leeds and Edinburgh in 1991 will mark the successful conclusion of seven years' work on the largest single project undertaken by British Rail since the 1955 Modernisation Plan. Authorized in 1984 — to the surprise of many — by a Conservative Government, the original £306 million scheme involved the electrification of 400 route miles. A further 27 miles from Edinburgh to Carstairs were added to this in September 1989, to enable East Coast trains to continue to Glasgow Central. For the first time in Britain, a fleet of trains capable of running at 140 mph has been introduced, and as early as September 1989 one of them achieved a speed of 161.7 mph down Stoke Bank, powered by a Class '91' locomotive, the most powerful design ever to run on our railway system.

To enable these services to operate, some 30,000 steel masts had to be erected to support 2,800 miles of overhead contact wire. Over a dozen Feeder Stations were required to supply power at 25,000 volts, while more than 100 bridges had to be raised to provide clearance for the wires. Major changes to some of the signalling systems were also required to immunize them from the effects of induced currents. Although not actually part of the electrification scheme, major changes were also made to the track layout in the station area at York, while in Newcastle the station was extended on the south side, and the trackwork extensively remodelled northwards over a distance of some 2 miles.

This book describes the work undertaken by British Rail to bring this scheme into successful operation. It is intended for the interested layman, rather then being aimed solely at the enthusiast, and also includes various aspects of the technical background to the work. The route itself is not described in detail, as that has already been included in my previous book, *Speed on the East Coast Main Line*, published by Patrick Stephens Limited in 1990. Although that contains a final chapter about the 1984–1991 electrification project, it deals primarily with the earlier diesel eras of the 'InterCity 125s' and the 'Deltics'.

Although, by international standards, the railways in Britain have lagged behind those in the rest of Europe when it comes to electrification, the East Coast Route has nevertheless been the subject of numerous electrification proposals over the years. Indeed, even from the windows of today's fleet-footed 'InterCity 125s' the knowledgeable traveller can still spot between Durham and Darlington the remains of an electrical Feeder Station for the country's first main-line electrification. Although that scheme did not directly involve the East Coast Route, the site was chosen over three-quarters of a century ago so that it could also, at a later stage, have supplied power for electric traction on the main line.

Speed on the East Coast Main Line led into the diesel age by reviewing the achievements of over a century of steam traction. It is thus appropriate for us to start our present story by describing those previous electrification schemes which have concerned the East Coast Route, as they provide an interesting insight into the way in which the railway planners have used developments in electric technology to transform what was already Britain's premier high-speed line.

P. W. B. Semmens
MA CChem FRSC MBCS MCIT FRSA
York

Part One

ELECTRIFICATION PRIOR TO 1984

Chapter One

EARLY ELECTRIFICATION SCHEMES

The Great Northern suburban proposals of 1903
During the early years of the twentieth century there was considerable world-wide activity in the application of electric traction to railways, with numerous proposals or schemes being put forward in Britain. These were aided by the passing of legislation by the government to permit railways to change to electric traction after obtaining Board of Trade permission, rather than having to get their own amending Act of Parliament. Interest was aroused too in the enthusiast world, and for several years *The Railway Magazine* published frequent articles describing the latest developments. One of those schemes, that covering the southernmost part of the East Coast Route, will be the first

On 1 July 1905, Great Northern 'Single' No 100 approaches Wood Green with the 6.10 pm departure from King's Cross. (LCGB/Ken Nunn Collection/H. L. Hopwood)

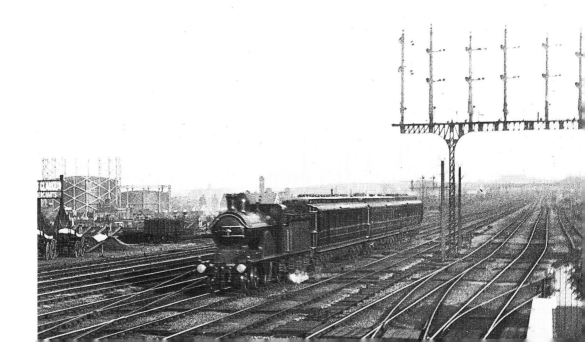

which we will consider in detail.

By 1903, the Great Northern Railway's suburban services in London were feeling the strain. They were operating a total of 3,526 train miles every day, with 54 inward workings being scheduled during the two-hour morning peak, which was appreciably more than those run by today's corresponding Network SouthEast services through Finsbury Park. Handling this traffic was stretching the capacity of the steam-hauled trains to the limit, and the Great Northern requested the firm of Dick, Kerr to put forward proposals to electrify its King's Cross suburban services. There is a copy of the resulting report, dated 29 June 1903, in the Library at the National Railway Museum, bound in green buckram with gold lettering, entitled *Scheme for the Substitution of Electricity for Steam Traction on the Suburban Lines of the Great Northern Railway Company.*

Figure 1 *The route diagram of the proposed Great Northern suburban electrification, taken from the Dick, Kerr report of 1903.* (Courtesy National Railway Museum, York)

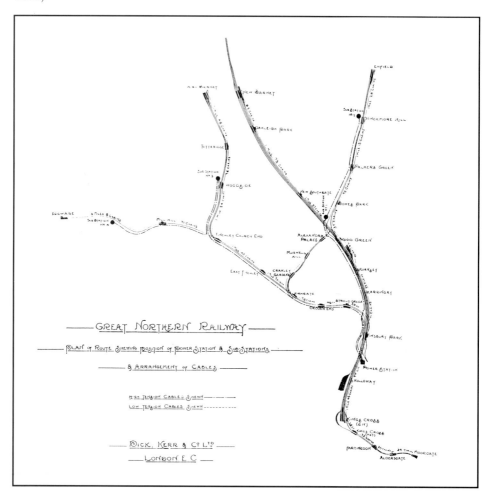

The lines covered are shown in Figure 1, which is taken from the report, and the 28 route miles concerned extended over much shorter distances than we now recognize as the King's Cross suburban area. Along the two routes served by today's Class '313' inner suburban EMUs, the 1903 proposals only extended as far as New Barnet and Enfield, the latter line finishing there in those days, prior to its 1910 extension to Hertford. The scheme also covered the Edgware, High Barnet and Alexandra Palace branches, the trains for which left the main line at a flying junction just north of Finsbury Park. This has been demolished for many years now, and the lines themselves have also disappeared from the BR map. The branch to Alexandra Palace was closed in 1954, and much of the other route mileage had been handed over to London Transport from 1939 onwards. The Northern Line burrowed up to join the one-time GNR branch south of Highgate, so by 1940 electric trains were running through to High Barnet. The following year tube stock also reached Mill Hill East, but has so far never continued beyond this point as Edgware was already served by the other Northern Line route from Camden Town.

The 1903 electrification was to have been carried out at 650 volts dc, using a four-rail system. No recommendation was made as to whether to insulate the return rail, or cross-bond it to the running rails, although the latter arrangement would have reduced the electrical resistance of the whole circuit by a third. Two sites were considered for the power station. One was at New Southgate, where coal could be equally easily delivered by main-line trains, and a well was available for water. It did, however, have disadvantages compared with the preferred location alongside the Great Northern's existing 'Electric Lighting Station', situated on the up side of the line half a mile south of Finsbury Park. This was because a very unusual form of power generation was proposed. Half of the current would be generated as dc, and would be fed directly into the third rails on the tracks outside. The rest would be produced as three-phase ac from 25 Hertz alternators, and distributed by high-tension cables to the other four Substations, where it would drive rotary converters supplying dc to the track. To form a ring main, a 650-volt cable link was to be installed through the grounds of Alexandra Palace from the end of the branch to the main line at Wood Green station (which, just to confuse the issue, was renamed Alexandra Palace in 1982).

The trains for the new system would have been modified from existing Great Northern four-wheeled non-corridor stock. Two different formations were planned, as shown in Figure 2. The 'standard' formation comprised 12 vehicles, with three motor coaches, one at each end and the other in the middle of the train, the last of these not needing a driving compartment. Both types were to have been converted from ordinary steam-hauled coaches by fitting them with electric bogies. A diagram of the former is given in Figure 3, showing the vacuum brake equipment, but not the electrical control gear and resistances, which would have been mounted alongside the brake cylinder on the underframe. To work the New Barnet–King's Cross services, 16-coach formations were to have been used, and these had an additional four-coach section, complete with one further motor coach at the outer end, added to one of the standard sets.

Figure 2 *Diagrams of the two types of electric train proposed for the 1903 Great Northern suburban electrification. Reproduced from the original Dick, Kerr report.* (Courtesy National Railway Museum, York)

Fully loaded, one of the intermediate power cars was estimated to weigh just under 25 tons, and each axle would have been driven by a 100-hp motor. Within an overall length of 32 feet it had seats for no fewer than 72 passengers, squeezed into six compartments, each of which was no more than 8 feet

Figure 3 *A diagram of one of the two types of motor coaches proposed by Dick, Kerr for the 1903 Great Northern electrification. This one has space for use by the driver or guard at the ends of the train, while the other was of the intermediate variety, with six instead of four passenger compartments.* (Courtesy National Railway Museum, York)

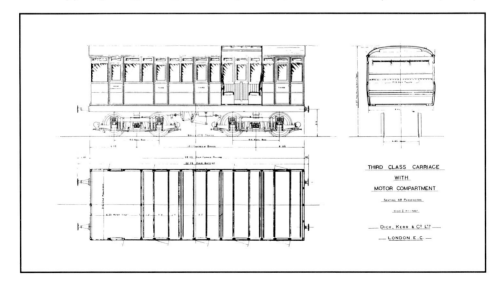

$11^{1}/_{4}$ inches wide between the internal pillars, and 5 feet 2 inches between the near-vertical seat-backs. By comparison, one of the present-day Class '313' trailers seats 84 passengers within overall dimensions of 65 x $9^{1}/_{4}$ feet and provides a very different ambience to that of the turn-of-the-century stock. However, while there will be few who can remember what it was like to be a GN commuter at that time, my general impression from the diagrams is that there was remarkably little difference in the standards of passenger accommodation between them and the 1930s 'Quad-Art' sets. These survived the end of steam traction on the King's Cross suburban services, and were hauled by diesel locomotives, such as the 'Baby Deltics', in the early 1960s. When built by Gresley they were designed to be capable of being converted into electric multiple-units.

One of the 12-coach electric trains would have seated 708 passengers, with the capacity of a 16-coach Barnet 'Flyer' being no less than 972. These figures compared with the seating capacity of 656 for an existing 11-coach steam-hauled train, which slightly exceeded the length of a 'standard' electric set. One of the 16-car trains was 493 feet long, so could still have been accommodated within all but one of the existing platforms on the line. The figure given for the length of the 16-coach train in Figure 2 is 493 feet $1^{3}/_{8}$ inches, which represents one of the worst examples I have met of spurious accuracy in a railway engineering dimension! Any single buffer could probably change its length by up to an inch depending on the compression of its springs, and along the train there were no fewer than 30 pairs of these in contact. This is quite apart from the possibility of the headstocks being bent by the occasional rough shunt!

The Great Northern's specification for the electrification scheme was to enable them to increase their carrying capacity by 40 per cent, without any changes to the track or signalling. It was nevertheless intended to decrease the headway between successive trains from 3 to 2 minutes. That limitation was fixed by operating requirements, rather than signal spacings, so the ability to reverse the electric trains in the terminal platforms was a big step forward, eliminating the need for numerous light-engine movements.

Historically one of the unusual features of the Great Northern suburban system has been that many of the trains have not used King's Cross, either as their southern terminus, or on their way to or from Moorgate via the Widened Lines. For most of the day on Mondays to Fridays, our present Class '313s', for example, leave the main line at Finsbury Park, and dive down into what was built as the Great Northern & City Railway in 1904 (later becoming London Transport's Northern City Line). Back in 1903 many of the suburban services north of Finsbury Park were operated by trains from the North London Railway, running to or from Broad Street, and these workings were expected to continue after the GN electrification. A remarkably high proportion of passengers changed trains at Finsbury Park, a figure of 80 per cent being quoted for 1905.

The proposed timetable for up trains during the morning peak after electrification is given in Figure 4, the North London services having their train numbers shown in brackets. It will also be noted that there were several

TIME TABLE FOR PROPOSED ELECTRIC

UP TRAINS.

No. OF TRAIN.	14	(21)	33	28	6	15	34	16	(12)	9	29	(1)	21	22	(2)	(35)	13	1
New Barnet	...	...	...	7 55	...	...	...	...		...	8 5	...	...	...	...	...	...	...
Enfield	...	...	...	...	...	...	8 8	...	8 0	...	...	8 5	8 10	...	...	8 12	...	
Wood Green	...	...	8 2	8 4	...	...	8 8	...	8 10	...	8 13	...	8 15	8 20	...	8 18	8 22	
High Barnet	7 45	...	...	...	7 53	...	7 55		Steam train from Hatfield.	...	...	...	...	...	...	...	...	
Edgware	...	7 49	...	...	...	...	...			...	...	...	...	...	...	...	8 10	
Finchley (Church End)	7 51	7 57	...	...	...	8 2	...	8 4		...	...	...	...	...	...	...	8 16	
Alexandra Palace	...	...	...	...	...	...	...	...		...	...	...	...	...	...	...	...	
Muswell Hill	...	...	...	8 3	...	...	...	...		8 10	...	8 13	...	8 16	...	...	...	
Highgate	8 0	8 3	...	8 7	8 8	...	8 10		8 14	...	8 17	...	8 20	...	...	8 23	
FINSBURY PARK arr.	8 6	8 9	8 9	8 11	8 12	8 14	8 15	8 16	8 17	8 17	8 19	8 20	8 22	8 24	8 25	8 25	8 27	8 29
,, ,, dep.	8 7	...	8 10	8 12	8 13	8 15	8 17	8 17	8 19		8 20	8 21	...	8 24	8 25	...	8 26	8 30
York Road	...	...	...	8 17	...	...	...	8 22		...	...	8 26	...	...	8 30	...	...	
KING'S CROSS (G.N.R.)	8 12	...	8 15	...	8 18	8 20	8 22		8 24	...	8 25	...	8 29	...	...	8 31	...	8 35
MOORGATE	...	...	...	8 24	...	...	...	8 29		...	...	8 33	...	8 37	...	...	...	
REMARKS.		Returns empty, starts again from High Barnet 8.51.	To Broad St.	Returns empty, starts again from Wood Green. 8.38.		Returns empty, starts again from Muswell Hill 8.58.		Returns empty, starts again from Wood Green 8.38.		To Broad St.			To Broad St.	Returns empty, starts again from Enfield 9.13.		To Broad St.	Returns empty, starts again from Wood Green 9.25.		To Broad St.

UP TRAINS (Continued).

No. OF TRAIN.	32	10	(16)	3	33	11	(17)	14	(3)	27	37	20	12	34	(12)	38	(4)
New Barnet	8 50	...	...	...	...	...	...	...	...	...	9 5		...	...	...	9 14	
Enfield	...	...	8 48	...	...	...	8 51	...	...	8 57	...		...	...	9 7	...	
Wood Green	8 55	...	8 58	...	9 2	...	9 4	...	...	9 7	9 13		...	9 15	9 17	9 22	
High Barnet	...	...	...	...	...	...	...	8 51	...	...	8 57	Steam train from Hatfield.	...	...	...	...	Steam train from Cambridge.
Edgware	...	...	...	8 47	...	...	...	...	...	...	...		...	...	...	...	
Finchley (Church End)	...	...	...	8 54	...	...	...	9 0	...	...	9 6		...	...	...	...	
Alexandra Palace	...	...	...	...	...	...	...	...	...	...	...		9 9	...	...	9 15	
Muswell Hill	...	8 53	...	...	...	9 0	...	...	9 4	...	...		9 12	...	...	9 20	
Highgate	...	8 57	...	9 1	...	9 4	...	9 6	9 8	...	...	9 12	9 16	...	...	...	
FINSBURY PARK arr.	9 2	9 3	9 5	9 6	9 9	9 9	9 10	9 11	9 14	9 11	9 17	9 18	9 21	9 22	9 24	9 26	9 27
,, ,, dep.	9 3	9 5	...	9 7	9 10	9 12	...	9 14	...	9 15	9 18	9 20	9 23	9 23	...	9 27	9 29
York Road	...	...	...	...	...	...	...	...	...	9 20	...		9 29	...	...	...	
KING'S CROSS (G.N.R.)	9 7	9 10	...	9 13	9 15	9 17	...	9 19	...	...	9 22	9 25	9 28	...	...	9 31	9 33
MOORGATE	...	...	...	...	...	...	...	...	...	9 27	...		9 35	...	...	...	
REMARKS.				To Broad St.	Returns empty, starts again from Wood Green 9.32.		To Broad St.		To Broad St.				Returns empty, starts again from Wood Green 9.44.	To Broad St.		To Board St.	

Figure 4 *Proposed morning peak timetable for up trains in the 1903 Great Northern Railway suburban electrification report.* (Courtesy National Railway Museum, York)

additional GN steam-hauled trains which originated at Hitchin or further afield. During the two hours between 8 and 10 am, this new service would have given an overall increase of some 57 per cent in the number of seats available to Finsbury Park, as shown in Table 1 (page 20), which is again taken from the 1903 report. It should be emphasized that the figures given for the number of passengers actually refer to seats, and those in the columns headed 'Electric' also include the Great Northern and North London steam-worked services referred to above. This period on a weekday was the busiest time on the line, and determined the number of electric trains required, the

SERVICE FROM 8 to 10 a.m. (Table No. 2.)

Note: —Broad Street trains are separately numbered and their numbers shown thus ( ).

30	23	(18)	17	(14)	37	33	(8)	(19)	24	38	34	6	25	13	(15)	(9)	31	18	26	9	19
8 14	...		8 19	...	...	...	...	8 26	...	...	...	...	...	...			8 42	...	...	...	...
...	8 14		...	...	8 19	...	...	...	8 25	...	...	...	8 30	...	8 32		...	...	8 40	...	...
8 23	8 25		8 28	...	8 30	...	8 33	...	8 35	8 35	...	8 38	8 40	...	8 42		8 50	...	8 50	...	...
...	...		8 15	...	...	...	...	8 20	...	...	...	...	...	...		8 31	...	8 34	...	...	8 39
...	...		8 24	...	...	...	...	8 29	...	...	...	...	8 30		8 40	...	8 43	...	...	8 48
...	...		...		8 28	...	8 35	...	...	...	8 31		8 38	...	8 36		...	...	...	8 48	
...	...		8 30	...	8 32	...		...	...	8 38	8 38		8 42	...	8 41		8 46	...	8 49	...	8 52	8 56
8 30	8 32	8 34	8 35	8 36	8 37	8 38	8 40	8 41	8 43	8 43	8 43	8 45	8 47	8 47	8 50	8 50	8 51	8 52	8 54	8 55	8 57
8 31	8 33	8 35	...	8 37	...	8 39	8 41	...	...	8 44	8 45	8 47	8 50	8 48	8 51	...	8 53	...	8 55	8 56	8 58
8 36	...	...	8 42	...	...	...	...	...	8 49	...	...	8 53	8 56	...	...	...	9 2	...	...	...
8 43	8 38	8 40	...	...	8 44	8 46	...	...	8 56	8 50	8 52	8 55	9 0	9 4	...	9 8	...	8 59	...	9 9	...

4	21	(10)	35	23	6	(5)	33	(20)	36	(6)	22	(11)	13	31	34	35	18	17	24	(7)	(2)
...	...	...	...	...	...	...	...	9 24	...	...	...	...	...	9 37	...	...	...	...	...	...	...
...	9 13	...	...	9 18	...	...	...	9 32	9 34	...	9 28	...	...	...	9 45	9 44	9 47	...	...	9 41	...
...	9 23	...	9 25	9 28	...	...	...	...	...	9 20	9 38	...	9 25	...	...	...	...	9 34	...	9 51	...
...	...	9 10	...	...	9 15	...	...	...	...	9 29	...	...	...	...	...	...	9 33	...	...	...	9 53
9 9	...	...	...	...	9 24	...	...	...	...	...	...	9 34	...	...	...	...	9 41	9 43	...	...	10 0
9 16	...	9 19	...	...	...	9 28	...	...	...	9 34	...	9 38	...	...	...	...	...	...	9 48	...
9 23	...	9 25	...	...	9 30	9 32	...	9 35	...	9 38	9 40	9 49	9 49	9 51	9 54	9 54	9 56	9 58	9 52	10 7
9 29	9 30	9 31	9 32	9 35	9 36	9 36	9 38	9 39	9 41	9 42	9 45	9 46	9 50	9 50	9 52	9 55	9 55	9 57	9 58	10 14
9 30	9 31	...	9 33	9 36	9 38	9 38	...	9 40	...	9 42	9 45	9 46	9 51	9 56	...	10 0	...	10 4	...
9 35	...	...	...	...	9 44	...	...	...	...	...	9 51	...	...	9 54	9 57	10 0	...	10 2	...
9 42	9 36	...	9 38	9 41	...	9 42	...	9 45	...	9 47	9 49	...	9 58	...	10 3	...	...	10 7	...	10 11	...

(Vertical column notes, reading across: "Steam train from Hitchin." / "Returns empty, starts again from Enfield 9.18." / "To Broad St." / "To Broad St." / "Returns empty, starts again from Wood Green 9.2." / "To Broad St." / "To Broad St." / "Returns empty, starts again from Wood Green 9.15." / "To Broad St." / "Steam train from Hatfield." / "To Broad St." / "To Broad St." / "Returns empty, starts again from New Barnet 9.37." — lower half: "To Broad St." / "Returns empty, starts again from Wood Green 9.47." / "Steam train from Dunstable." / "To Broad St." / "To Broad St." / "Steam train from Cambridge." / "To Broad St." / "To Broad St." / "To Broad St." / "To Broad St.")

total coming to 58, of which three would have been of 16 coaches for the New Barnet services.

Train performance is covered in great detail in the report, and a number of interesting points emerge. The traction motors proposed were the Dick, Kerr No 100 Type 'A', which were referred to as having a rating — possibly a 1-hour one — of 100 hp. Their characteristic curve showed that they could actually produce a maximum of 165 hp, which would be achieved at 8 mph with 33-inch diameter wheels and the gear ratio proposed. However, they were not rated at this in the configuration suggested for the Great Northern scheme, where they would have been installed in pairs on the bogies, as shown in Figure 5. Starting with them connected electrically in series, the change-over to the parallel configuration would have taken place after about

Table 1: No of trains and passengers capable of being carried to London (Finsbury Park) from 8 to 10 am with steam and electric trains in 1903

Time	8 to 9 am					9 to 10 am				
	No of trains		No of passengers			No of trains		No of passengers		
Route	Steam	Electric	Steam	Electric	Increase (%)	Steam	Electric	Steam	Electric	Increase (%)
From New Barnet ...	4	6	2,624	4,512	71.9	4	5	2,624	4,596	75.15
„ High Barnet ...	4	6	2,624	4,248	61.89	5	7	3,280	4,956	51.09
„ Enfield ...	7	10	4,592	7.080	54.18	6	8	3,936	5,664	43.9
„ Alexandra Palace	6	8	3,936	5,664	43.9	6	9	3,936	6,372	61.89
„ Edgware ...	2	3	1,312	2,124	61.89	2	3	1,312	2,124	61.89
„ Wood Green ...	4	6	2,624	4,248	61.89	4	6	2,624	4,248	61.89
Total ...	27	39	17,712	27,876	57.38	27	38	17,712	27,960	57.85

Total from 8 to 10 am			
No of Trains		No of Passengers	
Steam	Electric	Steam	Electric
54	77	35,424	55,836

6 seconds, at 8 mph. Under these conditions, with all the resistances in the circuit, each of them would have delivered 150 hp, which would have been maintained up to about 18 mph while the notching was completed.

One of the standard trains had a designed maximum tractive effort of 34,749 lbs force (lbs.f). Running fully loaded, the weight of the three motor coaches totalled almost 73 tons, which would have given an adhesion factor of 0.21, rising to 0.25 if there were no passengers travelling in the motor coaches. By comparison, with a nominal tractive effort of 32,909 lbs.f., and a total adhesion weight of 66 tons, the corresponding factor for an 'A3' 'Pacific' was 0.22. Drivers of the latter had a very difficult task in preventing them from slipping excessively when leaving King's Cross. In spite of the better weight distribution on the bogie axles of the electrics, it would have been unlikely that the motormen of the proposed 1903 multiple-units could have used full power up the 1 in 107 through the smoky tunnels at the exit from the terminus.

At higher speeds with the 1903 stock, the Back Electro-Motive Force would have caused the current to fall rapidly, and, with no field-weakening, the balancing speeds were quite low, as shown in Table 2. At 41 mph the horsepower being produced by a standard train was down to 400. The advances in electric traction that took place in the following 75 years are well demonstrated by the fact that in 1978 I noted a Class '313' out-distancing my Class '47'-hauled train, which was doing 65 mph between New Southgate and Oakleigh Park up the long 1 in 200 gradient to Potters Bar.

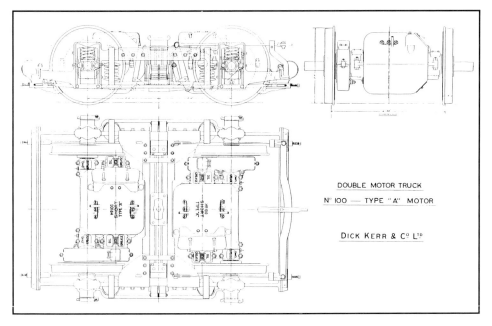

DOUBLE MOTOR TRUCK

N° 100 — TYPE "A" MOTOR

DICK KERR & C° L^{TD}

Figure 5 *Diagram of the Dick, Kerr power bogie for the 1903 Great Northern Railway suburban electric train conversions.* (Courtesy National Railway Museum, York)

Overall the empty power/weight ratio of 6.2 hp/ton for one of the 1903 standard trains would have been not all that much lower than the corresponding figure of 8.6 for a Class '313' set, which provides a reminder that it is not wise to use this factor to compare performances of very dissimilar types of motive power, whether separated by age or type of traction. For a given train there is also a trade-off between the initial acceleration and the balancing speeds if the engineers change the ratio used for the step-down gears between

Table 2: Balancing speeds for the proposed Great Northern electric trains

Gradient (1 in)	Balancing speed (mph)
Rising	
60	26.8
100	30.8
200	35.0
300	37.4
400	38.0
Level	41.2
Falling	
200	50.0
100	50+, with power off

the motor and its driven axle.

Back in 1903, Dick, Kerr went into the performance of electric trains in appreciable detail, plotting speed and current for each section of the different routes. As would be expected from the figures given in Table 2, speeds were not very exciting, even on the New Barnet expresses, while the stopping trains were shown as reaching their highest speed — 50 mph — in the tunnels outside King's Cross, 40 seconds before the stop. This was after calling at Holloway, where there was a station until 1915, and one wonders if it really would have been possible to cut 2 minutes off the 7-minute steam timing for the run in from Finsbury Park, inclusive of a 20-second halt at Holloway. Even so, appreciable time savings were predicted for the all-stations trains, the largest cut in the running times being of 9 minutes in each direction between King's Cross and High Barnet, and 6 minutes on the down trip to Alexandra Palace. The New Barnet 'Flyers', with stops at New Southgate and Finsbury Park, would have saved only 2 minutes in the up direction and 1½ in the down, compared with their existing steam equivalents. The projected high speeds through the tunnels, plus the low balancing speeds, made the performance more akin to that of urban rapid-transit units rather than suburban trains.

The report does not give any figures for the capital cost of the electrification proposals, and the case was not sufficiently attractive for the Great Northern to go ahead with it, but the information it contains provides a very interesting example of railway electrification practice at the turn of the century. Great Northern commuters did, however, benefit from improvements that took place when the steam-hauled services were extensively revised in 1905. This followed the arrival of Ivatt's Class 'L1' 0-8-2 tanks, the prototype of which had appeared in 1903, and represented a big advance on his 4-4-2Ts, which had previously worked the King's Cross suburban services. The extra power and adhesion of the new design was particularly useful on the steeply graded High Barnet line. Two years later they were to be joined by his Class 'N1' 0-6-2Ts, and Gresley's larger-boilered versions of these — the 'N2s' — were to see steam out on the King's Cross suburban services.

The opening of the Great Northern & City tube line to Finsbury Park in February 1904 also gave passengers an alternative route to Moorgate, and in the first six months of the following year it handled a total of 6.4 million passengers. The 1903 electrification scheme would have left the North London working its trains over the Great Northern by steam, so it is not surprising that it, in turn, considered electrifying its main line in the following year. However, it was not until 1911, after the NLR had amalgamated with the London & North Western, that electric trains actually appeared, and one of the 1916-built motor coaches used on its line — but never on the Great Northern — is now preserved in the National Collection.

The North Eastern Tyneside electrification of 1904

We now move northwards to Newcastle, where the North Eastern Railway's Tyneside suburban lines were successfully electrified in 1904, the official inauguration taking place on 29 March. Public services started on the same day between New Bridge Street station in Newcastle and Benton, and the whole of the system was successfully changed from steam to electric traction overnight between 30 June and 1 July of that year. This made the North Eastern Railway the first main-line company in Britain to introduce a complete electrification scheme. The first trial trip with an electric train had taken place in 1903, the date for that notable event having been fixed for 27 September, which was not to be the last major railway occasion along the East Coast Route to be celebrated on an anniversary of the opening of the Stockton & Darlington Railway.

A map of the original plans is given in Figure 6, but changes were made during the work. As a result, the line running westwards from Gosforth to Ponteland was never electrified, and was to lose its passenger service in 1929. The semi-circular line from Manors Yard down to Quayside was also electrified, and a pair of Bo-Bo electric locomotives purchased from Brush continued to work this steeply graded stretch for 60 years before being withdrawn. They were able to start a 150-ton train on the 1 in 27 gradient, and accelerate it to 10 mph, while, on the level, they could reach 14 mph with a load of 300 tons.

At the 1904 annual meeting of the British Association for the Advancement of Science, held at Cambridge, a comprehensive survey of the Tyneside electrification was given in one of the papers, which was delivered by Charles Merz and William McLellan, those Tyneside pioneers who did so much to develop electric supply systems and railway electrification. Entitled *The Use of Electricity on the North Eastern Railway and upon Tyneside*, it showed how advanced that area was with the provision of such public supply systems. From its inauguration in 1890, the capacity provided by the Newcastle-upon-Tyne Electric Supply Co had risen steadily to nearly 2,700 hp by 1900, but consumption then took off, with the result that they had to increase their installed horsepower to no less than 38,000 in the next three years. Much of this was used in the heavy industry which clustered along the banks of the river, a map in the paper showing more than 65 major companies whose works, employing some 40,000 men, used electrical power. The area's self-suffiency in coal supplies was also demonstrated by the inclusion of another map, marking the location of well over 200 collieries situated between the middle of Co Durham and Morpeth.

With the availability of considerable power generation capacity on Tyneside, the North Eastern Railway opted to purchase its electricity, rather than generate its own. To provide the railway's requirements and meet the rising demand from elsewhere, the Newcastle-upon-Tyne Electric Supply Co supplemented the capacity already available from its Blaydon and Neptune Bank Power Stations by building a new one at Carville, on the north bank of the river. The supply company had strong views about the economies of size and its beneficial effect on electricity costs was later to make other companies envious of the North Eastern Railway's ability to obtain cheap power. The electricity was supplied to the third rail at 600 volts through four Substations, with a total capacity of 15,000 hp. The largest of these, at Pandon Dene, just north of Manors station, contained four 1,100-hp rotary converters, each of

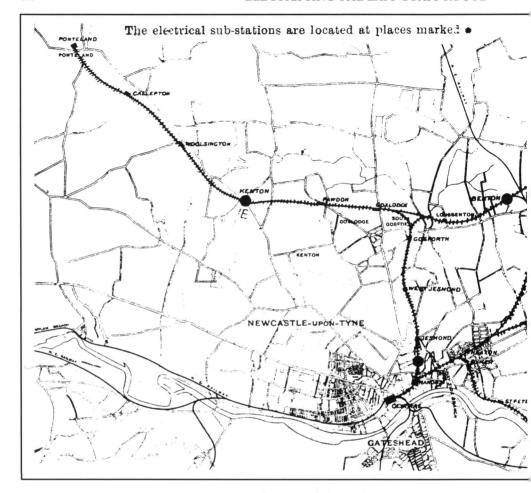

Figure 6 *Map of the North Eastern Railway's proposed electric lines on Tyneside.* (The Railway Magazine)

them capable of handling overloads of 200 per cent for short periods.

The stock used for the passenger services was designed to be operated in multiple, although it was not formed into coupled sets as we know them. By 1910 the North Eastern had a fleet of 106 electric vehicles, all with open saloons, 62 of them being motor coaches. They ran in formations of between one and nine coaches, which meant that some of them had to have driving controls at both ends. In the main, trains were made up with motor coaches and trailers in equal proportions, although the 1904 diagram reproduced in Figure 7 shows a three-car set with only a single trailer. Electric parcels vans were also to appear, and these were used to carry, amongst other things, fish from ports such as Tynemouth and Cullercoats. They were also capable of being operated in pairs at opposite ends of rakes of ordinary coaches equipped with through control wires. In this guise they were used on holiday specials to the coast, as well as on regular workmen's trains on the Riverside

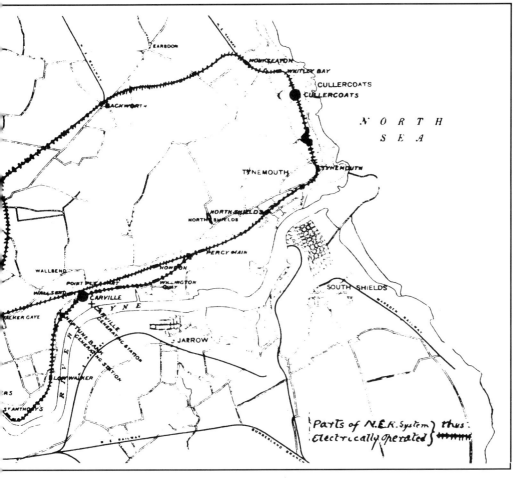

line, with a remarkable selection of old six-wheeled coaches marshalled between them.

As well as going in for the installation of large-capacity generating sets, Merz and McLellan also advocated the use of higher-power EMUs, because this markedly reduced the power consumption by permitting drivers to coast without losing time. Their British Association paper showed the classic comparisons between steam and electric suburban stopping trains, and also the effect of providing the electrics with greater installed power. Even at the quite modest speeds achieved by 1904 electric trains, on a flat-out run over a one-mile stretch between stations, they were able to save 40 seconds on the 3-minute timing required by steam. If the electric was to start coasting at 30 mph, after a minute, it would still clip 20 seconds off the usual operating time for a steam train, which would need the regulator to remain open for 140 seconds to reach 29 mph, before coasting and braking to a stop. By installing more power in the electrics it was possible to cut just over 20 seconds from the motoring time for a one-mile section. In spite of maintaining the same overall time and scheduled average speed, the higher-powered unit would use

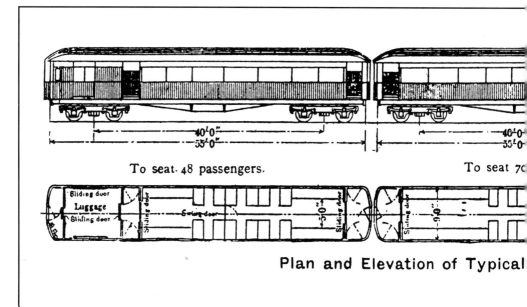

To seat. 48 passengers.   To seat 7c

Plan and Elevation of Typical

Figure 7 *Diagram of a three-coach Tyneside electric train of 1904.*(The Railway Magazine)

only five-sixths of the power.

From 1910, after the short connecting line from New Bridge Street to Manors had been built, the basic service was a circular one, being worked in and out of the electrified bays at the east end of Newcastle Central station. As can be followed from Figure 6, in the clockwise direction this ran via Manors, and then northwards to Gosforth, before turning east to reach the coast at Whitley Bay. After serving the coastal ports, resorts and dormitory towns, the trains turned back up the river at Tynemouth, joining the main East Coast Route at Heaton to continue through Manors back into Central station. The running time for the 20.1 miles, inclusive of stops at virtually all the stations, was approximately an hour.

Tyneside, like many other large industrial areas, had seen the development of many electric tramway lines, and these had siphoned off virtually all the railway passengers making journeys of two miles or less on parallel routes. The NER actually lost 4 million passengers — 40 per cent of its total — in two years. However, these only represented about 10 per cent of those who used the new trams, the rest being 'entirely new traffic generated by the increased facilities afforded'. In the words of Merz and McLellan, the North Eastern Railway adopted electric traction '. . . not so much with a view to retaining the short-distance passenger, as to developing suburban traffic, and for dealing as efficiently as possible with a frequent inter-urban service over some 40 miles of line.'

The basic circular service was thus stepped up from approximately hourly, in the case of steam, to quarter-hourly. This increase in frequency, coupled

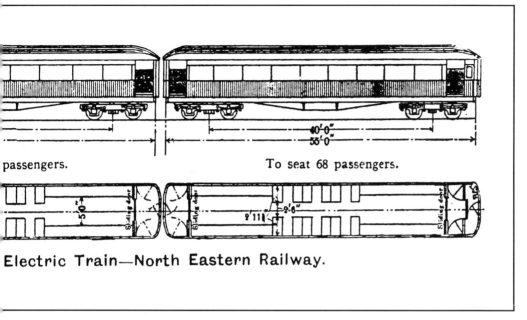

passengers.   To seat 68 passengers.

Electric Train—North Eastern Railway.

with a 20 per cent saving in time, considerably added to the railway's appeal as a mode of transport. On the other hand, as has been the case with the recent introduction of the 'Express' services on BR, the trains were shorter, decreasing from 6.5 coaches in steam days to an average of 3.1 with the new electrics. There were additional short-distance workings at peak periods, but the services along the Riverside line via Walker were less frequent, running mainly at shift-change times to suit those employed in the factories alongside the route.

While the majority of services between Newcastle and the coast ran via the circular route described, there were a few expresses which used the East Coast Main Line between Heaton and Benton, where they diverged to the right to pick up their usual route. This shortened the distance as well as enabling some quite fast running to take place, particularly with up trains on the 1 in 295 descent southwards from Benton. A few years ago Lt Commander E. Corlett described to me how he occasionally used one of these trains in the late 1920s:

'I was at school in Jesmond, and can vouch for the modest speeds of the Tyneside electrics. From memory, the average speed start-to-stop between Jesmond and Monkseaton was something like 21 mph. Allowing for stops it was 27 mph. However, the high point, if one missed the 8.20 from Monkseaton in the morning, was to get the Businessmen's Express which left at 8.30. Of course, it was more than our lives were worth to take a regular's seat! It did give us schoolboys a vantage point because we had to stand in the end aisle and so could time the train. The 8.30 express took the Benton spur on to the main line and so saved three-quarters of a mile and 10 minutes to Manors, whence we used to run like hell back to Jesmond to get to school for nine o'clock. The great thrill was to clock 40 mph between the spur and Heaton.'

Although the electric service was a great improvement for most users, there was some difficulty with first class passengers. In early 1905 *The Railway Magazine* reported that 'passengers ready and willing to pay first class fares are in revolt', having earlier referred to 'the democratic "one-class" train'. This is rather odd, as 24 of the first 88 electric vehicles included first class seating. The matter came to a head on 9 January when there was a well-attended protest meeting at the Station Hotel. It was chaired by no less a personage than the Duke of Northumberland, who proposed five motions condemning the railway's tactics. He claimed that the fault was entirely that of the Directors, 'whose ideas seemed to be that the public were like so many cattle or sheep'. The resolutions were carried unanimously and the meeting formed itself into an association to secure the redress of its grievances.

A month later the magazine gave some figures from which it was claimed that the company's accounts for the second half of 1904 showed that £6,300 had been lost because of the absence of first class fares on the electric trains, which had only generated £9,100 in additional receipts. Figures were given for the cost of electrifying the line and obtaining new stock, but the latter did not tie up with those quoted elsewhere. On the strength of these it was claimed that the electrification lost £10,875 during the six months concerned. Without having access to that particular set of accounts, I cannot help feeling that the figures, as presented, could well have been misleading, and probably originated from the users' association in an attempt to bolster their grievances! As the North Eastern Railway had undertaken the electrification with a view to stimulating traffic in the longer term, the first six months' results would, in any case, hardly be typical of how it was hoped they would develop.

A longer-term picture did emerge in 1913 from the chapter 'Electric Traction on Railways', which was contributed to Volume 6 of *Modern Railway Working* by Philip Dawson, the Consulting Electrical Engineer for the London, Brighton & South Coast Railway. The vital comparison is given in Table 3, which has been reproduced verbatim from the 1913 work:

Table 3 North Eastern Railway electrification results

Items	Half-year ending 1903 (Steam	Half-year ending 1905 (Electric)	Percentage increase
Gross earnings	£129,000	£151,000	17.1
Running costs	£42,761	£47,779	11.7
Ratio of costs to receipts	33.2%	33.8%	—
Locomotive costs per train mile	14.5d (6.0p)	7.75d (2.8p)	—
Passengers carried	2,844,000	3,548,000	24.8

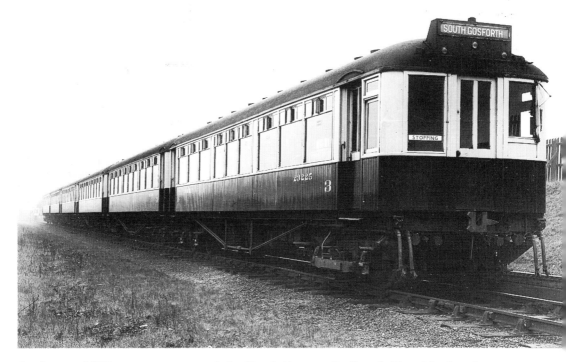

In August 1918, over a quarter of the North Eastern Railway's Tyneside electric vehicles were lost in a fire at the car sheds. They were replaced during 1920–2 with new coaches built at York, which had semi-elliptical roofs instead of the previous clerestory type. A six-car set of the new stock is shown in this photograph, taken in LNER days, after the leading driving motor coach had acquired a '2' prefix to its number. (National Railway Museum, York)

It will be seen that passengers had increased by a quarter within two years, although the gross earnings were not up in the same proportion. There was a significant reduction in the locomotive costs per train mile, in spite of the fact that Philip Dawson considered that those for steam traction were somewhat low. This was because, with this form of traction, it was not possible to abstract the costs for locomotives on suburban workings from those of the whole fleet. While not directly disproving the specific arguments put forward by the protestors in 1905, this information does show that the North Eastern had improved its financial position following the change in motive power, and most passengers on Tyneside had certainly benefited. In the longer term, the rising demand required the construction of a further 35 electric coaches by 1915, and passenger totals had topped the 10 million mark again two years earlier.

Details of some other aspects of the electric services were included in an earlier paper, given by C. A. Harrison, the North Eastern's Chief Engineer, to the Institution of Civil Engineers' symposium on railway electrification. On the operating side he mentioned that the railway was scheduling 15 electric trains out of Newcastle Central during the peak evening hour, each of them carrying over 500 passengers. Five of them were booked to leave at one-minute intervals, and only two terminal platforms were required, which meant that station operations were eased considerably. During the summer, as many as 100,000 people a day had been taken to the seaside, and had returned home during a three-hour spell in the evening. In steam days the last unfortunate passengers on Bank Holidays had been known not to arrive back in Newcastle until 2 am.

In the 1930s, considerable changes took place on the Tyneside electric system, with the arrival of 64 new articulated two-car EMUs built by Metropolitan Cammell to Gresley's instructions. Of all-steel construction, they were much faster than the originals, and the time round the circle was cut appreciably. In 1950 it was down to 53 minutes, in spite of an extra station having been built at West Monkseaton. The line to South Shields was also electrified in the 1930s, resulting in the third rail being laid over part of the celebrated diamond crossing at the east end of Newcastle Central station. The best of the old vehicles were extensively refurbished for the South Tyneside lines, and these, in turn, were replaced by a batch of BR two-car non-corridor sets in the early 1950s. The latter included a very limited amount of first class seating, and, when they later joined the rest of the class in the Southern Region, these were down-rated. Knowledgeable travellers, aware of the numbers of the former Tyneside sets, could thus seek out what appeared to be an ordinary red-upholstered second class compartment, but ride in first class comfort. As far as is known, the Southern commuters did not follow their North Eastern predecessors in complaining about the absence of first class accommodation!

The reason for the return of these Eastleigh-built 1950s sets to the south of England was the abandonment of electric traction on the South Tyneside lines in January 1963, a considerable set-back to the cause of railway electrification. The reason given was that the large fixed costs associated with electric traction made it impossible to continue the services, which had seen passenger journeys fall from $3\frac{1}{2}$ to $2\frac{1}{2}$ million between 1956 and 1961. Dr Beeching is said to have been disillusioned by electrification, or perhaps by the way the work on the West Coast Route was being carried out. In the light of subsequent information on the relative operating costs of diesel and electric multiple-units, it is hard to believe that cost statement as it stood. Major renewals of some of the electrical supply equipment may have been needed, and there was certainly a surplus of DMUs following all the contemporary branch line closures, while the new EMUs could be redeployed on the Southern. The real reasons behind the abandonment are not clear, but one suggestion at the time was that the change-over was intended to be a warning to the electrical supply industry about the price the railways were prepared to pay for power.

Although the South Tyneside line changed to diesels, with slightly longer journey times, the articulated Gresley EMUs continued to operate over the original system north of the river. Their days, however, were also numbered, and they too were replaced by DMUs in the summer of 1967. Ironically that was the same year that the government produced a White Paper outlining its national plans for dealing with increasing urban traffic and fostering better public transport. The legislation that followed saw the formation of the Tyne & Wear Passenger Transport Executive (PTE) in 1969, and one of the earliest studies commissioned by that body was to lead to the construction of the Tyne & Wear Metro. Its Act was obtained in 1973, and construction began the following year. In central Tyneside it mainly follows new alignments, either underground, or on viaducts or bridges, including a new one across the Tyne. Clear of these areas, for most of the time the trains operate over tracks that were once part of the 1904 electrified system, although the Metro's running lines are almost entirely separated from those of BR.

Today's articulated Metrocars, in their distinctive yellow and white livery, are classed as Light Rapid Transit Vehicles, and operate from 1,500-volt overhead wires, rather than the third rail. They even serve Bankfoot, on the Ponteland branch, which was never reached by their North Eastern predecessors. When the Metro was opened, the PTE was also directly running the buses, so their routes were designed to feed the trains at interchanges like Heworth and Four Lane Ends, and they did not operate road services crossing the river bridges. Even though deregulation now enables any operator to run buses wherever it may be found profitable, the Metro continues to play an extremely important part in keeping Tyneside on the move, with the rail/bus interchanges still being advertised and well used. Parliamentary authority for a new line from Bankfoot to the Airport was obtained in 1989, and the new branch, with an intermediate park-and-ride station at Callerton alongside the A696 bypass, is due to open in January 1992.

The York–Newcastle proposals of 1919

The first proposal to electrify a main-line stretch of the East Coast Route was put forward by the North Eastern Railway just after the end of the First World War. The report by Vincent L. Raven, the Chief Mechanical Engineer, and H. A. Watson, the General Superintendent, is dated October 1919, and consists of just 18 pages, including two coloured diagrams. Although this seems a modest document for such a major scheme, it only represents the tip of the iceberg as far as the work that was put in on the proposal is concerned, much of it by Merz & McLellan, the consulting engineers for the project.

It was not, however, the North Eastern's first main-line railway electrification scheme, as the company had converted its Shildon–Newport freight line during the war. Authorized in 1913, it was partially experimental, having the advantage that 'as it was purely a mineral line, no dislocation of passenger service would result from any failures'. At that time there was a steady flow of coal eastwards from the concentration yard at Shildon to the Erimus sorting yard at Newport. Situated just west of Thornaby, between the River Tees and the passenger lines to Middlesbrough, Newport split up incoming trains for the numerous small works on Tees-side. Completion of the electrification was delayed by the war, but the ten 1,100-hp Bo-Bo locomotives went into operation in July 1916, and had worked virtually all the traffic over the line for the three years prior to the appearance of the 1919 Report.

One of the North Eastern Railway's Bo-Bos waits to leave Newport for Shildon with the Dynamometer Car on a test run. In 1920 No 8 had been fitted with a De Normanville clear-view screen in the cab window. Widely used on ships, the rapidly-rotating disc flung the water droplets outwards, thus giving the driver a clear view. (National Railway Museum, York)

The 1,500-volt dc overhead system was used, with two Feeder Stations being provided for the 18½-mile route. These took power direct from the electricity supply company and fed it into the overhead wires after rectification. They thus differed from Substations, where the power for the overhead wires or third rail came from a railway-owned distribution system, usually at a lower voltage than the supply company's system. One of these Feeder Stations was at the east end of the Erimus Yards, but the other was built close to the over-bridge which took the electrified line across the East Coast Route on the skew, just over a mile north of Aycliffe. It had thus been sited where it could also potentially be used for any future electrification of the north-south trunk line.

The 1919 proposals were on a much larger scale than those for the mineral line, and involved the electrification of just over 80 miles of the East Coast Route between Newcastle and York, plus the Northallerton–Stockton–Ferryhill loop. This latter section included a stretch of the Shildon–Newport scheme, and this connection would have enabled all the freight traffic between the East Coast Route and the Erimus Yards to be electrically hauled. Over the area concerned, train working was, in those days, largely self-contained, which would mean that a minimum number of additional motive power changes would be required because of the extra form of traction. At the same time it was a busy area, and there were good electricity supplies available, the NER, as we have seen, already taking its power on Tyneside from local commercial systems, rather than generating its own.

In several respects, the plans were extensions of the railway's existing practice, since it had had 15 years' experience of passenger workings, as well as the shorter spell of freight train operation. It had already used overhead and third-rail systems, and a combination of both types was proposed for the new scheme. Third-rail was much cheaper to install, at approximately £2,850 per track mile, compared with £4,340 for overhead wires. On the other hand, the maintenance costs went the other way, being £93/year/track mile for third-rail (up from £50 in 1910), and only £74 for the overhead. The advantages and disadvantages of the two types of supply were discussed in the report, and the decision was made to go primarily for third-rail, but with overhead wires being installed in a number of yards and stations.

It was expected that 282 track miles would be equipped with the third rail, and 115 with overhead wires. The third rail would be fully protected, but the details of how this would be done for a 1,500-volt system are not included, although it was stated that the Consulting Engineer was preparing a special report on this subject. Three years earlier Metz & McLellan had produced such a system for the Central Argentine Railway, using a very deep, asymmetric, U-section rail, mounted on its side, which might have proved difficult to roll in the steel mills. Thought was given to the problem of the pick-up shoes re-engaging with the rails after a gap, which would have to be done at far higher speds than those that prevailed on the Tyneside suburban services. The complex conductor rail section would certainly have made it difficult to provide three-dimensional entries at the ends of these sections, compared with those that are now widespread on the Southern Region and regularly traversed at speeds of 100 mph. To check the proposed system in 1919, some tests were made at Strensall with dummy third rails and shoes fitted to the bodies of one of the NER's 4-4-4 tanks.

In the 1919 Report there is a diagram showing how the two different types of electrification would be applied at Thirsk Junction, where the layout used to be very different from what it is now. Then there were just two tracks between a pair of station platforms. At the York end was the junction with the non-electrified line from Melmerby, while south of that point running loops were located on both sides of the main line. All these tracks, including the crossovers, were to have been equipped with third-rail supplies, like the four-track section continuing northwards towards Northallerton. There were extensive yards on both sides of the line beyond the north end of the platforms, and most of these were to have been given overhead wires. The only major stretches of track not electrified were at the north end of the gravity sorting yard on the up side.

The electrification would have continued through York station to Dringhouses signal box, which served the sidings where the North Eastern exchanged freight trains with 'Foreign Companies' (the pre-grouping companies were very insular!). It was proposed to electrify all the running lines, as well as most of the relief sidings, although some of the platforms at Eaglescliffe were excluded. Presumably the outer sides of its two island platforms were primarily used by the Darlington–Saltburn services in those days, as was still the case at the end of steam. At ordinary 'Roadside Stations', the principle was adopted of only electrifying one or two sidings for horsebox traffic, while in large goods yards the supplies were limited to the shortest practicable stretch at the inlet end of the sidings. On the other hand, it was proposed to take the wires into a number of collieries and quarries situated within a couple of miles of the main line, after suitable arrangements had been made with their owners, whose property the connections were.

Seven Feeder Stations were expected to be sufficient to rectify the electricity from the existing large power companies in the area, and supply it to the tracks. The 1913 one at Aycliffe, built for the Shildon–Newport scheme, would not, after all, be utilized, as the electrification of the Stockton loop made it better to place the next one north of Darlington at Ferryhill, where it could feed both of the lines it was now intended to equip. It was hoped to supply power to the lineside at a cost of 0.708d (0.295p) per kilowatt-hour, the supplies in the North East at that time being cheaper than in other parts of the county. The Feeder Station capacities and cabling were designed to be able to cope with a 50 per cent overload, which it was expected would be enough to handle any likely increase in traffic.

To haul the trains, three types of locomotive were planned. The existing Bo-Bo type from the Shildon–Newport line was considered to be suitable for freight traffic on the main lines, and was expected to be able to average 30 mph, the same speed as slow passenger trains, which would reduce the number of signal checks and the need to put the freights into loops. As a result it was hoped to improve the utilization of the locomotives and crews. For shunting work it was proposed to use locomotives fitted with batteries to enable them to make short forays away from the electrified lines, but it was intended to continue with steam for work in yards. It was also recommended that the goods loops at Bradbury, Ferryhill and Newcastle Central station should be lengthened to enable the electric locomotives to work trains of up to 80 wagons. This represented an increase of 60 per cent in their length, and would have markedly improved the crews' productivity.

For the passenger trains, it was stated that there were three types available which were currently used on high-speed services in the United States, and it was proposed that these should be studied further by Raven and the consulting engineer. Details of various different designs are shown in R. A. S. Hennessey's excellent book *The Electric Railway that Never Was: York–Newcastle 1919* (Oriel Press, 1970, ISBN 0 85362 087 3), which also included an extensive bibliography of this scheme.

For the 1919 Report, the future train service after electrification was studied in detail, to provide an indication of the number of electric locomotives required. Because the passenger traffic had been considerably reduced during the war, the calculations were based on the steam service operating in May 1914. On the other hand, for the corresponding freight calculations, the actual traffic flows on 27 March 1919 were taken. It was considered that 142 trains could have been operated electrically, and a new timetable was made to see how few electric locomotives would be required, taking into account their superior performance. The outcome of this simulation gave the following figures for the number of locomotives required:

Type	Steam	Electric	Saving
Passenger	54	29	25
Freight	155	80	75
Total	209	109	100

Between them the steam locomotives would have worked 13,888 train miles on each weekday, and 5,064 on Sundays. Allowing for shunting and light-engine trips, the annual mileage came to 5,071,585, and would have required 678,746 enginemen's hours. The predominance of freight traffic on the North Eastern is clearly demonstrated by the fact that only 37 per cent of the total mileage involved passenger trains, while the slower speed of the freights meant that they occupied 73 per cent of enginemen's hours. From these figures it was calculated that the operating costs came to £462,213, to which had to be added £177,485 for Repairs and Renewals, plus £19,167 for Depreciation (based on 5 per cent per year over a locomotive's 35-year life). Even if the loops had not been lengthened, and there had been no consequent reduction in the train miles, the average daily mileage expected from the electrics was a very modest 127 — less than one round trip between Newcastle and York!

Compared with these figures for steam, the use of electric locomotives would have altered the annual mileage only marginally, but their superior performance would have given a reduction of almost a quarter in the enginemen's hours, even without any single-manning. The power consumption was worked out in detail, with East Coast expresses being assumed to use 17.5 kilowatt-hours/mile, and an 800-ton freight, 23.3. The annual power bill would have come to £231,841, which was slightly greater than that for the steam locomotives (£228,693), although to be comparable the latter had to be increased by £13,270 per annum for water. (The passenger electric locomotives were to have been equipped for steam heating, but the cost of the water for their boilers appears to have been too small to be worth including.) Overall, the electrification would thus have reduced the operating costs by 16 per cent to £388,549. Adding in the lower figures for Repairs and Renewals, and Depreciation, gave a total of £472,387, compared with £656,865 for steam.

The Civil Engineer estimated that the cost of electrifying the tracks would be £1,302,800. Even in those days work would have been needed on the signalling to immunize it from induced electric currents. £71,800 was to have been spent modifying the track circuits between York and Newcastle, while the automatic signals on the Alne–Thirsk stretch would have required alterations costing a further £22,000. Maintenance costs for the electrification equipment would have amounted to £65,443 per annum, inclusive of a small charge representing the additional expense caused by the presence of the electric equipment during the normal renewal of 12 miles of permanent way each year.

Taking everything into account, and making no allowance for any increased passenger business, the calculations showed that, for a capital outlay of £1,396,000, there would be an annual saving of £121,025, which represented just over 8½ per cent. In today's financial climate that would be a reasonable rate of return for such a scheme, but 80 years ago interest rates were much lower. It was even better than the nominal return on the North Eastern's own shares, with dividends totalling 7½ per cent in that year. On the strength of this it might have been expected that the scheme would go ahead, but the years immediately after the First World War were difficult ones for the country and the railways, and there were still many important points to be clarified in the proposal. Raven did, however, obtain authority to build an express passenger electric locomotive, and its design and manufacture were duly put in hand.

With such a major step forward in technology, the new locomotive, carrying the number 13, was not outshopped from Darlington Works until May 1922. This visually-impressive machine, weighing just over 100 tons, was a 2–Co–2 design, with the six 300-hp motors rigidly mounted in the central body section. Pairs of them powered the three driving axles through quill drives, the ends of which transmitted the tractive effort to the driving wheels by means of coil springs. These driving wheels were the same diameter as those on the NERs express passenger steam locomotives — 6 feet 9 inches — and had a complicated pattern of spokes to distribute the tractive effort to the rims. The electrical equipment was provided by Metropolitan-Vickers from its Trafford Park works, and thus came from a predecessor of GEC Alsthom, which has supplied the Class '91s' for the present electrification. The specifi-

The first electric locomotive for the East Coast Main Line — Raven's 2–Co–2, No 13, for the North Eastern Railway, as turned out of Darlington Works in 1922. Each of the four motors of today's Class '91s' has a higher continuous power output than this 1922 locomotive, which weighed a third as much again as the new InterCity 140 mph design. The unusual spoke design on the driving wheels can be seen, together with the coil springs which transmitted the tractive forces to them from the quill shafts. (National Railway Museum, York)

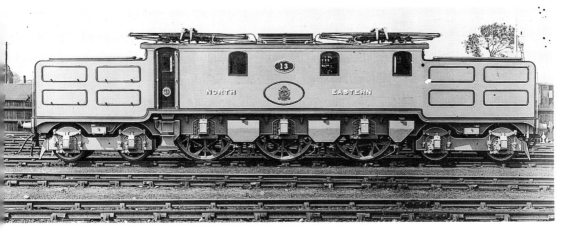

cation called for the locomotive to be able to restart a 450-ton train up a 1 in 78 bank, which was a gradient that did not exist on the NER main line. However, the final climb through St Margaret's Tunnel towards Edinburgh Waverley is inclined at this figure, so clearly the North Eastern was thinking ahead with its new express locomotive. The locomotive cost £27,767 — a considerable sum for its time — and was, furthermore, over-budget to the tune of nearly 40 per cent. Allowing for 65 years' inflation, the cost was equivalent to £1 million at 1987 prices, which makes an interesting comparison with the Class '91s'. When the contract for those 31 locomotives was signed in late 1986, their cost was given as £1.1 million each.

Finished in the standard NER express passenger livery of apple green, and fully lined out, No 13 ran a number of trials between Shildon and Newport, although the speed limitations on this freight-only line did not really give it the opportunity to display its full capabilities. Photographs nevertheless exist of it pulling a 17-coach train, including the North Eastern Railway's Dynamometer Car, which later in its life was to be whisked down Stoke Bank at 126 mph behind *Mallard*. At 65 mph, No 13 had a tractive effort of 8,400 lbs.f. (3.75 tons force), which was comfortably in excess of Churchward's aim of 2 tons force at 70 mph which he required from his express passenger 4–6–0s for trains such as the 'Cornish Riviera'. The corresponding drawbar horsepowers work out at 1,460 and 840, giving the electric a 75 per cent advantage over the best express steam locomotive of the day.

By the time No 13 had been tested and found to perform satisfactorily, the climate for the electrification scheme had changed considerably. R. A. S. Hennessey describes in detail the reasons for this, many of which pre-date the grouping of our railway companies, which is erroneously believed by many to have been the cause of its abandonment. The copy of the 1919 Report in the Library at the National Railway Museum contains numerous manuscript alterations to the costing figures in the appendices, but there is also a separate sheet of typewritten figures, which puts the proposals in a very different light.

Coming from the Chief Engineer's Office at Darlington, it is dated 9 June 1921, almost a year before No 13 emerged from the Works, and the comparative cost figures for steam and electric traction are very different from those in the original report of two years earlier. There is no covering commentary, so the reasons for the changes are not immediately obvious, but all the figures are much lower than the earlier versions. For each category of the costs, the percentage reduction is much the same for both schemes. Repairs and Renewals and Depreciation, are both exactly half what they were two years earlier, but, compared with the former figures, Enginemen's Wages are down to 46 per cent for steam and 42 per cent in the case of electrics. Coal and water have dropped to 44 per cent of the 1919 figure, and the Electrical Energy costs are estimated to have fallen to 43 per cent. This latter figure is based on the neatly entered manuscript alteration, which drops the expenditure on electrical energy from £147,350 to £100,531.

These changes in the annual costs must have been due to alterations in the amount of traffic over the route, as railway operating expenses in this country had generally doubled between 1913 and 1919. As a result of the strike in

September 1919, they were to rise still further to three times their pre-war level. Capital expenditure schemes must always be justified in the light of current conditions, and the lower levels of traffic over the line by 1921 had dropped the annual saving to £61,885. This made the rate of return a much less attractive 4.4 per cent, even assuming that the cost of the electrification work had not risen. So, before No 13 had even turned a wheel, the case for electrifying the York–Newcastle stretch of the East Coast Route had disappeared. Successful though the trials of the 2–Co–2 were, there was nothing for it to do, although it did appear in the 1925 Cavalcade for the Centenary of the Stockton & Darlington Railway, where it had to be hauled by a steam tank locomotive. It continued to languish in the paint shop at Darlington until 1947, when it was moved to the Gosforth Car Sheds, only to be scrapped three years later.

From 1935 onwards, No 13 had been joined in store at Darlington by the ten Bo-Bos from the Shildon–Newport line, which had reverted to steam traction. The scrapping of this pioneering main-line electrification could be seen as an argument against the use of that type of traction in this country. However, the reason for it, which is not well known, was the major change that had taken place in the pattern of coal movement in Co Durham. The coal measures in the county dip towards the east, so it was natural that they should have been exploited initially where they were shallowest, in the Bishop Auckland–West Auckland–Shildon triangle. At the time of the Stockton & Darlington Railway's 150th Anniversary celebrations, I got Don Wilcock to prepare for me a map of the mines there, and, as shown in my book *Exploring the Stockton & Darlington Railway* (Frank Graham, 1975, ISBN 0 85983 006 3), there had been more than 60 of them at one time or another in that small area.

Coal wagons from all these mines were worked into the yards at Shildon, and a considerable proportion was forwarded to Tees-side, being hauled by the Bo-Bos from 1916 onwards. The early mines were among the first to be worked out, and at the same time the dipping strata caused flooding problems for others nearby. Improvements in mining technology had enabled deeper mines to be dug, until the largest came to be situated on the coast itself, with their working faces stretching out below the waters of the North Sea. In addition to this marked change in the location of the main working pits, the factories consuming coal on Tees-side grew in size, and it became more economic for the LNER to operate block trains straight through from colliery to steelworks.

The result of this was that by the end of 1934 the yards at Shildon were only handling a seventh of the traffic they had dealt with in 1913. They had consequently been reduced to single-shift working for the previous two years, with a corresponding lack of activity along the electrified route, and the LNER had to take the drastic step of closing them both down. Gresley terminated the contract for the power supply from 31 December 1934, and the yards finished operating a week later. Some of the overhead electric structures were reused as gantries when Hull was resignalled, and the locomotives were stored. Later in the 1930s it was intended to use the latter for banking purposes on the line over Woodhead when electrification of that route was being planned. After this scheme had been held up by the war, one of the locomotives was rebuilt, but it was not considered suitable for the climb over the Pennines, so spent its final days as pilot in the Carriage Sheds at Ilford. No 13 presumably might also have been used on passenger trains on the Woodhead line, and it would have been fascinating to see it in action below the dark moorlands surrounding that route. It was, however, appreciably less powerful than the Co-Cos eventually built for the passenger services there, and they finished their working lives in Holland anyway.

The 1931 Study by Metz & McLellan for the LNER

Moving onwards, the next serious examination of a scheme to electrify part of the East Coast Route took place at the beginning of the 1930s, and again involved work by Metz & McLellan. It was one of the exercises carried out for the Ministry of Transport's 'Committee on Main Line Railway Electrification'. At the end of its deliberations it produced what is always referred to in railway circles as the 'Weir Report', named after Lord Weir, who led the study. However, the electrical industry uses that reference for his 1925 Report on the national electricity system, which had also benefited from the same distinguished chairman.

The 1931 Weir Report is a detailed study of the whole question of railway electrification, and each of the two case studies by Merz & McLellan occupies more pages in the appendices than there are in the whole of Raven's and Watson's full report for the North Eastern Railway in 1919. Another member of the committee was Sir Ralph Wedgwood, the Chief General Manager of the LNER, who doubtless ensured that the consultants were given every facility during the course of their investigation.

As will be seen from Figure 8, the area covered the Great Northern main line to Peterborough, as well as quite a large proportion of that company's former lines in Lincolnshire. The East Coast Route as we know it was included as far as Doncaster, with an extension to Leeds. Cleethorpes was reached via Louth and Grimsby, while the two major freight centres of Colwick and Whitemoor were also connected to the electrified network. In all it covered a total of 492 route miles, giving a scheme that was intended to be 'fairly representative of the British Railways as a whole'. Its route mileage exceeded that of the 1984–1991 East Coast Electrification project.

One of the decisions the Weir Committee had to face was to decide what constituted a 'main line', and its final definition amounted to everything except 'suburban lines in London and round about important provincial towns . . . with the exception of some spur or branch lines carrying little traffic'. As far as the committee was able to establish, all the existing suburban electrification schemes had been successful from the technical and economic points of view, and had substantially improved the service to their communities. It worked on the assumption that the railway companies would continue the conversion of other similar lines, although there seemed no obvious move by any of them to electrify any more of their main lines. The Shildon–Newport stretch was the only one in Britain to qualify for inclusion

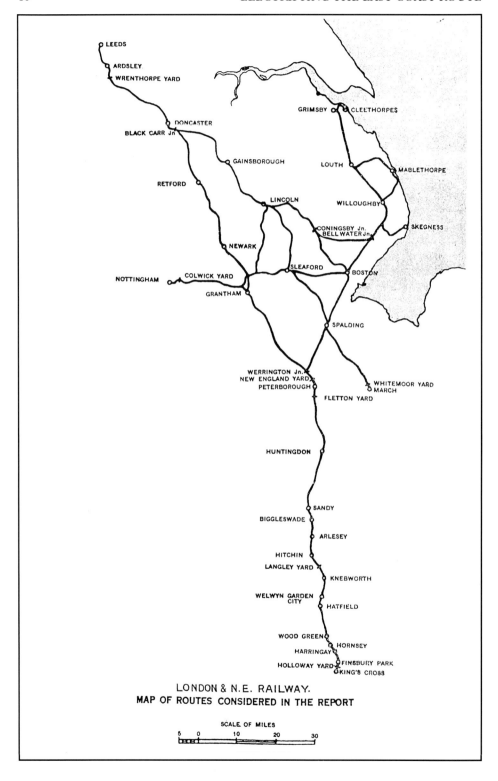

LONDON & N.E. RAILWAY.
MAP OF ROUTES CONSIDERED IN THE REPORT

SCALE OF MILES

in the main-line category, and that was not far from closure because of radical changes in traffic flows, as we have already seen.

The King's Cross suburban area thus fell outside the remit of the report, and was specifically excluded from the Weir study by Merz & McLellan, who assumed that the services over the 20.6 miles from King's Cross to Welwyn Garden City had already been electrified. In 1930 the LNER had actually resolved to do this in principle, given an adequate grant from the government. Although this was not ultimately forthcoming, work was carried out for the railway company by Merz & McLellan, and the scheme included the widening of the Greenwood–Potters Bar bottleneck. Even with the suburban services already electrified, an additional 22.39 miles of track in the King's Cross area would have had to be energized for the main-line scheme, with just over 47 more out as far as Wood Green (Alexandra Palace in today's nomenclature). This provides an indication of the massive length of sidings and secondary running lines alongside the first 5 miles of main line out of the terminus associated with what we would now refer to as InterCity, Parcels and Railfreight operations. In all there were no fewer than 1,312 miles of running lines in the area of the study, and just over 600 miles of sidings of one sort or another.

The Weir Committee did not have to go into the best method of carrying out the electrification. This had been decided in 1928 by a committee under the Chairmanship of Sir John Pringle, although this was not actually confirmed by the Minister of Transport until 1932. The recommendation was for two alternative standards, both of them using direct current. One was the existing third-rail system, with a maximum voltage of 750; the other used overhead wires, which would enable the voltage to be increased to 1,500, except under special circumstances, when the wires might carry up to 3,000 volts. Effectively the outcome of the report was to make 1,500 volts overhead the new standard, away from existing third-rail systems, and within four years such an arrangement was in successful operation along the 8.7 miles of the Manchester, South Junction & Altrincham line, which was partly owned by the LNER.

On the LNER it was proposed to use electric locomotives and multiple-units for passenger traffic, the latter form of traction producing just over a third of the train miles. On the other hand, goods traffic could only have been handled by locomotives, and their annual train miles would have totalled 4.44 million, 30 per cent up on the corresponding figure for locomotive-hauled passenger trains. For long-distance passenger trains a locomotive weighing 110-115 tons, with four driving axles and a leading and trailing truck, was considered suitable. Capable of a maximum speed of 75 mph, it would have had a one-hour rating of 2,400 hp. This sounds remarkably like a stretched version of the North Eastern 2–Co–2 No 13. A drawbar pull of almost exactly 2 tons at full speed was assumed, which seems a very modest target. As has already been mentioned, Churchward got that out of his steam 4–6–0s a

Figure 8 *Diagram from the 1931 LNER report by Merz and McLellan.* (Courtesy National Railway Museum, York)

One of Gresley's 'P1' 2–8–2s, No 2393, blasts its way through Sandy on 8 June 1933 with a train of 100 loaded coal wagons for London. Under the 1931 electrification proposals, these trains would have been worked by a pair of Do-Do electric locomotives. (G. H. Soole Collection, National Railway Museum, York)

quarter of a century earlier, and by 1931 Gresley's adoption of long-travel valve gear had put his 'Pacifics' well in advance of anything that one of the Swindon designs could produce. The proposed 1–Do–1s were considered capable of working the heaviest trains on the existing timings, and it was not thought worthwhile to provide a smaller design for the shorter, 350-ton trains.

For the heaviest goods trains, which weighed as much as 1,220 tons, an eight-axle locomotive weighing 144 tons was considered necessary, with each wheel being provided with twin brake blocks to enable it to stop an unfitted train from 25 mph in 1,000 yards on a descending 1 in 200 gradient. These Class A machines were to have had the Do-Do wheel arrangement, while a closely related Class B, Co-Co, design, using the same traction motors, was also proposed. Massive though the former were, it was considered that pairs of them would have to be used in multiple on trains of more than 900 tons. This was an expensive way of providing head-end braking, but the idea of using a number of braked wagons as a 'fitted head' was not around at that time. Both classes would be limited to a maximum of 35 mph, which meant that they would not be suitable for express goods trains. These would be worked by Co-Cos with a higher gear ratio and a vacuum exhauster, referred to as the Class B1s. With a maximum speed of 60 mph, they would also have been suitable for hauling excursion trains, and so were the electrical equivalent of the Gresley 'K3s'. Some of them would thus have needed train-heating boilers. For shunting work, a 60-ton Bo-Bo was proposed, with four 160-hp motors and a tractive effort of 20,000 lb.f. This would have been more versatile than our present-day Class '08s', being capable of making trip workings between yards. All sidings would be electrified, which was considered to be less expensive than the North Eastern's 1919 solution of cutting back on the wiring and using locomotives equipped with batteries as well as collection gear.

Table 4 gives details of the number and cost of the electric locomotives and trains necessary to meet all the traffic requirements in the area under consideration in the report. The EMUs would have been converted from existing coaching stock, with a maximum speed of 60 mph, and marshalled into three-car sets, so that after electrification there would have been 440 locomotives

Table 4: Electric locomotives and multiple-units proposed in the 1931 LNER Electrification Study[1]

Type	Number	Individual cost (£)	Class cost (£)
Passenger locomotives	35	16,259	568,750
Motor coach equipments[2]	258	5,130	1,323,540
Trailer coach equipments[3]	516	420	216,720
Goods locomotives			
Class A	32	11,570	370,240
Class B	193[4]	7,860	1,516,980
Mixed traffic locomotives			
Class B1	28	11,490	321,720
Class B1 with boilers	14	12,000	168,000
Goods shunting locomotives	75	7,080	531,000
Passenger shunting locomotives	63	7,780	490,140
		Total cost	5,507,900

[1] In the original report there is an anomaly between this table and the text of the appendix. The latter refers to the Class A goods locomotives as having the Do-Do wheel arrangement, but, in the table, this class has a much lower individual cost. It is thus presumed that the figures were accidentally crossed over, and this has been corrected in the version reproduced here.

[2] The price includes the extra cost of providing motor bogies instead of ordinary carriage bogies, and wiring and fitting coaches for electric heaters.

[3] The price includes the cost of alterations to the coach bodies, and wiring and fitting coaches for electric heaters.

[4] This total includes 15 locomotives for ballasting and departmental trains.

and 258 multiple-units. These would have displaced no fewer than 925 steam locomotives, which were similarly itemized by wheel arrangement, from the 35 'Pacifics', with an average age of 4.96 years, down to the 1.08-year-old Rail Motor. It is interesting to note that the same number of electric express passenger locomotives was proposed as 'Pacifics' they replaced. By post-nationalization standards, this seems remarkably generous, even allowing for the speeds of the trains remaining the same, and indicates that the motive power people of that time thought that the electrics would require as much time each day being serviced as was the case with steam locomotives.

Figures were given for the engine miles in goods and passenger service for both forms of traction. Unfortunately no specific allocation of the different steam classes to the two types of service is given, but it is reasonable to assume that the bulk of the passenger mileage was to be achieved by the 35 'Pacifics', 23 4–6–0s, 80 'Atlantics' and the 96 4–4–0s. On this assumption, their average mileage on trains came to 32,000. If the 14 boiler-fitted Class B1 electrics spent half their time on passenger work, the corresponding annual train mileage for the new locomotives worked out very much higher, at 91,000, an increase of almost 200 per cent. On the other hand, each of the 258 EMUs was expected to average a mere 15,000 miles per year, which presumably reflects the large number of leisurely timed stopping trains in those days. Overall, the number of engine miles on trains, including those for multiple-units, was assumed to remain the same, at 7,631,333 per year. A more valid comparison of the utilization of the two different forms of motive power might therefore be to compare the steam figure with the overall one for electric locomotives plus the EMUs. That brings the proposed average annual mileage down to 25,000, or less than was already being achieved with steam. As we will see later in our story, the utilization of today's electrics is vastly superior to that which was being proposed 50 years ago.

As was frequently the case when electrification was being considered, alternative ways of dealing with the cost of the new motive power were given. According to the LNER Chief Accountant, almost £4 million had already been charged for the depreciation of the units displaced, which would have reduced the net cost from £5.5 million to a mere £1.5 million. The alternative was to consider how much money would be saved by not having to replace the existing steam locomotives. Over the period 1925–9, the LNER replaced an average of 132 locomotives a year, at an average annual cost of £514,767. The 925 steam locomotives made redundant by electrification would thus have been equivalent to seven years of ordinary renewals. Assuming that the electrics would have taken three years to be introduced, it was calculated that, at 5 per cent compound interest, the net expenditure on the new motive power would be £741,697 per year over this period, making a total of £2,225,000. However, the railway was currently only replacing 1.8 per cent of its locomotive stock each year, which was appreciably less than the number that would have to be renewed to maintain the average age of the fleet at the desired $33^1/_3$ years. If allowance was made for this, the net cost of the electrics came down to just £2 million.

To the above figure had to be added the cost of the electrification work.

Table 5: Estimated capital expenditure for the LNER 1931 Electrification Study

Item	Cost (£)
Track equipment	5,542,400
(1,355.62 miles of running track and 589.26 miles of sidings)	
Alterations to ways and works	
Tunnels, bridges and structures	165,028
Telegraphs and telephones	49,689
Signals	286,432
Track circuits	87,200
Alterations to running sheds and repair shops	118,000
Control and maintenance offices, stores and staff quarters	48,500
Spares and materials for motive power and track equipment	246,000
Alterations to auxiliary power and lighting installations	119,074
Contingencies, engineering expenses and interest on capital	755,000
Total, excluding motive power	7,417,323
Locomotives and multiple-units	2,000,000
	9,417,323
Less credits for assets displaced	771,000
Net capital outlay	8,646,323

This was estimated to come to nearly £7¹/₂ million, made up as shown in Table 5. Rather surprisingly, the average cost of the electrification equipment per mile of track was appreciably lower than the corresponding figures for the NER York–Newcastle scheme. Those for the LNER scheme were based on 'schedule rates taken from recent contracts for similar work of large magnitude'. As many of these would have been for overseas countries with different wage rates, the report was careful to say that they were 'adapted for the conditions of manufacture and erection in this country'. They should thus have been reasonably accurate, while the 1919 estimates were more speculative. Unfortunately in 1931 we were not given the split between the costs for electrifying sidings and running lines that we have for the earlier scheme, although the ratio of the two different mileages are very similar. With the cost of the electric motive power added in, the scheme would have involved an outlay of nearly £9¹/₂ million. However, there was also a credit of £771,000 for assets 'displaced by electrification', which brought the net cost of the electrification down to £8,646,323.

The comparative operating costs for steam and electric traction are given in Table 6, which has been condensed from the figures given in the report. Experience in costing railway electrification schemes has clearly moved on very considerably, and, wherever appropriate, each of the figures reproduced in my table was divided into three sub-headings for passenger, goods, and shunting plus departmental traffic. One of the most interesting points is the

Table 6: Comparative annual working expenses for the LNER 1931 Electrification Study

	Cost (£)	
Item	Steam	Electric
Locomotive fuel	524,869	586,620
Water for locomotives	37,108	300
Lubricants for locomotives	10,909	3,880
Locomotive stores	43,676	23,460
Locomotive crews' wages etc	671,665	318,464
Locomotive cleaning, boiler washing, etc	112,220	39,570
Supervision	28,395	18,400
Locomotive repairs	438,693	187,420
Maintenance of engine sheds	14,532	5,800
Maintenance of train lighting sets	17,028	—
Guard's wages, etc	169,145	140,392
National Insurance, etc	32,218	14,900
Maintenance and operation of substations	—	35,800
Maintenance of track equipment	—	97,380
Auxiliary power supplies and maintenance	103,487	57,994
Depreciation of locomotives and track equipment	55,965	103,900
Totals	2,258,910	1,634,280
Difference in favour of electrification £624,630		

figure for the cost of crews for the locomotives, which was reduced to less than half. As the number of trains being run was assumed to have been the same, this must have implied that the LNER hoped to work all the electric trains with only a driver. While this was accepted practice with multiple-units, it was stated in the main report that 'similar arrangements would be adopted on shunting locomotives and, subject to certain limitations, on train loco-motives'. The railway company's thinking had thus progressed from that of the North Eastern just over a decade before, and it had already been working its steam railcars with just a driver and fireman — and no guard — since 1925. It is interesting to speculate whether the economic conditions in the 1930s would have permitted such a change to take place, because if it had, and the work had gone ahead, many subsequent electrification schemes would have been much more easy to justify.

On the figures in the report, these Merz & McLellan proposals for the LNER would have given a return of 7.22 per cent on the net cost of the scheme. The price of coal had a significant effect on the economics, an increase of one shilling (5p) per ton giving an extra 0.225 per cent return. In the same report, the consultants also costed the electrification of the West Coast Main Line between Crewe and Carlisle, together with one or two offshoots, the most important of which was the route from Weaver Junction to Liverpool. Some 123 route miles and 843 track miles were involved, and the net capital outlay was estimated to have been £5,123,370. Savings were much less, however, at £127,766 per year, which gave a mere 2.5 per cent return on capital, approximately a third of that for the LNER scheme.

Neither of these proposals went ahead, and, although the terms of reference of the Weir Committee did not call on it to produce any definite recommendations, it did point out the economic advantages of pressing ahead with a comprehensive scheme for the electrification of this country's main lines. This should 'preferably be carried out as a united co-operative scheme by the railway companies, in order to obtain the best results from the technical, constructional and supply standpoint'. In the difficult economic conditions of the 1930s nothing of this sort took place although, later in the decade, the availability of low-interest government finance did enable the LNER to come up with electrification schemes for the Liverpool Street–Shenfield stretch of the Great Eastern system and the Woodhead route across the Pennines. Both were held up by the Second World War, but work restarted after the end of hostilities. When the latter was completed in the 1950s it became the country's first fully electrified main line, with frequent heavy freight trains alternating with passenger traffic. However, it was to close completely in 1981, like the Shildon–Newport scheme nearly half a century earlier, the victim of declining traffic demands for coal.

Chapter Two

THE BR MODERNISATION PLAN PROPOSALS

The Second World War caused great physical and social upheavals to this country and its railways, and, after peace had been restored, other aspects of post-war rehabilitation, generally speaking, had precedence over the railways. Following nationalization of the railways in 1948, the LNER's two electrification schemes out of Liverpool Street and across the Pennines were completed in 1949 and 1954, the latter after the construction of a new three-mile tunnel at Woodhead. In 1955, however, the BR Modernisation Plan was announced, which included major plans for further electrification. To oversee this work, an Electrification Committee was formed under the chairmanship of S. B. Warder. It held its first meeting in May 1955, and the first of its reports was produced just under two years later. In the interim, however, a decision was reached which had a fundamental effect on the whole future of electrification on this country's railways away from the Southern Region and London Transport.

It was in October 1955 that the British Transport Commission accepted the recommendations that the direct current 1,500V standard, as put forward by Pringle in the 1920s, should be replaced by a higher-voltage alternating current system, with the overhead wires energized at 25kV from the country's 50 cycles per second public supply system, referred to these days as 50 Hertz (Hz). There are two important advantages in having a railway that is electrified in that particular way. The first is that the voltage derived from an ac supply can readily be altered by means of a transformer, and the other is the ability to tap into the ordinary electricity system serving industries and homes throughout the country, without having to build Substations at frequent intervals along the track.

The railway electrification engineer has to optimize two competing factors. He needs a rugged traction motor, but he must get the power to it as cheaply as possible. The former necessitates relatively low voltages being used inside it, but transmission losses and distribution costs increase as the voltage is lowered. The limitation on the maximum voltage that can be used in the motors, which have to operate in all weathers under very punishing physical conditions, has set an upper limit of about 3,000V for direct current railways. With alternating current, voltage reduction can be achieved quite simply with a transformer carried on the train, so the overhead line can be energized at a much higher tension. This produces another potential problem, however, as variable-speed ac traction motors do not operate well on a standard industrial supply of 50 or 60 Hertz, although at lower ac frequencies this can be done reasonably satisfactorily. As a result, a number of railways throughout the world have been electrified using $16^2/_3$ or 25 Hz supplies. The provision of these often requires dedicated generation capacity, and German Railways (Deutsche Bundesbahn) still has power stations of its own, with limited interchange between its own supplies and the national distribution system. By contrast, the dc motor is robust, although this is at the expense of overall system efficiency, and its high-speed performance is also limited.

Although German Railways standardized on a $16^2/_3$ Hz system, their Hoellenthal line in the Black Forest was experimentally electrified off the industrial 50 Hz system, following some earlier work in Hungary. After the Second World War, this part of Germany lay within the French Zone, and the SNCF became interested in the technical possibilities of this form of electrification. As a result it installed such a system on its own 55-mile stretch from Aix-les-Bains to La Roche-sur-Foron, in the Alps south of Lake Geneva, and carried out experiments with locomotives using both ac and dc motors. In the light of the results, SNCF then decided to adopt a 50 Hz system for its major electrification scheme between Thionville and Valenciennes in the north-east of the country, the first section of which came into operation in July 1954. This decision was taken in spite of the recent completion of the Paris–Lyon electrification at 1,500V dc, carried out with the assistance of Marshall Aid. Again, locomotives with ac and dc motors were built for the services in the north. The development of robust mercury-arc rectifiers small enough to install on railway rolling-stock produced a reasonably satisfactory way of supplying power to series-wound dc traction motors, which had been almost universally used on suburban electric railways throughout the world.

The scene was thus set for a major change in direction for electrification on British Railways. Although BR had reaffirmed the use of 1,500V dc on the Liverpool Street and Woodhead schemes in the late 1940s before authorizing their completion, technology altered rapidly during the first half of the 1950s. So, as already mentioned, in October 1955 the British Transport Commission agreed to adopt a 50 Hz ac system for the electrification schemes being carried out as part of the Modernisation Plan. This was announced publicly the following March, and a report on the subject was made available in June when the decision was approved by the Ministry of Transport. To give some idea of the savings that could be obtained, the capital costs of supplying power from the Central Electricity Authority's 132kV grid to the motive power on the Euston to Liverpool and Manchester electrification scheme was estimated to decrease from £38.6 million to £29.3 million by switching to ac. Some extra costs were involved with the motive power and signalling, but the overall difference in the figures came out at £5.8 million. To this had to be added an annual saving of £1 million in run-

ning costs. What was not quantified at the time was the bonus that was about
to result from further technical progress taking place with solid-state silicon
rectifiers. These devices greatly simplified the construction and operation of
ac locomotives using the dc traction motors. As a result, this principle was
adopted very widely by railways throughout the world until the thyristor
came into use during the last 15 years or so, which, in turn, opened up a
whole series of further possibilities for railway electrification.

There was, however, one feature of the 1955 proposals which differed considerably from those that had been adopted on the other side of the Channel.
This was the use of sections of overhead line energized at 6.25kV to reduce
the amount of civil engineering work necessary to provide clearance for the
high-voltage wires. In this country the railways that merited electrification
ran through numerous conurbations, where bridges and tunnels occurred
very frequently at sites where they could not easily be raised. It was thus more
economic to build motive power that was capable of running on both voltages, rather than lifting the significant number of overhead structures which
had an adequate clearance for 6.25kV, but not for the full 25kV. At the time
that this decision was made, a 25kV wire had to have a static clearance of at
least 11 inches from the roof of a vehicle or the underside of a bridge,
although this could drop to 8 inches as a train passed and the pantograph
forced it upwards. On the other hand, clearances for 6.25kV were only half
that figure, making them the same as for 1,500V dc, and such clearances had
been adopted fairly widely on the railways when bridges had been rebuilt during the previous two decades.

Ac electric trains could operate at full power on either systems, as the pri-
mary windings of the transformers were in four sections. On 25kV these were
connected in series, but were automatically switched to parallel when the pantograph was in contact with a 6.25kV catenary. In the light of 30 years' experience, it has now been proved that the reduced clearances provided for
6.25kV are also adequate for 25kV, and all the remaining sections of line that
were once electrified at 1,500V dc and 6.25kV have now been converted to
25kV, the last of the latter being changed over in June 1989. However, all this
still lay in the future in 1955, and some of the problems with our early electrification schemes stemmed from the use of these twin voltages.

From the point of view of the East Coast Route, the Modernisation Plan
included the electrification of the line from King's Cross to Leeds, with a possible extension from Doncaster to York. In competition with this for
resources and finance was the London Midland electrification over the busier
routes from Euston to Liverpool and Manchester, as well as several suburban
schemes throughout the country. By the time the 1957 report of the
Electrification Committee had appeared, the following ac schemes had
already been approved and work had begun:

Manchester–Crewe
Colchester–Clacton
Glasgow Suburban (Stage I)
Enfield–Chingford

London, Tilbury & Southend
Conversion of Liverpool Street–Shenfield and Chelmsford–Southend to ac

The report outlined the time scale for the schemes included in the Modernisation Plan, together with others stretching into the future as far as 1990, although those for more than five years ahead were admitted to be somewhat tentative. They were listed in three categories: Category A comprised the Modernisation Plan routes, plus a number of additional ones, all due to be fully electrified by 1970, while Categories B and C covered the periods '1970-1980', and '1980 onwards'.

Table 7 gives some idea of the work involved in these proposals, and lists the number of electric track miles that were expected to be commissioned each year, excluding any third-rail electrification on the Southern Region. It should be noted, however, that the schemes from Waterloo to Salisbury, and on to Exeter, due for commissioning by 1967 and 1970, were presumed to have been at 25kV overhead, and are thus included in the table. The maximum length of single track due to be electrified in any one year was in 1967, when 871 miles were to be involved. From the maps and tables it is not possible to determine the exact timing of the various Eastern Region schemes, nor of those north of the Border. This was because some lines in East Anglia were to have been electrified in the same 1961–70 period, as well as the West Coast Route southwards from Glasgow to Carlisle (the Weaver Junction–Carlisle gap was not planned to be filled until 1974).

It was, however, clearly intended, by the time this report was produced, that the East Coast Electrification was going to extend all the way to Edinburgh, and, like the NER's 1919 proposals, would have included the Northallerton–Stockton–Ferryhill loop, with the line to Middlesbrough thrown in for good measure. In Scotland, electric working would also by 1970 have been in operation over two routes between Edinburgh and Glasgow. One was from Waverley to Glasgow Queen Street, which carries today's intensive diesel passenger service, and the other was over the second North British line between the two cities via Bathgate and Airdrie, which has long since been severed between the two last-named places. South of Doncaster, the GN&GE Joint Line from Doncaster to March was to have been included in Category A, together with the continuation to Ely, where it would have joined the wires over the second route from Liverpool Street to Norwich. The important freight centre of Colwick was also to be connected electrically to the main line, as were Grimsby and Hull, the latter being linked to Leeds as well as Doncaster.

One of the interesting things in the report is the high priority given to the East Coast Route. A firm completion date of 1970 had already been fixed for the whole of the London Midland main line scheme, with the last two years being occupied with the North Staffordshire loop. The completion of the rest of the scheme would have taken place in 1968, when electric services would start between Rugby and Euston. Over on the eastern side of the country, firm plans had not been worked out, but the electrification of the whole of the East Coast group of lines was similarly proposed to be completed by

Table 7: 1957 Electrification Committee's proposals

Year	Single track miles to be commissioned (ac only)	Locomotives required	Multiple-units required
1958	67	13	74
1959	262	43	222
1960	350	35	163
1961	550	147	162
1962	512	155	165
1963	650	220	190
1964	650	183	195
1965	800	243	110
1966	800	240	110
1967	871	220	105
1968	675	160	60
1969	642	160	52
By 1970	*6,829*	*1,818*	*1,608*
1970	671	152	52
1971	475	148	42
1972	475	142	39
1973	504	141	39
1974	567	141	39
1975	458	141	39
1976	417	140	39
1977	475	140	39
1978	408	140	39
1979	387	140	38
1980	367	140	38
1970-1980	*5,204*	*1,565*	*404*
1981	312	106	17
1982	250	85	12
1983	250	83	12
1984	250	83	10
1985	250	83	10
1986	183	70	7
1987	183	70	7
1988	183	70	7
1989	183	70	7
1990	183	70	7
1980 onwards	*2,227*	*650*	*82*
Grand totals	14,260	4,033	2,094

These figures have been taken from diagrams in the BR report, rather than
tables, and may thus include small scaling errors.

1970. In every year from 1958 to 1969 a greater or equal length of track was due to be electrified in the Eastern Region as on the London Midland, but the former also included lines in East Anglia which were not directly associated with the East Coast Route. It should also be remembered that at this time the North Eastern Region was a separate entity; its electrification plans were confined to the East Coast Route, and so were all additional to the mileage converted by the Eastern Region.

Before leaving Table 7 it is worth commenting on the number of electric locomotives it was proposed to obtain. Over the whole 33 years, more than 4,000 were to have been placed in service, with as many as 240 being built in a single year (1966). In 1980 the actual number of electric locomotives owned by BR was 301, and, including the diesel-electrics, their total locomotive stock was only 3,379. Even adding the APT and HST power cars would not have lifted the total to that proposed for the electrics in 1957, but it must not be forgotten that the slimming exercises of the Beeching era had not taken place then, although some branch lines were already being closed.

With electrification of the East Coast Route taking such a high priority in the 1957 report, it is not surprising that it should have its own master plan, which was set out by the Eastern and North Eastern Regions in June 1959, under the title *Report on the Modernisation and Electrification of the East Coast Main Line between King's Cross and Newcastle and Certain Associated Lines.* This was a much more business-orientated document, and its summary makes very interesting reading.

> The East Coast main line is a vital trunk route. Its potential earning capacity is not being fully realized because few major improvements have been carried out for many years. Apart from a change in traction, route modernization is long overdue.

> It is proposed to modernize and electrify the lines mentioned in the published Modernisation Plan with projection of electrification to Newcastle and over certain feeder lines. The total route mileage to be electrified is 415.

> The proposals are based on an assessment of the traffic that could be attracted to the fully modernized and electrified route by about 1970. Provisional timetables for that volume of traffic have been compiled; locomotive and rolling-stock requirements have been calculated from the draft timetables and the necessary improvements to track, stations and signalling planned in some detail.

> The estimated increases in traffic have been related to 1956-7 levels, on the assumption that the current trade recession is temporary and that, after a pause, industrial expansion will be renewed. On this basis, it is estimated that, by 1970, passenger earnings should increase by 35 per cent and freight and parcels earnings by 20 per cent, giving an increase of £10.5 m in gross earnings.

If the assumptions in respect of industrial output are falsified by events, the volume of traffic forecast for the East Coast main line will not readily be achieved. But if the route is not modernized, its share of competitive business will almost certainly fall and potential industrial and residential developments will not be realized.

The passenger timetable after electrification will provide substantially augmented regular-interval services between London and all provincial cities and towns of importance, at average speeds of 70 mph or more between the principal cities. Pullman and other named expresses will be run in addition to the basic services.

In conjunction with the rationalization of the marshalling yard network and the concentration of freight at fewer depots, faster and much more reliable freight services will be possible.

The motive power and passenger rolling-stock estimates call for 188 electric locomotives and 62 four-car multiple-unit sets. In comparison with present stocks, 420 steam locomotives and 350 passenger coaches would become redundant.

The route modernization proposals include a number of track widenings, especially on the GN main line; flyovers at certain junctions; modern power signalling installations with continuous track circuiting on the principal lines; and a general raising of speed limits by track improvements. The number of signal boxes will be reduced from 344 to 104. On the fast lines between London and Newcastle, 100 mph will be permitted over 150 miles, 90 mph over 54 miles, and 80 mph over 44 miles; of the remaining 20 miles, only 7 will be restricted to less than 60 mph.

The proposals are broadly estimated to require a net outlay of £105.0m (of which £80m would be net additional investment) as under:

	Net outlay (£m)	Net replacement cost of assets displaced (£m)	Net additional investment (£m)
Route modernization	56.1	12.0	44.1
Equipment for electrification	31.0	—	31.0
Motive power units and depots	18.4	13.5	4.9
Total	105.5	25.5	80.0

The estimates of outlay include everything needed for complete modernization except:

(a)   the amalgamation of the Leeds passenger stations

(b) buildings, etc at the new King's Cross and Peterborough stations
(c) marshalling yards, freight concentration depots and the like
(d) maintenance depots for hauled stock
(e) telephone exchanges and trunk equipment

There is not likely to be any significant change in the annual costs of maintaining the track and signalling. Despite substantial increases in traffic, annual movement/haulage costs are expected to fall by about £1.5m.

The estimated improvement in net revenue is placed at £12m, made up of:

	(£m)
Increase in gross earnings	10.5
Reduction in movement/haulage costs	1.5
Improvement	12.0

The improvement in net revenue will give a return, soon after electrification, of 11% on the net outlay and 15% on the net additional investment.

The modernised system would be capable of carrying, at little additional cost, a greater volume of traffic than is forecast for 1970 or thereabouts, and assuming a subsequent expansion of personal travel and industrial output the longer-term return on net investment might well rise to 20% or more.

Compared with the technical report of two years earlier there had been a number of changes, the most important of which was that electrification would be confined to the East Coast Route proper and only extend as far north as Newcastle, including the Northallerton–Newport–Ferryhill lines. Grantham–Colwick was to be electrified, but the extension from there into Nottingham Victoria was not considered to be economic until other electrification in the area was carried out. To connect Colwick with the north, a new electrified curve was to be built at Barkston, which would have enabled the Bottesford–Newark line to be abandoned. The overhead wires would also have been extended from Retford to Rotherwood, to connect with the 1,500V dc line from Manchester to Sheffield via Woodhead, which it was proposed to convert to ac. A separate scheme was being developed for the King's Cross suburban services, including the Northern City line to Moorgate. At the Newcastle end, the electrification would extend as far as the carriage depot at Heaton, although the electric locomotives would be based at Gateshead.

The report provides an interesting reminder of how early the rationalization process had started on the East Coast Route, as the number of intermediate stations between Hitchin and Doncaster had by 1959 already been reduced to those which appeared in the timetables in the mid-1980s (before the new Network SouthEast station at Arlesey was opened in 1988). The main long-distance train services were also following a substantially regular-interval pattern, leaving King's Cross at approximately hourly intervals for Leeds and Newcastle. After electrification, these arrangements would have been developed, and the following pattern was proposed in the down direction from King's Cross to these destinations.

Newcastle
Hourly, with alternate trains running through to Edinburgh or Glasgow. Most trains calling at Peterborough, York and Darlington.

Leeds and Bradford
Hourly, calling at Peterborough, Doncaster and Wakefield, where the Bradford portion would be detached.

Hull and Sheffield
Two-hourly, calling at Peterborough, Retford, Doncaster and Goole. The Sheffield portion would be detached at Retford, and call intermediately at Worksop. In some cases these coaches would continue to Bradford, calling at Penistone, Huddersfield, Brighouse and Halifax.

Sheffield and York
Two-hourly, calling at Peterborough, Grantham, Newark, Retford and Worksop. The York portion would also call at Doncaster and Selby.

Grimsby
Two-hourly, calling at Hitchin, Huntingdon and Peterborough, and then principal stations in Lincolnshire.

Peterborough
Two-hourly, calling at Hitchin and then all stations to Peterborough.

Consideration was also to be given to providing through trains to Lincoln off one or other of the last two services. In addition to these regular-interval operations, extra workings would be scheduled for such trains as the 'Elizabethan', 'Tees-Tyne Pullman', 'Yorkshire Pullman', 'Sheffield Pullman', and one through working to Harrogate.

Table 8 gives an outline of the fastest provisional running times between King's Cross and the principal places served by the new services. As recounted in my earlier book *Speed on the East Coast Main Line*, the East Coast route had led the post-war speed renaissance with steam, and by 1954 had an aggregate of 2,098 miles at over 60 mph, start-to-stop, out of a national total of 4,356. The fastest schedule in 1958 was with a down morning business express, which was booked to average 67.5 mph between Hitchin and Huntingdon. The proposals for the electrics were well ahead of this, with a best average of 78.0 between King's Cross and Doncaster in the down direc-

Table 8: Express passenger train timings in the 1959 East Coast report

King's Cross to	Distance (miles)	Fastest average scheduled speed			
		Down		Up	
		(h m)	(mph)	(h m)	(mph)
Peterborough	76¼	1 00	76.3	1 03	72.6
Doncaster	156	2 00	78.0	2 01	77.4
Sheffield	161½	2 18	70.2	2 35	69.2
Leeds	185¾	2 35	71.9	2 35	71.9
York	188	2 31	74.7	2 39	70.9
Bradford	193¼	3 05	62.7	3 02	63.7
Hull	196¾	3 13	61.2	3 15	60.5
Newcastle	268½	3 48	70.7	3 45	71.6
Edinburgh	393	5 40	69.4	5 36	70.2

tion. The contrast was most marked with the London Midland's requirement embodied in the specification for its first batch of electric locomotives. This referred to an average of 67 mph between London and Manchester, with one intermediate stop of a minute, although this was with a trailing load of 475 tons. Although the London Midland was to improve its average speeds, the East Coast Route was already establishing its attitude to high-speed travel in the post-Modernisation era, which has kept in in the forefront of Anglo-Scottish speeds for so long.

One of the interesting aspects of the East Coast proposals in 1959 was the use of multiple-unit stock for several of what we would today consider to be the prime services, including the one to Leeds and Bradford. Such units are well suited to work trains for multiple destinations, and some of the disparity between up and down timings in Table 8 may have resulted from the order in which the sections departed from the point of division and arrived back there to combine. The Class '309' EMUs for the Liverpool Street–Clacton services, with their 100-mph capabilities, were to appear in 1961, and those which would have been provided for the longer-distance East Coast services were probably intended to be generally similar.

The East Coast electric locomotives were to have been 'the 3,300-hp standard type ordered for high-voltage ac electrification on British Railways'. For the Manchester–Crewe pilot scheme on the London Midland, 100 prototype Bo-Bos were ordered, of five types (Classes '81' to '85'). They were all built to the same general performance specification, but included many differences from the various manufacturers. They were all provided with fully-spring-borne motors, but many of these gave trouble, and when the 100 Class '86s' were ordered for the full service, the very retrograde step was taken of going back to the nose-suspended variety, which played havoc with the LM track over the years.

The electric timetable for the East Coast Route was worked out in considerable detail, and several years ago Alan Parker sent me details of the hourly sequence out of King's Cross from 07.54 onwards. This started with a multiple-unit for Leeds, which covered the traditional racing stretch between Hitchin and Huntingdon at a flying average of 94 mph in the course of its 59-minute booking to Peterborough, After a 3-minute stop, it then took 62 minutes to Doncaster, and reached Leeds at 10.34. Next away from the terminus was the 08.00 locomotive-hauled express for Edinburgh. It had identical timings to Retford, but did not stop at Doncaster, so reached York, via Selby, at 10.30. This train was followed by the 08.06, with portions for Sheffield, Hull and Cleethorpes. It stopped additionally at Grantham, Newark and Retford, where the Sheffield coaches were detached before continuing after a 6-minute stand. At Doncaster the Hull section was away first, but managed a locomotive change in 5 minutes. The Cleethorpes section followed after a further 4 minutes.

After this the next train to reach Doncaster was the 07.00 'Stopper' from King's Cross, which had been overtaken by several subsequent services while it continued along the existing or additionally proposed stretches of slow line. It took 1 hour 33 minutes to Peterborough with six stops, which should be compared with the 1 hour 19 minutes allowed for the up journey with today's off-peak Class '317s', which make eight calls (the present down trains are allowed an extra 8 minutes). The overall times for the two portions to Leeds and York were 4 hours 15 minutes and 4 hours 22 minutes. The last of the trains in the hour concerned was the 08.46 for Sheffield, taking 1 hour 40 minutes overall. It reached Peterborough in the even hour, where there was a smart connection from the next 'Stopper' from King's Cross, which left at 08.12.

Important though the 1959 East Coast Electrification report was, it had already been overtaken by events. In 1955 English Electric had started operating its prototype 'Deltic' 3,300 hp diesel-electric locomotive on the London Midland Region, and discussions with the British Transport Commission two years later struck a very responsive chord with Gerry Fiennes, then Line Traffic Manager at King's Cross. Two years earlier he had read a paper to the Railway Students Association (now the Railway Study Association), suggesting that to compete with air over distances of up to 300 miles, the railways needed to achieve end-to-end averages of 70-75 mph. With alternative means of transport getting steadily faster, the East Coast authorities could not afford to wait 12 years until the electrification was completed in 1970 to achieve these standards. The plans in the pipeline for the diesel locomotives intended to replace the East Coast 'Pacifics' would not have given the required speeds, so a case was made out for the purchase of 22 'Deltics'. The contract was signed in early 1958, with delivery due to start in the spring of 1960, but the first of the class to arrive on the East Coast Route were almost a year late.

Meanwhile, difficulties had arisen with the London Midland electrification scheme. Against a background of falling receipts and rising wages, the cost of the scheme escalated, and technical problems reared their heads with some of the early ac motive power operating elsewhere. The first of the stylish 'Blue Trains' for the Glasgow suburban services had to be withdrawn after serious transformer failures, caused in part by the twin-voltage equipment installed.

There were also difficulties with the multiple-units operating out of Liverpool Street. Again some of the problems were due to the need to operate on a 6.25kV supply as well as 25kV, although, as with the 'Blue Trains', trouble was also caused by the faulty operation of the mercury-arc rectifiers. Two major steps forward did, however, result from the subsequent investigations. The change-over to solid-state silicon rectifiers was speeded up, and a further look at the clearances required for 25kV overhead wires enabled these to be reduced, thus eliminating the need for any 6.25kV sections on the lines from Manchester and Liverpool to Euston. They did, however, remain for the time being on the other lines where they had already been installed.

The 1959 plans for the East Coast Electrification included several sections which would have been energized at 6.25kV. On the Eastern Region it was proposed to use this lower voltage between King's Cross and Potters Bar, and through Stoke and Peascliffe Tunnels. The engineering work necessary to achieve the required clearances in all the tunnels on these stretches was estimated to be £4 million for 25kV, compared with just £100,000 for the lower voltage. Up in the North Eastern Region, 6.25kV was also to be used through the Tyneside conurbation from Birtley to Heaton, and in the Eaglescliffe–Stockton–Thornaby area on Tees-side, where there were numerous overbridges carrying busy urban thoroughfares or other railways. The

The scale of the structures used for the overhead wires on the West Coast Route in the 1950s and 1960s is apparent in this photograph of the Ford Motor Company's train from Dagenham to Halewood in March 1966. (National Railway Museum, York)

changes in clearances that arose from the investigations into the multiple-unit failures, referred to above, were not recommended until 1962. By that time the East Coast proposals were on ice, so the effect of these changes was not recorded. However, when we come to consider the wiring work for the current East Coast Electrification we will see how the electrical engineer has been able to reduce the clearances for 25kV still further as a result of the experience obtained during another quarter of a century's operations on our electrified lines.

I have not referred to the comprehensive range of improvements to the track and stations that were also listed in the 1959 Electrification Report, as many of these were carried out very successfully during the 'Deltic' era. Although those diesel-electrics had the same nominal 3,300-hp rating as the Bo-Bo electrics that had been planned, there were considerable differences between the effective output of the two sorts of motive power. For a start the electrics were lighter and capable of producing higher outputs at the wheel rim for short periods, since the power limit was determined by the maximum temperature rise allowed in the traction motors. With a diesel-electric, the power output is quoted at the flywheel of the prime mover, and some is then lost by inefficiencies in the electric transmission. In spite of this, the 'Deltics' were to improve on many of the electric schedules shown in Table 8. Their finest hour came towards the end of their 21-year reign, when they were scheduled to work the 'Flying Scotsman' in both directions between London and Edinburgh in 5 hours 27 minutes, inclusive of a Newcastle stop. On the down 'Hull Executive' their 1979 timing from King's Cross to Retford involved an average of 91.4 mph, which was the fastest locomotive-hauled schedule in the country at the time, the West Coast electrics included. These achievements of the 'Deltics' were not due to their power alone, but to the way in which the East Coast authorities had set out to improve the speed profile of their track to give faster services.

From the time of the arrival of the fleet of 'Deltics' on the East Coast Route, plans for electrification were at least moribund, if not completely dead, and this was not the only argument to be used against further main-line electrification at that time. BR's difficult economic situation prompted such critical investigation in the early 1960s, and one of the financial reappraisals was by the Stedeford Group, which comprised four industrialists, including Dr Richard Beeching. He personally was opposed to the London Midland electrification scheme, and considered that diesels could do the job more cheaply, but the Group's final recommendation to the Minister of Transport, Ernest Marples, was to continue with it, particularly as the full maintenance costs of diesels became apparent. It was, however, decided to concentrate the country's electrification resources on that scheme, and accelerate its completion. The lines from Euston to Liverpool and Manchester, including the West Midlands and Potteries loops, came into operation in April 1966, and the frequent, regular-interval InterCity services were worked by 25kV Bo-Bos. Although these were now permitted to reach speeds of 100 mph — a significant improvement on the 90-mph figure in the original submission — over on the East Coast Route, the 'Deltics' had already been doing that for the

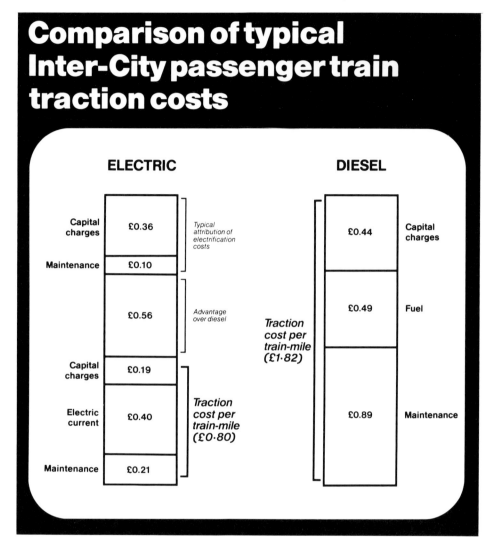

Figure 9 *A late-1970s comparison of diesel and electric traction costs for InterCity trains.* (BR)

previous two years. Against this background, with Dr Beeching subsequently becoming Chairman of British Railways, main-line electrification in this country was in for a lean time. The third rail did, however, reach Bournemouth in 1967, the authorization for that electrification being received a few months before Lord Beeching returned to ICI.

Chapter Three

THE KING'S CROSS SUBURBAN ELECTRIFICATION OF 1971–77

In the 1959 report on the East Coast Main Line electrification, discussed in the previous chapter, reference was made to the work being carried out in parallel for the corresponding King's Cross surburban scheme, which was actually authorized in 1960. The Eastern Region was to have taken over the Great Northern & City underground line, and route its newly electrified services from Hertford North via Finsbury Park into Moorgate. However, only a few small works were carried out before the scheme was abandoned as part of the switch to diesels that characterized the Beeching era.

Moving on a decade, in August 1971 Peter Walker, the Secretary of State for the Environment, announced that the Government had authorized the electrification of 70 route miles from King's Cross to Royston, via both the Welwyn and Hertford North routes. A grant of 75 per cent would be made towards the £35 million infrastructure costs. The objects of the scheme were to reduce the losses on the interim diesel service, replace unsatisfactory and ageing rolling-stock, create conditions which would enable the railways to benefit from future population developments and stimulate rail travel to relieve road congestion.

As in 1959, the scheme involved BR taking over the Great Northern & City line from London Transport, and working some of the trains into Moorgate. These were the Inner Suburban services, which were to run as far out as Welwyn Garden City and Hertford North. The Outer Suburban trains would take the main East Coast Route to Hitchin and then continue to Royston on the Cambridge line, where they would connect with diesel multiple-units. As originally envisaged, there would not normally have been any services over the northern half of the Hertford Loop, although that was to be electrified for use in emergencies. The full electric services did not come into operation until the autumn of 1977, the long time-scale relative to the modest route mileage involved being due to the fact that the electrification work

Figure 10 *Schematic route diagram for the Great Northern suburban electrification of 1971–77.* (BR)

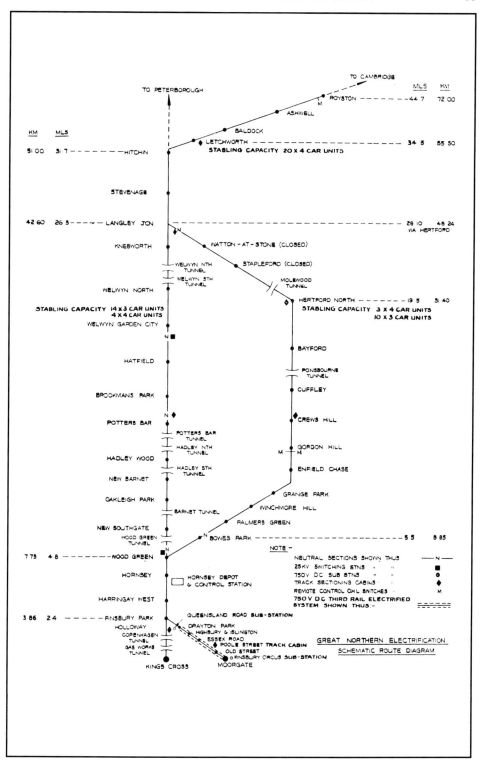

GREAT NORTHERN ELECTRIFICATION
SCHEMATIC ROUTE DIAGRAM

was carried out in parallel with the main-line resignalling and track rationalization between King's Cross and Sandy. This was an essential preliminary to
the inauguration of the East Coast 'Intercity 125' services in 1978.

The quadrupling of the Greenwood–Potters Bar stretch, mooted in the
Merz & McLellan scheme of 1931, had been completed in 1959, but a lot of
civil engineering work was nevertheless involved in connection with the electrification and track rationalization. This stretched out as far as Welwyn
Garden City, where a flyover was constructed to enable the Inner Suburban
trains to turn back without having to cross the fast lines on the level. A second
flyover was built just north of Copenhagen Tunnel, and the track layout
changed at Belle Isle, betwen Copenhagen and Gas Works tunnels, to facilitate electric trains reaching the surburban platforms on the west side of the
main station at King's Cross. This was a replacement for an existing flyover
which had previously only provided access to the King's Cross Freight
Terminal. As a result, it was possible to simplify the track layout at King's
Cross and increase many of the speed restrictions. During the work, the tracks
were removed from the eastern bores of Gas Works and Copenhagen tunnels,
and the connections to the Widened Lines severed, over which some peak-
hour diesel workings had continued to serve Moorgate.

The electrification of the Inner Suburban services thus had to be completed first, because it was necessary to get these trains out of the terminus. This
then facilitated the major 'Throat Clearing' operation, as the public relations
people named it, which was carried out over an eight-week period starting in
January 1977. Since the abortive plans for the 1960 scheme, the Great
Northern & City's sub-surface platforms at Finsbury Park had been taken
over by the Victoria Line when that was built, so the London Transport services from Moorgate had been cut back to Drayton Park. It was thus necessary to construct two new connections from the East Coast Route south of
Finsbury Park, within sight of the Arsenal football stadium at Highbury, in
addition to modifying the tunnel sections for BR stock. The changed clearance requirements for 25kV electric wires meant that it was no longer necessary to use 6.25kV through the tunnels south of Potters Bar, but there was no
way in which a catenary could be threaded from Drayton Park to Moorgate
through the former London Transport tunnels, which, although larger than
those for normal tube lines, were not up to full main-line dimensions.

To provide the through workings, a completely new type of electric multiple-unit therefore had to be developed. These were the aluminium-bodied
Class '313' three-car sets, built by BREL at York, with GEC Traction equipment which is able to operate from a 750V dc third-rail system as well as from
the 25kV ac overhead. Drivers switch from one system to the other by pressing the appropriate button in the cab while the train is standing at Drayton
Park station. Once this has been done, the change-over is entirely automatic.
The end vehicles are power cars, each of which is provided with four 110-hp
dc traction motors.

On the third-rail system, each car uses the pick-up shoes on its bogies, and
the current is fed to the traction motors through the usual dc control gear,
consisting of starting resistances and series/parallel connections. When work-

ing on 25kV ac, the power is collected by the pantograph on the roof of the intermediate trailer, and the main cable is ducted through the passenger saloon to the underfloor transformer. The output from this is rectified and fed into a bus line running the length of the train, where it is supplied to the motor control equipment in the ordinary way. When running on the dc system, the bus line is isolated because government regulations do not permit such an item on underground trains operating through single-bore tunnels. Speeds are restricted to 30 mph in the tunnels, but the motors are provided with field-weakening to permit a maximum speed of 75 mph in the open. Their balancing speed up the 1 in 200 ruling gradients on either side of Potters Bar is approximately 65 mph.

Fully automatic couplers are provided at the outer end of each power car, enabling sets to be joined or split by the driver in the cab, and up to three units can be operated in multiple, although not more than two are normally used together, even in peak hours. Seating is all standard class, with a basic 2+3 arrangement in open saloons; these units were also to introduce the somewhat unfortunate layout which provided relatively few rows with an unimpeded view out of the windows. While this is not too much of a disadvantage on a surburban commuting train which spent a large proportion of its journey in tunnel, the subsequent application of a similar layout to the first 'Sprinters' used on scenic lines such as that along the Cambrian Coast was not a good move. It is significant that one of requirements by Chris Green —

A pair of twin-voltage Class '313' multiple-units as used on the King's Cross Inner Suburban services, working a train for Moorgate. (BR)

Managing Director of Network SouthEast — for the new generation of 'Networkers' was that the same arrangements should not be perpetuated.

Power-operated sliding doors are provided, and these later enabled the units to go over to Driver Only Operation (DOO), after the required radio links had been provided between drivers and the control centre, together with mirrors or television monitors on the platform ends so that the driver could ensure that passengers were clear of the doors. To comply with Department of Transport requirements for evacuation in single-line tunnels, each of the power cars has an end-door, and these gave them a distinctly owl-like appearance before the coming of Network SouthEast livery removed the yellow 'cheeks' from the front corners.

On the other hand, the Class '312' units for the Outer Suburban services were much more traditional in design, being based on the Class '310s' introduced in 1965 for the stopping services on the Euston-Birmingham route. They were, however, geared for a maximum speed of 90 mph, compared with 75 for the earlier units, and on the long 1 in 200 descents of the GN main line were frequently recorded as reaching 100. Although provided with buckeye couplers, these do not include the brake pipes and electric control connec-

The first of the original Class '312' multiple-units for the King's Cross Outer Suburban services to Royston. (BR)

tions, which had to be joined or disconnected by hand whenever units were coupled or uncoupled. Although a single four-car set with slam doors can be used in DOO mode, multiple-unit operation of this type is not permitted, so they have now been cascaded away from the King's Cross area.

Initially 26 units were provided for the Outer Suburban services and 64 for those on the Inner Suburban workings into Moorgate. A new maintenance facility was constructed for them all at Hornsey, on the up side of the main line. The Depot Manager was also responsible for the overhead equipment and the power supply arrangements, the control room for the latter being located there. Two Feeder Stations were necessary for the 25kV system, and are located at Welwyn and Wood Green (as the latter was known at the time, before being renamed Alexandra Palace). On the 750V dc stretch there is a railway Substation at each end of the underground section.

Hornsey depot's responsibilities have changed since the late 1970s, but in 1978 52 out of the 64 Class '313' units were in traffic on an ordinary week-day, and all of them received a daily clean. During the day 35 of them were dealt with, the initial arrival coming in for cleaning after the morning peak at 08.47, and the first re-entering service for the evening rush at 16.10. This work was carried out on the two most westerly tracks inside the six-road inspection shed. As each unit arrived it went through the washer, and was then directed either to the storage sidings or to the cleaning or maintenance tracks. There was a 14-day cycle for traction maintenance, with defective components being exchanged to enable the items to be sent away for over-haul to benefit from economies of scale. The wheel lathe in its separate building could deal with up to 12 axles in an eight-hour shift. This enabled tyres to be reprofiled without sending the sets to one of the main works, which effective-ly provided an extra two units in service, and amply justified the cost of the lathe and its associated facilities. At that time it was the only such installation on BR capable of guaranteeing the quality of tread profile required for wheelsets on trains that ran at over 100 mph; the APT-P even visited Hornsey for attention.

As originally planned, there were three inner Suburban trains per hour off-peak in each direction to Hertford North and Welwyn Garden City, calling at all stations, which meant that there was a train every 10 minutes between Moorgate and Wood Green. At Highbury & Islington there are cross-plat-form connections between BR trains and the Victoria Line, and the easiest way of reaching King's Cross main line station from the northern suburbs is usually by this route. Under the tighter financial regime of Network SouthEast, the off-peak traffic on these services did not warrant such a fre-quent service, and for much of the day it has been cut back to half-hourly, although this makes a long gap when a train is cancelled. On the other hand, a Huntingdon train now provides a regular hourly service over the northern half of the Hertford Loop. Outer and Inner Suburban trains connect at Welwyn Garden City, but the service pattern has become much more com-plex since the electric workings have been extended to Peterborough and Cambridge. After about 21.00, and at weekends, the Inner Suburban services have now been diverted to King's Cross, enabling the Great Northern & City line to be closed. All the platforms at King's Cross were electrified, and it soon became common to find both sorts of EMU in the main station at quiet times of the day.

The ability of the Class '313s' to operate on third-rail as well as 25kV has enabled the surplus units from the Great Northern Inner Suburban services to be cascaded elsewhere in the London area, some of them onto the North London Line. Since the closure of Broad Street, the basic third-rail service runs through from Richmond to North Woolwich, but the dual-voltage capacity of the Class '313s' was required for a few peak-hour workings in and out of Liverpool Street. Other sets are used on the London Midland's Euston–Watford dc services, where they have replaced older slam-door stock, after being fitted with additional shoe-gear and 750V bus lines to enable them to bridge the longer gaps between the conductor rails on this route.

Although there were some teething troubles with the doors, motors and automatic couplers on Class '313' units, the Great Northern Suburban Electrification quickly became a showpiece for BR, both out on the tracks and at the impeccably run Hornsey depot. In September 1978 I attended a presentation on railway electrification at Hatfield, which concluded with an inspection of the maintenance depot, our party being sandwiched between visitors from Queensland and Norway during adjacent weeks. With the

Hornsey Electric Control Room, with the mimic control panel in the background. The space available for later use when the wires extended beyond Hitchin can be seen. (BR)

authorization of the Bedford–St Pancras electrification in 1976, the Hornsey Electrical Control Room was being adapted to deal with this system as well, and on the occasions of such visits the mimic panel would be labelled up to include the Midland main line to Sheffield as well as an extension of the electrification northwards along the East Coast route.

One of these VIP visits was to have a considerable influence on the whole future of railway electrification in this country. At the request of Sir Peter Parker, the then Chairman of BR, the Eastern Region Public Relations Department organized a visit to the line for the Secretary of State for Transport, Bill Rogers. He was received at King's Cross, and taken to the new signal box where the system was explained and the region's future plans were outlined. The party then joined one of the Outer Suburban Class '312' units, which the Secretary 'drove' on its fast run to Welwyn Garden City. On alighting there he was introduced to the leading citizens of all the local authorities served by the new electrification, who had gathered for the occasion, together with the press. The enlarged party then returned on one of the Inner Suburban Class '313s' to Moorgate, where they walked up to the Circle Line platform to board one of latest London Transport units for the short run to Liverpool Street. Emerging from the station, the party progressed across Liverpool Street itself between the ranks of the City of London police, and

The interior of the new King's Cross signal box in 1978, showing the control panels which regulate trains over 83$^1/_2$ route miles. (BR)

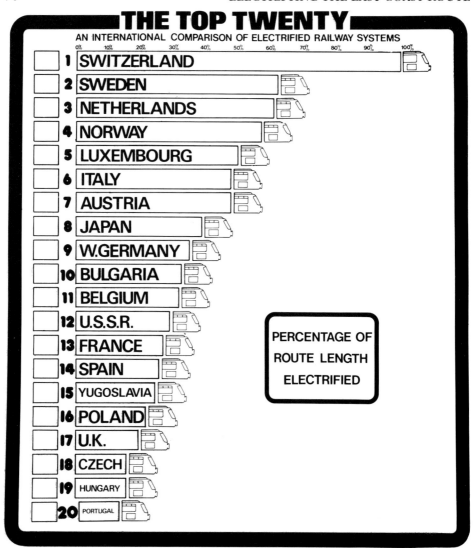

Figure 11 *A diagram showing Britain's poor position in the world railway electrification league, as used during the campaign for more investment in electrification in the late 1970s.* (BR)

adjourned to the Great Eastern Hotel — then still part of BR — for a reception and lunch. During the course of the morning it had become clear that the Secretary of State's attitude to BR's operations was softening, spurred on, in part, by the reactions of the local civic leaders to their new electric services. This continued during the subsequent informal conversations, and in his speech after lunch, Mr Rogers, to the surprise of his staff, came out very warmly in favour of what BR wanted to achieve. As a result it was agreed to set up joint discussions between BR and the Department to look at the way in which further electrification could be progressed in this country.

PART TWO

THE 1984–91 INTERCITY ELECTRIFICATION TO LEEDS, EDINBURGH AND GLASGOW

Chapter Four

THE OUTLINES
OF THE PROJECT

On 27 July 1984, five days before that summer's parliamentary recess, Nicholas Ridley, then the Secretary of State for Transport, authorized the go-ahead for the electrification of the East Coast Route, a £306m scheme which was to be BR's biggest single project since the Modernisation Plan. While the news was not actually greeted by the ringing of the bells at York Minster, the celebrations in the Eastern Region General Manager's mess at the Royal York Hotel certainly went on well into the night. Although that particular proposal had been approved within two months of its submission, the decision-making process can be traced back to the dialogue that had started between BR and the Department some five years earlier.

As mentioned in the previous chapter, in the light of the energy crisis at the end of the 1970s, and Britain's poor standing in the international league for railway electrification, a series of joint discussions had been set up between BR and the Department of Transport. Before these got going, however, the 52-mile Bedford–St Pancras–Moorgate scheme had been authorized in 1976. That was a special case, since the existing Class '127' diesel multiple-units, used for the suburban services over the line since 1959, were reaching the end of their working life on passenger duties, which made electrification much easier to justify financially. The £80 million scheme included the link from Dock Junction, St Pancras, down to the Widened Lines, and on to Moorgate in the City, which had a five-year existence as the 'Midland City Line' before becoming part of 'Thameslink'. The start of public services was delayed for nearly a year until April 1983 by the protracted dispute with ASLEF over Driver Only Operation, but by that summer the full capabilities of the new 90-mph Class '317' units were being demonstrated over the Chiltern switch-backs of the Midland Main Line.

Meanwhile, a lot of studies had been carried out to prepare the case for electrifying the East Coast Route, and some work actually took place along the track. Foundations for the overhead electrification masts were put in northwards from Hitchin as far as Huntingdon, the justification for this advance work being to keep the specialized construction teams in being after

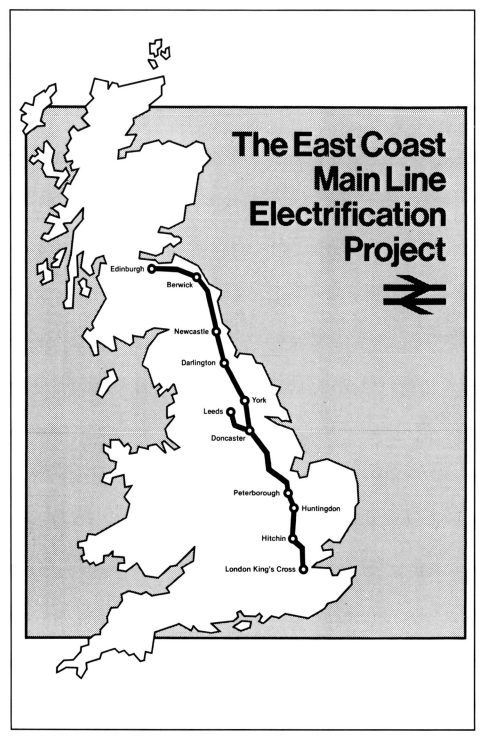

Map of the electrification of the East Coast Route under the 1984 proposals. (BR)

Table 9: Electrification schemes authorized between 1981 and June 1983

Date authorized	Title	Location	Length (route miles)	Cost (£m)
1981				
December	Anglia (East)	Colchester–Norwich/Harwich	75	62
1983				
March	Ayrshire	Glasgow–Ayr/Largs	39	80
October	Hastings	Tonbridge–Hastings	31	31
1984				
January	Anglia (West)	Bishops Stortford–Cambridge	25	20
	Southminster	Wickford–Southminster	16	3
June	Romford	Romford–Upminster	4	3

they had completed the wiring for the Bedford–St Pancras scheme. These operations stopped as soon as the Anglia (West) scheme had been approved and the contracts had been let for the construction of its overhead line equipment. By this time concrete foundations spread along the lineside of the East Coast Route for some 27 miles, the central hole in each for the mast being formed from a plug of polystyrene foam, which remained in place.

In spite of BR's on-going labour problems, by June 1984 no fewer than six electrification schemes had been authorized, as listed in Table 9, but the 'Big One', represented by the East Coast Route, had not so far received approval. In 1982 BR had put forward proposals for the electrification to Leeds and Newcastle to be approved in principle, but this never got off the ground because of the economic recession at that time. A year later the first stage, to Leeds, was formally proposed, but this, in turn, was scuppered by the turn-down in Western Region carryings, which meant that WR could part with some of its HSTs to the Midland Main Line, thus pre-empting the post-electrification cascade from the East Coast Route which had formed part of the economic case.

However, Anglo-Scottish business had been growing on the eastern side of the country, and the prospect of having to change motive power at Newcastle was likely to have been an even bigger handicap than it had been on the West Coast Route prior to 1974. The Class '50' diesel locomotives used in pairs up to that time north of Crewe would have been some 15 years older had they been drafted to the East Coast Route, and would still have been limited to 100 mph. The alternative of putting an HST power car on each end of a northbound train at Newcastle after detaching the electric locomotive would have been likely to require even more time, and would have been costly and complicated. So the idea of extending the electrification all the way to Edinburgh was then considered, and was found to improve the overall case, as well as giving a better service for the passengers. Although electric traction at a maximum speed of 125 mph was not expected to give much saving over existing HST schedules, reliability problems with the latter's hard-worked power cars had by that time started to make themselves felt. This was another factor taken into account with the submission, which was already strongly based on the higher costs of diesel maintenance compared with that for 'straight' electric traction.

The final approval was coupled with what *Modern Railways* referred to as 'the rather elusive InterCity Review', which formed BR's comprehensive survey for passenger traffic into the 1990s. What was not known at the time was that the deal struck with the Government stipulated that InterCity would not receive any subsidy after April 1988. BR was already committed to getting InterCity into profit, a principle going back to Anthony Crosland's White Paper of 1976, but this had not previously been laid down with such a stark time-scale. Although BR had to fund the £306m electrification out of revenue, the £14m lower running costs and £2-10m increase in revenue expected would give a good return on the money, and make a contribution to the overall improvement required. The savings would come from a 60 per cent reduction in maintenance costs, a 25 per cent lower fuel bill and reliability increases of 50-70 per cent.

In the autumn following the scheme's approval, the Prime Minister, Mrs Margaret Thatcher, paid a visit to the National Railway Museum. After she had toured the historical exhibits, she was handed over to Bob Reid, the BR Chairman, for a private discussion about the electrification plans with him, Cyril Bleasdale, the Director of the InterCity sector, and Don Heath, the Project Director. The visual aids used on that occasion were subsequently published by BR, and provided a clear indication of the magnitude of the scheme and its objectives.

The East Coast Route then served a population of 21 million, and InterCity's market share of passenger journeys to and from South-East England was as follows:

Area	Market Share %
East Midlands	18
Yorkshire	34
North East	38
East Scotland	36

The task of bringing the electrification into operation for the benefit of the community, the passengers and the railways involved the items listed in Table 10, while the phasing of the expenditure and work is shown in Figures 12 and 13 (page 78). At a time when unemployment was high, another of the scheme's benefits was that it would create or safeguard some 3,000 jobs. Half of these were in the rolling-stock construction industry and a further 500 on the railway itself. The other 1,000 were spread over the construction, signalling and electrification industries.

By the summer of 1990, the new Chairman of BR, Sir Bob Reid, was able to report that the £420m East Coast Electrification was on time and *within budget*. There are various reasons for this change in total cost, one of them being that inflation was excluded from the original figure, which, over a six-

Table 10: Investment involved in the East Coast Electrification Scheme (1984 figures)

Item	Cost (£m)
Civil Engineering	35
127 bridges to be raised or reconstructed	
Signalling	27
400 miles of optic cable to be laid	
4 new telephone exchanges	
Immunization of	
1,000 track circuits	
1,000 signals	
600 point machines	
Electrification equipment	112
200,000 tons of concrete	
33,000 masts	
1,400 miles of contact wire	
1,400 miles of catenary wire	
14 Feeder Stations	
Locomotives and rolling-stock	
62 electric locomotives	62
4 suburban trains	4
324 coaches	66
Total	306

year period, would represent getting on for 25 per cent. In addition, several related schemes have subsequently been tacked on to the original project, including two extensions of the overhead wiring. One of these is the short stretch from Leeds station to Neville Hill Depot, costing £1.8 million, to enable the electric locomotives to haul their own coaches to and fro to be stabled and serviced.

The second extension is much longer, and covers the 27 miles of the one-time Caledonian Railway's line from Edinburgh to Carstairs on the West Coast Route. This will link up the two Anglo-Scottish electrified lines, and also enable through electric workings to Glasgow from the East Coast Route. For some years now there have been comparable HST services, but these follow the former North British route through Falkirk to Queen Street station in Glasgow. Space there is limited between the buffer-stops and the tunnel portal, which makes a 2+8 'InterCity 125' difficult enough to handle. The position would have been significantly worse than with the longer electric trains, particularly after the authorization of the ninth coach for each set, to be referred to later. As a prelude to these workings, from autumn 1990 the first through HST started operating over this route, after the bulk of the electrification work had been carried out during the summer.

On the other hand, although the 'InterCity 225s' will run through to Forster Square station in Bradford without changing motive power after the route from Leeds has been electrified, the finance for that project will be provided by the West Yorkshire Passenger Transport Authority. Further south

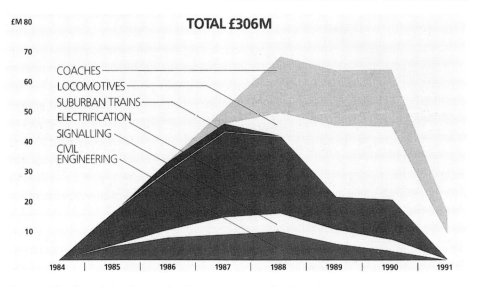

Figure 12 *The original spread of investment on the East Coast Electrification Scheme.* (BR)

Figure 13 *The original programme for the East Coast Electrification Scheme.* (BR)

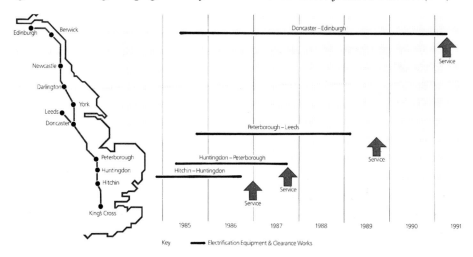

still, after several unsuccessful attempts, authorization was finally obtained in March 1987 for the £2.5 million scheme to extend the wires from Royston to Shepreth Branch Junction, where they join up with the line from Liverpool Street to Cambridge. This was justified on its own account, largely because of the cost of maintaining a small fleet of elderly diesel multiple-units, and is now worked as an integral part of the King's Cross suburban system, which extends as far as Peterborough. The hourly fast services are scheduled to average over 60 mph between King's Cross and Cambridge.

As originally authorized, each of the 31 new electric trains for the East

On 23 March 1987, the inaugural electric train ran to Cambridge from Liverpool Street, with David Mitchell, then Minister of State for Transport, as chief guest. After the record run to the university city, he waved off the first works train for the Royston–Shepreth Junction electrification. By way of a gentle hint, it was hauled by Class '47' No 47 576, named King's Lynn, *to remind everyone that Network SouthEast was busy making a case to extend the wires to that town!*

Coast Route was to consist of a Class '89' Co-Co electric locomotive with nine improved Mark III coaches and a Driving Van Trailer (DVT). As will be described in Chapter 8, this was changed very shortly afterwards, the new plans being to use a Bo-Bo locomotive and a new design of coach, the Mark IV. Both were to be able to run at speeds of up to 140 mph, and the combination is known as 'InterCity 225' (while the existing 'InterCity 125' designation refers to the speed in mph, the new train is metric, and 225 km/h equates in round figures to 140 mph). This change proved to be more expensive than the original plans, and the length of each train was therefore trimmed back to eight Mark IV coaches. However, in the light of increased traffic demands, a case was made to add a ninth vehicle to each of the 31 sets, at a cost of £8.7m, and this was also separately authorized by the Department of Transport in June 1989.

A number of important East Coast HST services run through to destinations off the main route, and it was originally proposed that motive power for these would be changed at the points where they left the electrified system. One of the problems with this was always the provision of suitable diesel power, quite apart from the time taken for the change-over. Coupled with the growth in traffic, there is now a case for some of the HSTs to be retained for these workings, and services like the 'Highland Chieftain' for Inverness will continue to be worked in the same way as present, the diesel power cars in that case running for nearly 400 miles 'under the wires'. The 31 'InterCity 225' sets will thus mainly be confined to the electrified 'core' of the East

Coast Route, where maximum use can be made of their high-speed capabilities.

The original scheme also included the purchase of 31 mixed-traffic electric locomotives, which were to have been up-dated versions of the Bo-Bos built for the West Coast extension to Glasgow in 1973–4. An earlier batch had already been authorized for the London Midland Region, and they were initially referred to as Class '87/2'. Rapid developments taking place with thyristor drives for locomotives justified so many changes in the design that their designation was altered to Class '90'. The East Coast batch are intended primarily for freight work, which has meant that the coming of the Channel Tunnel has had an effect on the number required. To permit BR locomotives to operate freight trains from as far away as Scotland and northern England all the way through the tunnel to the Frethun terminal in France, a new type of locomotive was necessary, capable of taking power from the Southern Region third-rail dc system as well as from the 25kV overhead. Twenty of these Class '92' two-system locomotives were authorized by the Department of Transport in May 1990, and this will result in only 21 Class '90s' being allocated to the internal East Coast electric services.

There have also been a number of major engineering works, which, although carried out in conjunction with the East Coast electrification, have been justified as separate projects. The most notable of these have been the resignalling and track remodelling in the areas of two of our great Victorian stations, at York and Newcastle. Their power-operated signal-boxes dated from the 1950s, although some of the preliminary work at the former location dated back to before the Second World War. Since that time the whole pattern of train working has altered out of all recognition, with multiple-units taking the place of many locomotive-hauled trains, while many services which once used some of the platforms have disappeared as the lines they served have been closed. Another change has been the very short time now allowed for station stops on our faster services, which has again reduced the number of platforms required. There was clearly a case for rationalizing these stations' operational facilities at a time when the signalling was being renewed and the tracks wired for electric traction, and this has been done in both cases. There have been relatively few changes at Leeds, but the station had been extensively rebuilt and resignalled since the Second World War, at the time of the closure of Leeds Central station.

Other engineering activities, such as the work on the viaduct at Durham, were more of a maintenance character, although cost of reconstructing over-bridges to provide clearances for the overhead wires fell on the electrification project. In the course of the next four chapters we will be studying these and many of the other facets of the engineering work connected with the East Coast electrification in more detail.

Chapter Five

PROVIDING THE POWER

In our present-day private lives we are so used to being able to obtain electricity at the turn of a switch that we largely take the supply for granted. The advantages of railway electrification from the passengers' point of view are also well known, and it is widely appreciated that overhead wires or energized third rails have to be provided before this type of motive power can operate. However, these outward forms of the supply system only represent the tip of the iceberg, and there are considerable problems when it comes to providing a reliable and economic supply along the full length of a trunk railway route, such as the one from London to Edinburgh.

As we have already seen, railway electrification schemes in this country go back to the turn of the century. Although the horsepower installed in the trains of those days was modest, by contemporary standards their operation nevertheless required quite a substantial power supply. In many places there was no suitable local generation capacity available, either because of the overall demands, or because of the specialized supply needed. It was thus often necessary for the railway companies to build their own power station.

For example, the pioneering City & South London — the first 'tube' line in the capital — had its own generators at Stockwell, while the Waterloo & City's power station was beyond the terminus at the southern end of its line. Elsewhere, notably in the Newcastle area, reliable commercial supplies were available locally from very early on, so the North Eastern Railway was able to obtain power from the North-Eastern Electric Supply Co for its pioneering suburban electrification on Tyneside. These power stations were thermal ones, and were, in the main, fired with coal, although the generators at Heysham Harbour, used for the Midland's 1908 line to Lancaster, were driven by gas. In all probability this was producer gas, obtained from coke.

Since those days the position has changed considerably. First of all came the construction of the National Grid in the years between the two World Wars, being completed in 1935. This connected the various small power stations throughout the country with overhead lines at 132,000 volts (132kV), supported on pylons. Its main purpose was to link all the separate commercial and municipal systems, and enable them to be operated as a whole, backing each other up so that each local installation did not need to have as much spare plant to cover 'outages' due to maintenance or breakdowns.

The National Grid also played an important role in standardizing the use of 50-Hertz alternating current throughout the country, which enabled consumers to move their appliances from one house to another without any problems. Another significant development in 1935 was the passing of the Electricity Supply Act, which permitted the railway companies to purchase power supplies directly from the Central Electricity Board. The Grid at this time was, however, limited in scope, because the transmission of power was only economic over relatively short distances.

In the years following the Second World War, the demand for electricity increased very considerably, and the generating stations were nationalized, putting them and the Grid all under the control of comprehensive authorities. These were the Central Electricity Generating Board (CEGB) in England, and, north of the Border, the South of Scotland Electricity Board (SSEB) and the North of Scotland Hydro Electric Board. At the time of writing, these are in the process of being privatized, but, as far as the electrification of the East Coast Main Line is concerned, it was the CEGB and SSEB which were involved in the planning of the necessary power supply, and we can ignore the subsequent split of the CEGB into the National Power, Power Gen and National Grid companies.

To meet the increasing post-war demand, numerous new power stations were built, their individual size steadily increasing as technology developed. Each of these had to be connected to the National Grid, the distribution capacity of which had similarly to be increased to handle the higher loads. Power-line technology was also moving on, and by 1953 it was possible to use a voltage of 275kV for a new section of the Grid being constructed. An even greater change was to follow in 1963 when the present-day 400kV Supergrid *transmission* system started to be built. By using multiple conductors at this very high voltage, strung high above the ground from lofty pylons spaced well apart, it became more economic to move energy around the country in the form of electricity than as coal.

The biggest concentration of coal-fired power generation in the country is situated quite close to the East Coast Route, in South Yorkshire, Humberside and the Trent Valley. Good supplies of coal are located nearby, while plenty of cooling water is available from the river systems of the area. Comprising eight stations, their total output is 10,000 megawatts, which enables them to supply over a quarter of the nation's power requirements. Many of them are visible beside the East Coast Main Line, which is crossed by the unending stream of 'merry-go-round' coal trains linking them to the collieries.

The 400kV transmission lines have also played an important role in connecting the remotely sited nuclear power stations with the main areas of consumption, while other new technology has enabled the British and French electricity systems to be linked under the Channel. All these developments have permitted the operation of the whole system to be optimized, with the national supplies being generated from an optimum combination of coal, oil, gas and nuclear stations, not forgetting the pumped-storage systems in North Wales. However, as we will see, not all the resulting changes have been to British Rail's advantage, mainly because the 132kV Grid has lost its original status. Much of it has been transferred to the local Electricity Boards, and now forms part of their local distribution networks.

We will be discussing the electrics of the new East Coast motive power in more detail in a later chapter, but it is worthwhile at this stage to examine briefly the developments in electric systems on the railways, since these have an effect on the supply system required. The advent of the thyristor, which consists of a control grid added to a solid-state rectifier, enabled a single device to combine rectification with control of the voltage, using a microprocessor that switches it on for only part of each cycle. The simple thyristor was then followed by the development of the Gate Turn-Off variety, or GTO. These permit the control system to switch the passage of electricity through each device on and off extremely rapidly at will. By combining several of them into an 'inverter' it is now possible to produce a *three-phase* alternating current supply on the locomotive or train, which can be then used to power very compact synchronous or asynchronous motors. The torque produced by the latter can be easily controlled by varying the frequency of the inverter output, and it also becomes feasible to use the traction motors to brake the train regeneratively. In this way energy is returned to the supply system, which makes it more efficient than the rheostatic type, where it is just dissipated in resistances. The development of the inverter, however, came too late to be considered for incorporation into the design of the Class '90s' and '91s' for the East Coast Route.

For any railway electrification scheme, power has to be fed into the supply system at intervals along the track at Feeder Stations or Substations. The position of these is determined by the acceptable voltage drop between each, which in turn depends on the supply voltage and the nature of the traffic. On the older Southern third-rail system, the Substations were originally not more than $3^1/_2$ miles from each other, and often much closer. Any wider spacing made it difficult to ensure that the circuit-breakers at both ends would always detect a short-circuit on the track or a train, and trip out the supply, regardless of where it occurred. This in itself was a function of the voltage-drop along the conductor rails. When the Bournemouth line was electrified in the mid-1960s, it was possible to adopt a spacing of $4^1/_2$ miles after special controls had been developed to make a circuit-breaker also simultaneously trip the one at the opposite end of the electrical section, but the scope for further extensions of the spacings between Substations is limited.

The cost of a Substation or Feeder Station is quite considerable, so the fewer that are required the better. With the 25kV overhead electrification system they need be no closer than 25-40 miles apart, depending on the traffic load. Although the equipment needed to handle the higher voltage is clearly somewhat more expensive, rectifiers, as used in a dc Substation, are not required. Another important consideration is the availability of bulk high-voltage supply, and clearly this cannot be obtained from the CEGB every 3 to 5 miles. A dc railway thus has to have its own very expensive power cables along the tracks, which are such a familiar lineside feature on the Southern Region.

Reference has already been made to this country's first long-distance 25kV electrification scheme from Euston to Manchester and Liverpool, carried out under the Modernisation Plan of 1955. It covered the busiest main line in the country, through Britain's industrial heartland. It was thus well served by the 132kV National Grid, and there was a fair probability that the railway would pass close to a suitable CEGB Substation or Grid line every 30 miles or so. In the event, 12 Feeder Stations were provided for a total route mileage of more than 370, thus achieving the desired spacing. Each of these includes two transformers that step the voltage down from 132kV to 25kV, with the main circuit-breakers being situated between them and the bus line supplying the railway's own overhead wires. These breakers form the boundary between the spheres of authority of the CEGB and the railway, and the latter has its own switching equipment to protect and isolate the various sections of its catenary. As a rule, the two supplies at each Feeder Station are kept separate by neutral sections in the overhead lines, and each supply energizes the line half-way to the next Feeder Station, where there is another neutral section, with its associated Mid-Point Track Sectioning Cabin.

From the point of view of any electric supply industry, an installation for a major consumer must meet a number of technical requirements to prevent it from causing problems for all the other users. Firstly there is the question of the power-factor to be considered, which is a characteristic of all alternating-current circuits. A simple one will have a power-factor close to unity, but the more extensive the circuit becomes, the greater the possibility that the power-factor will decrease unacceptably. This is because the electrical inductance of the system can cause the current flow to lag behind the voltage. Happening every half-cycle, or 100 times a second, this can result in a significant loss of efficiency, the effect being known as 'wattless power'. The suppliers of electrical equipment thus have to take particular care to design it so that it has a power factor that is acceptable to the supply industry.

With ac electric railways there is yet another problem. Electricity is generated and distributed in three-phase form, which is why the current-carrying cables on overhead power-lines come in threes, plus an additional neutral or earthing conductor. To achieve maximum efficiency, the power taken from each phase must be the same. While most of our individual homes are only provided with a single-phase supply, the consumption of a series of houses is allocated between the three phases by the local Electricity Board, so balancing the demand.

Normally anyone who wants to run a motor of more than a few horsepower in an office or factory is provided with a three-phase supply. On the railways a single locomotive, such as a Class '91', can at times require over 6,000 horsepower, but, because it is in contact with a single overhead contact system, it can only be given a single-phase supply. There are three-phase railway electrification systems in existence, but they require twin overhead lines, with the third phase being provided by the rails. Quite apart from the cost of duplicating the whole catenary, there is the problem of keeping the two lots of wires apart at junctions, while still enabling passing trains to obtain power. It is not surprising that such arrangements are, these days, confined to specialized local lines like the Jungfraubahn in Switzerland, which, in spite of all its remarkable engineering, requires its trains to slow severely — from their maximum speed of 15 mph — every time they come to a junction.

On our 25kV main lines it is possible to go part way towards evening out the demand on the phases by powering adjacent sections from two different phases. They are isolated from each other by the neutral section in the overhead wires at each Feeder Station, as already mentioned. It is not possible to go further by using different phases on the up and down lines because of the connections between them at junctions and crossovers. Given these constraints, an electric railway will thus always produce some degree of imbalance between the three phases of the power supply system, but the magnitude of this has to be limited.

The London Midland's electrical load is modest compared with the general level of public demand in the same area, which means that the peculiar characteristics of a railway supply are 'swamped', and thus the electrification plans did not cause problems. Moving on 25 years and crossing the Pennines, the position had changed appreciably when it came to electrifying the East Coast Route in the 1980s. Not only is the coverage of the 132kV Grid system less dense on the east side of the country, but the coming of the new large power stations in South Yorkshire and the Trent Valley had seen much of the older and less efficient generation capacity being scrapped. As a result, the main function of the 132kV system has now become distribution, rather than transmission, the latter being the province of the 275kV and 400kV Supergrid. Although these lines stride across the East Coast Route in many places, likes files of six-armed Martian recruits roped together to keep them in step, they make only occasional connections with the older 132kV system, and the high cost of the railway tapping into them directly means that this is only done when there is no cheaper alternative. As a result of this change, many of the 132kV lines which have been handed over to the Area Boards now only carry a comparatively light load. At the same time, the standards set by the supply industry have also been tightened, and, as far as the East Coast Route was concerned, the situation also worsened because less public load is now connected to the critical parts of 132kV Grid system. An unacceptable situation could thus arise much more easily if some of the railway's supply points from the Grid were out of action for one reason or another.

With the introduction of thyristors for electric motive power, another type of disturbance had to be prevented from getting into the supply system. The rapid switching sequences of the microprocessors can induce additional frequencies, in the form of 'harmonics'. With the public electricity supply system now being required to power ever more sophisticated electronic installations, it is important for it not to be 'contaminated' by these harmonics feeding back through the transformers. However, this was a problem that the railways had already faced themselves, since they had to ensure that thyristor harmonics did not upset their own signalling systems, particularly the track circuits. The signal engineers were very concerned about this in the early days, but the

The completed wiring on the four-track stretch of line at Milepost 5, just north of York. In the background the 400kV Supergrid makes its way across the North Yorkshire countryside.

magnitude of the trouble turned out to be far less than feared.

With the possibility of the East Coast Route being electrified, BR started discussions with the CEGB in early 1981 for the 387 route miles involved from Hitchin to Leeds and Edinburgh. The initial plan was for ten double and three single circuit supply points from the 132kV system, plus a double-circuit one from the 275kV Supergrid. On detailed analysis, these original plans for the 80-mile stretch between Peterborough and Doncaster turned out to be unsatisfactory. In addition to the Feeder Stations at both ends, an intermediate one had been proposed at Staythorpe, but it was found that, with equipment isolated for attention, the voltage profile on the 25kV over-head lines would be unsatisfactory. To overcome this, the proposed Staythorpe Feeder Station was replaced by two, one just north of Grantham and the other at Retford.

On a 25kV electrification system there are usually several Track Sectioning Cabins between each of the Feeder Stations. At these points, remotely con-trolled switching equipment is provided for the power supply, enabling stretches of overhead line on either side of them to be isolated for mainte-nance work. The two sections of contact wire are brought together side-by-side at an 'overlap'. As electric trains do not run through from energized to earthed sections it is not necessary to go to the complication of providing neutral sections at every one of them, although there has to be one such installation between every pair of Feeder Stations. If this were not done, the railway's overhead wires would form part of the CEGB distribution system should both Feeder Stations come off the same phase, or, alternatively, they would form a short-circuit between two of the Grid's phases. Normally the intermediate neutral section is located roughly halfway between adjacent Feeder Stations. As shown in Figure 14, when a Feeder Station is out of service, the neutral sections on either side of it are bypassed, and its own neutral section acts as the mid-point section separating the supplies from either side.

North of Newcastle the rural nature of the countryside traversed by the railway made it difficult to find points where power could be obtained from the Grid. In particular there would be a gap of nearly 50 miles between the proposed Feeder Stations at Ulgham Crossing (near Widdrington) and Marshall Meadows, the boundary between the Eastern and Scottish Regions, just north of Berwick. This was half as long again as the usual distance between such installations, and special arrangements had to be made to overcome the problems that would arise if both supply lines were out of action at either of these points. At the northern end, the next Feeder Station was to be at Innerwick, 25 miles further on, and, if the Marshall Meadows Feeder Station was completely out of action, it could provide a satisfactory supply as far south as the Fenham Track Sectioning Cabin, just beyond Beal.

In the particular circumstances that apply north of Newcastle, the equipment at the Fenham Track Sectioning Cabin includes a neutral section, for use when the overhead line this far south is being supplied from Innerwick, but it is bypassed electrically in normal conditions when Berwick Feeder Station is operational. At the south end of the 'Northumberland Gap', a variant on this system was adopted. There was no suitable equivalent to Innerwick, so an additional Feeder Station was provided at Benton, but was fed from the Grid by a single circuit only. If Ulgham Crossing Feeder Station is completely out of use, the one at Benton can supply power as far north as

The electrical connections between the overhead wires and the switchgear at a Track Sectioning Cabin are quite complicated. This view shows the partially complete installation at Colton Junction, and, at the time the photograph was taken, the switchgear enclosures had yet to arrive and be positioned on the concrete foundation in the foreground.

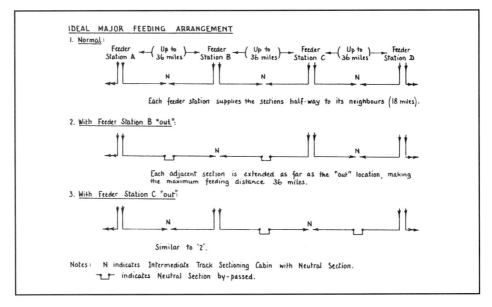

Figure 14 *Diagrams showing the way in which the Feeder Stations (A to D) and the neutral sections are arranged. There is one of the latter at each Feeder Station, as well as intermediately. The upper diagram corresponds to the normal condition, while the lower ones show how power is maintained when one Feeder Station is out of action for any reason.* (A. Goldfinch)

Figure 15 *Diagrams of the Feeder Stations and neutral sections for the 'Northumberland Gap', as described in the text. The normal situation is shown in the top diagram, while the next two correspond to the arrangements made when the Ulgham Crossing and Marshall Meadows Feeder Stations, respectively, are out of action.* (A. Goldfinch)

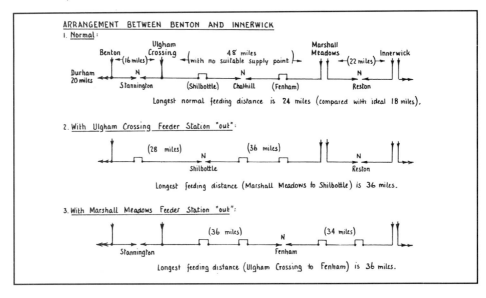

Shilbottle Track Sectioning Cabin. This is located just South of Alnmouth, and is equipped with the same facilities as the one at Fenham. These arrangements are shown in Figure 15.

During the period following the authorization of the East Coast Electrification, further studies were carried out by BR and the CEGB to determine how the characteristics of the proposed supply system would meet both the updated estimates of the railway load, and the tighter requirements of the electrical supply industry. These involved computer simulations, using new equipment and electrical estimating techniques, in addition to practical tests at existing supply points on the other electrified lines. The outcome of all this work, spread over five years, was that some reinforcement of the original plans was considered necessary, and steps were taken to provide this in time for the introduction of the full service in 1991.

The changes needed were quite extensive, many of them being involved with the Walpole Ring 132kV system in the Peterborough–Newark area, which presents the CEGB with particular difficulties. The plan for a Feeder Station at Staythorpe was re-activated, and this was supplemented by another at Bytham, while the original double-circuit arrangements at Peterborough were split, with two single-circuit Feeder Stations being installed a couple of miles apart at Nene and Bretton. Up in Scotland, the Portobello Feeder Station has been altered to be fed from the 275kV system, as the local 132kV grid is being phased out. The Marshall Meadows supply is also being taken off the 400kV Supergrid at Eccles, just north of the Border, using an auto-transformer to avoid installing equipment at the BR Feeder Station to overcome problems with harmonics. Harmonic filters are, however, being provided at the Benton and Ulgham Crossing Feeder Stations.

In addition to the three extra single-circuit Feeder Stations needed from the 132kV Grid, and the additional one from the 275kV system, BR also had to make a contribution to the cost of the auto-transformer installation at Eccles. The total price of the equipment at the power supply points was, in consequence, 25 per cent higher than the figure included in the original authorization, but this has been offset by cost reductions in other parts of the scheme.

Even with the system thus modified, it is recognized that there could be exceptional circumstances when the power taken by trains has to be temporarily restricted if certain key CEGB or BR equipment is out of action. The present proposal is that, in these conditions, when travelling at speeds of over 45 mph drivers could be instructed to operate their trains at half-power between certain pairs of neutral sections. However, once the full system has been commissioned, extensive tests are being planned jointly by BR and the electricity supply authorities to determine the exact constraints that will be necessary in practice.

Altogether there are 51 different switching stations (Feeder Stations and Track Sectioning Cabins) on the electric supply systems feeding the East Coast Route. These comprise 'package' enclosures, which are assembled, wired and tested in the factory before being moved to the lineside and lifted by crane on to prepared foundations. (In one case, an installation was actually

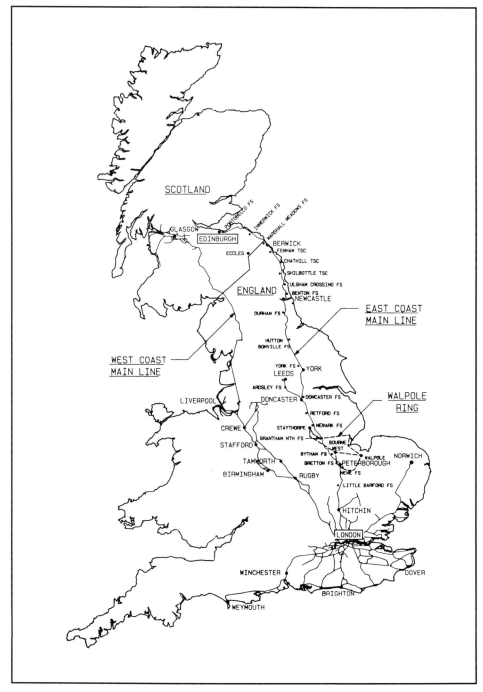

Figure 16 *Diagram of the Feeder Stations for the East Coast Electrification, showing the other electrified lines in Britain. It is based on a diagram accompanying Mr P. T. Williment's paper to the International Electrification Conference in York in 1989.* (Courtesy BR and the Institution of Electrical Engineers)

transported to the site by means of a barge on the Don Canal.) All the switching stations are supervised by three Electrical Control Rooms. Two of these already existed, at Hornsey (just north of King's Cross) and Cathcart (on the south side of Glasgow); the third is new installation at Doncaster. Although the commissioning of the newer of the existing ones, at Hornsey, only went back to 1976, the rate of technological change is such that the Doncaster one bears little resemblance to it. In this country the idea of centralizing control systems of this sort dates from the electrification of the Brighton line in the early 1930s, but their basic operating systems changed completely with the introduction of telephone-exchange-type electro-mechanical equipment in the 1950s, and latterly the development of solid-state control and indicating equipment.

In earlier installations control was exercised by electrical pulses of 50 volts dc, or musical tones, sent in sequence down the wires between the centre and the switching stations. Starting in the 1970s, the use of the computers enabled a very high-speed Time-Division Multiplex (TDM) system to be used to connect the Control Centre to each Switching Station, their use for this purpose antedating the application of similar technology to signalling systems. There are pairs of very high-speed, solid-state scanning mechanisms in the Control Centre and at each Switching Station, which are kept in step electronically so each function reports to its other half at frequent intervals. As soon as one of these comparisons shows a difference, the appropriate action is instituted. For instance, if a circuit-breaker in one of the Feeder Stations opens, this is immediately indicated to the controller and an alarm is sounded, while a change made by him to one of the settings is picked up at the remote location and acted upon. In the latest equipment the sequential mode of operation can be altered, with certain types of instructions automatically taking priority over less vital information.

As described earlier, the Hornsey Control Room was initially built to supervise the power supplies for the Great Northern suburban electrification of the late 1970s, but was extended in the early 1980s to cover the Midland electrification between Moorgate and Bedford. The technology of the time used a mimic control panel, which has switches and indicator lights at the appropriate places on the large wall diagram. Moving any of these switches causes the appropriate item of equipment on the lineside to operate, while the automatic operation of a circuit-breaker will cause its symbol on the panel to be illuminated and an alarm to sound. Even though these mimic panels take up a lot of room, additional spare space had been provided at Hornsey, in anticipation of the East Coast Electrification, to cover the electric system as far as North Muskham, just beyond Newark.

At this point the Doncaster Electrical Control Centre takes over from Hornsey, and supervises the power supplies for the line to Leeds and as far north as Chathill on the East Coast Route. This is a much larger system, which has been commissioned in three phases. The first came into operation in mid-1988, with the other two being commissioned in 1989 and 1990 respectively, even though there were still gaps in the catenary in the Newcastle area. Instead of a large mimic diagram on the walls, the controllers have work-stations where the information they require is provided by Visual Display Units (VDUs). These show coloured diagrams of the major power supply system, including the electrical connections and circuit-breakers at every Feeder Station and Track Sectioning Cabin, and it is possible for the controller to scroll along the line using a tracker-ball. Instructions are given to the equipment by means of a keyboard, and the changes then appear on the screens as they take place. Dummy circuit-breakers are provided for each of the Switching Stations along the track, and the integrity of the control system can be checked by causing these to operate, without upsetting the actual power supplies to the overhead wires. This has been a common feature in such centres for some time now, but the Doncaster one has a facility for each of the dummies along the line to be tested automatically in sequence.

The northern end of the system is controlled from the Centre at Cathcart, which was built some 30 years ago to serve the ac electrified lines in the Glasgow area, but was subsequently extended to cover the West Coast Route as far as Tebay, and then the Ayrshire Coast route. Its situation in Glasgow meant that, until the authorization of the Edinburgh–Carstairs electrification in 1989, it was not actually alongside the line it was to control, but that presents no difficulty with modern electronics and telecommunications links. Although its control equipment for the East Coast Electrification is even more modern than that at Doncaster, it uses its earlier mimic diagram, which was provided when it first opened. This has been altered to provide indications only, and will be retained only until its original equipment is replaced in the near future. Then VDUs will become the sole means of display and the mimic diagram will be removed. All operations taking place on the systems are recorded sequentially by a data logger, and in time it is hoped that the equipment will automatically issue the permit-to-work certificates which are required by staff who need to work on sections of the overhead wires after the necessary isolations have been carried out and the equipment earthed.

Communication between the Electrical Control Centres and the Switching Stations takes place over the BR signalling and telecommunications network, and utilizes both fibre optics and ordinary copper cables. Twin communication links are used between each centre and the lineside sites. The latter have their own internal computing system, which operates the local equipment using the local 240-volt supply, which is in turn backed up by batteries capable of providing a standby for at least six hours in case of a power failure. Provision also has to be made for a secure power supply for the Control Centres. At Hornsey there is a battery back-up, but elsewhere the input is duplicated, and fed through solid-state 'uninterruptable' supply units. At Cathcart the power comes from two different Area Board feeders, but at Doncaster there is only one local connection, the alternative source being the overhead catenary.

Having reviewed the particular problems of supplying power to the Feeder Stations along the electrified East Coast Route, and the solutions that have been adopted, in the next chapter we will consider the way in which it is transferred to the trains which have already run over parts of the line at speeds of more than 160 mph.

Chapter Six

RUNNING OUT THE WIRES

As well as organizing the supply of power to the lineside, the railway electrical engineers also have the far more extensive — and costly — task of installing a contact wire above each of the tracks to be electrified so that trains can draw the necessary current to power their motors. This is a complicated task, which not only involves the actual installation work, but, in the process, also interrupts the normal job of running the railway. However, since the early days of 25kV electrification in this country, BR and its contractors have made great strides in the way in which both aspects of the work are carried out, and the main facets of this will be described in this chapter.

Table 11 shows how the costs of installing the fixed electric equipment have changed since the first BR main-line 25kV electrification was undertaken. The figures are in pounds per single track kilometre, rather than being on a route-mile basis, since this removes the complications of trying to compare lines of very different character. There are well-established industrial indices for the effect of past inflation on materials and labour, and these have been used in the second column to correct the figures to those which would have applied in the first quarter of 1989. It will be seen that the cost has been vir-

Table 11: Reduction in costs of electrification equipment, 1956-88*

Scheme	Dates	Costs (£ per single track kilometre)	
		Actual	At first quarter 1989 prices
Euston–Manchester–Liverpool	1956-1967	13,800	127,000
Weaver Junction–Glasgow	1971-1974	15,300	91,000
Great Northern Suburban	1973-1977	25,400	78,900
Midland Suburban	1978-1982	42,900	74,600
East Coast Main Line	1984-1988	66,500 †	68,400

* Fixed equipment, excluding that at supply points
† At third quarter 1988 prices

tually halved over the last 35 years, and to these savings must be added those made by the railway operators themselves, who have made a considerable contribution, especially on the East Coast Electrification. The streamlining of layouts at numerous places, particularly at major stations like York and Newcastle, has appreciably reduced the number of track miles that require wiring. The traveller has often also gained, with speeds being raised as a result of the additional space which has enabled the civil engineer to redesign the track geometry.

One of today's electric trains has to be able to collect the equivalent of 6,000 hp from the overhead contact wire at full speed. This is done by the pantograph on the roof of the locomotive or power car, which has two met-allized carbon contact strips on its top surface. A force of approximately 20 lb.f presses these on to the bottom surface of a hard-drawn copper contact wire, which is just under half an inch in 'diameter'. As shown in Figure 17,

Figure 17 *Cross-section, life-size, of the BR 25kV contact wire.*

however, the section is not actually circular, but has twin grooves in the upper half to enable it to be gripped by the 'droppers' which support it from above. When new it has a cross-sectional area of 107 square millimetres, which means that it weighs almost 2 lbs per yard. Although referred to as a 'wire', in short lengths it is too stiff to be bent by hand. For satisfactory operation it has to be held firmly at precise heights above the track, and its lateral position must similarly be fixed. Neither must change unduly as the pantograph passes along it, nor must the contact wire be blown about by the wind or the slip-stream of a passing train.

At very low speeds it is possible to use just a single conductor, which is referred to as a trolley wire, but with such a simple arrangement the need for frequent supports to ensure vertical and lateral stability makes it economic in only a few instances. It is thus rarely used on BR's 25kV system, usually inside a fan of sidings where speed is low, or in a depot or terminal station where the roof structure can provide the support. Everywhere else the contact wire is suspended from a 'catenary' wire, so called because its shape approximates to that of a mathematical catenary curve. It consists of a cable twisted from seven strands of wire; two of these are aluminium-coated steel to provide the necessary tensile strength, while the other five are of aluminium. This is a more efficient conductor than copper, on a *weight basis*, and so provides the equivalent of an extra 40 per cent of the cross-section of the contact wire. The catenary is designed to sag between each of its supports, but the use of drop-pers of different lengths between it and the contact wire enables the latter to be given a precisely controlled sag in the middle of the span, which equates to the extra uplift caused by the passing pantograph at that point. In this way the extension of the pantograph above the vehicle does not have to change unduly quickly.

Both the catenary and the contact wire have to be tensioned to perform in the desired way, and on the Mark IIIB system each of them is subjected to a tension of 11 kN (1.1 tons force). To prevent this varying with the ambient temperature, the end force is applied by weights and pulleys, which compensate for the resulting expansion and contraction. In our climatic conditions such a system can deal with only just under $1^{1}/_{4}$ miles of wire, so the catenary and contact wires are divided into sections no longer than this. The ends of adjacent sections run parallel to each other, enabling the pantograph to change smoothly from one to the other. For the King's Cross suburban electrification the contact wires had only been tensioned to 8.93kN (0.9 tons force), which is adequate for speeds of up to 100 mph, so modifications have accordingly been made to the fast lines south of Hitchin to increase the contact wire tension to the higher figure needed for 125 mph.

At one time high-speed electric wiring used a pair of catenaries, one above the other, this being known as a 'compound catenary'. Another configuration used has been the 'stitched catenary', which has a second catenary wire for a short distance on either side of each support. The French adopted this for their first TGVs to Lyon, but have since changed back to a simple catenary for the TGV-*Atlantique*, where they set up a world record of 320 mph in May 1990. Although BR used a simple catenary system for the East Coast

On a Sunday in May 1988, a Class '317' for King's Cross approaches New Southgate on the 'wrong' line, passing an engineer's train on the up main. The workmen on the latter are modifying the overhead wires to increase their tension for higher-speed operation, as described in the text.

Electrification, on high-speed stretches the height of the masts has been increased by almost a foot, in case it should later be necessary to install a more complicated catenary.

There are various different ways of supporting the catenary wire, but BR's 35-year experience has enabled considerable simplification to take place, and this has been one of the main contributions to the lower cost. On single- or double-track stretches separate masts are used for each line. On each of these is mounted an insulated triangular cantilever structure, extending out over the track to support the catenary. These are now fabricated from galvanized steel tubes in place of the more expensive non-ferrous ones used on earlier schemes. The lower tube of the cantilever also supports the horizontal registration tube, which locates the contact wire horizontally by means of the steady arm. The latter is hinged at its fixed end to enable the contact wire to lift as the pantograph forces it up in passing. On straight stretches of track, where the equipment is not unduly exposed to high winds, the masts are normally positioned no more than 73 metres (80 yards) apart, but this can be stretched to 75 metres if any subterranean obstacles are discovered while the foundations are being excavated.

Perhaps the biggest change that has taken place in the design of the overhead equipment between 1956 and the present day is on multiple-track sections. Travellers on the West Coast route will notice how complex assemblies are used for this purpose, which, in turn, required very substantial portal structures, of fabricated steelwork, to support them (see the photograph on page 59). On the East Coast Route the present-day equivalent is much simpler, consisting of a single or double girder mast on each side of the track, with a 'headspan' stretched between them. This is formed from three spans of stainless steel cable, the upper one approximating to the shape of a catenary itself as it provides the support for the multiple sets of wiring. Below it are two horizontal cables which locate the top and bottom of the inclined tubes, one for each contact wire at that point. Each of these tubes contains an insulator, with the catenaries being supported immediately below these. The steady arm supporting the contact wire is pivoted from the lower end of the inclined tube, below the level of the bottom cross-cable. The old design of portal structure required the services of a crane to lift it into place, but a modern headspan can be fixed to the masts by men working from ladders.

This operation can even be carried out during a very brief track occupation between trains, after clearance has been obtained from the signal centre by telephone or radio. In places where there are long lengths of automatic signalling, between York and Northallerton for example, a system was introduced using a switch on one of the signals, which could be turned to put those on all the tracks to danger. When the timetable permitted, a railway operator turned the switch, and then gave the contractors the 'all clear' to begin work. By that time one end of the headspan had already been fixed to its mast, with pulleys having been slung similarly from the one on the other side of the tracks. The equipment was then spread out across the lines, and the other ends of the headspan wires were fixed to the lifting tackle to be hauled up into place, where they were fixed permanently by men working from ladders. As soon as this was complete, everyone got out of the way, and the signal switch was restored to normal so that trains could pass once more. Before this method of working was introduced, it was demonstrated to the Railway Inspectorate, and duly approved.

After the cantilevers and headspans are in position, the task of running out the wires can take place, starting with the catenary, and this is done from drums carried on one of the electrification trains. On ordinary double track, one end of the wire is fastened to a mast and the full 'tension length' unreeled as the train moves forward, being looped over pulleys temporarily fastened to the top arm of each cantilever. When the full length has been run out, it can be tensioned, and the pulleys then changed for permanent clamps. This sequence is not possible with headspans, as the catenary has to be threaded through each of them. In that case the drum wagon is kept stationary at one end of the length, and the free end of the wire is pulled out by the train, which has to stop at each headspan for it to be unclamped from the vehicle and threaded over the pulley on the inclined tube. There is another difference here too, as some of the construction pulleys are replaced by permanent ones, to accommodate the expansion that takes place towards the ends of each tension length. Following the fixing of the catenary, the droppers have to be put up and then comes the running out of the contact wire, which can always be done from a moving drum. This is clipped to the bottom end of the droppers and tensioned. Where there are crossovers, overlaps, low bridges or other places where the run of the wires is not straightforward, the appropriate items have to be inserted into the overhead equipment in the correct location. This is done either from a motorized trestle trolley on the track, or from ladders.

The contact wire must not be kept exactly above the middle of the pair of rails it serves, because this would cause severe local grooving in the pantograph contact strips. The alignment is therefore deliberately varied to make the contact wire sweep across much of the width of the pantograph to spread the wear. On straight track it is usual to achieve this by making alternate steady arms 'pull off' the contact wire in opposite directions. Since these arms are much more stable in tension, any horizontal pull by the contact wire is usually made away from the pivoted end. For the same reason, successive steady arms on sharp curves usually pull off in the same direction — away from the centre of the curve. The position of the contact wire can thus vary laterally for 400mm (15³/₄ inches) on either side of the centre-line of the passing pantograph. This allows for any tolerances in the alignment of the track and overhead equipment, and for the sway of the locomotive. It is now customary to minimize the effect of the latter by using anti-roll bars on the bogie(s) nearest the pantographs. Although the normal Mark IIIB catenary had successfully been used by the APT when it set up the British rail speed record of 162.2 mph in 1979, a few small changes in design were made to cope with the expected future running at 140 mph on the East Coast Route. Longer steady arms were fitted, and these are more deeply curved to allow greater pantograph uplift. In addition, hoops attached to these straddle the registration tubes in place of the previous wire windstays, or uplift stops are fitted.

It is also very important to ensure that the lateral position of the contact wire at mid-span is as near the centre-line of the rails as possible. This is where the maximum sideways displacement will occur in high winds, and these can blow from either side of the line, although local topography may make the gusts stronger in one direction than another. The procedure is therefore to adjust the staggers at alternate registration points to give a zero offset in mid-span under calm conditions. If this cannot be achieved on a particular curve with the planned layout of masts, that stretch has to be redesigned with additional masts, which cut down the unregistered lengths of contact wire. This is done during the design state, before any installation work is done out on the track other than any surveying which may be needed.

When the first Mark III catenary was installed over Shap, some problems were experienced with high winds blowing the contact wire off the side of the pantograph. The latter then rose to its full height and was damaged when it hit the next supporting structure or span wire, which also suffered in the process. Such happenings have also occurred on the first of the French *Lignes à Grande Vitesse*, where one of the TGV power cars has been known to cocoon itself in over 1,000 metres of contact wire before coming to a stand. On both sides of the Channel, appropriate changes to the configuration of the overhead conductors and the applied tension have now overcome this problem of excessive 'blow-off'. On the other hand, it is not possible to protect them completely from vandalism, flying debris or falling trees, the last of these being the major cause of trouble during the severe gales that struck this country during the winter of 1989-90.

Rogue pantographs can also damage the catenary, in particular by losing part of a carbon contact strip, which can unclip the contact wire from the droppers. A lot of work has been done to minimize this problem, and some interesting results emerged from a study into a spate of such happenings on the Great Eastern lines in 1989. It was found that the occurrence was not detected when the locomotive with the faulty pantograph caused the initial damage, and the wires did not come down until after many subsequent trains had passed, perhaps on the following day, which complicated the identification of the actual locomotive or multiple-unit responsible. As part of the general investigation into the effects of lateral winds and variations in the characteristics of individual pantographs, special equipment has been installed on the West Coast Route near Cheddington to record the behaviour of the overhead line equipment as each pantograph passes it. Accidents apart, experience has shown that Mark IIIB equipment, including the contact wire, experiences very little wear or other deterioration, and has a projected life of at least 50 years. By contrast, some of the French 1,500V dc suburban contact wires have had to be replaced after only two.

Any high-voltage equipment has to use insulators of various sorts, the main types on our 25kV systems being of porcelain construction. In certain places glass-fibre rods are used, notably at neutral sections. When our first ac electrifications were carried out, these installations were well over 100 yards long, and consisted of a number of overlapping lengths of catenary to prevent pantographs, particularly a succession of them on a long multiple-unit train, bridging the gap. This complicated the choice of lineside locations for the switching gear, and also increased the possibility of a train becoming 'gapped', with its pantograph in contact with the dead section of line. Many years ago a new type was developed, utilizing two lengths of glass-fibre rod, with ceramic beads strung on it, separated by an earthed section of ordinary contact wire. As 'seen' by a passing pantograph, such an installation has the same diameter and dynamic behaviour as the normal contact wire. Its overall length is only 4.5 metres (14³/₄ feet), so there is no need for the multiple overlaps.

The overhead wires provide the power for the train, but the electricity has also to return to the transformers at the Feeder Station. In the first instance this passes through the locomotive's wheels into the running rails, which have to be fitted with traction bonds to take the current through points and crossings and between tracks. Then, as shown in Figure 18, booster transformers are used to induce the current into an aluminium return conductor, which is mounted on the masts, but insulated from them. This is done to produce an inductive field opposite from, and approximately equal to, the current flowing through the contact wire. It thus minimizes the overall effect on any nearby metallic signalling or telecommunications cables, whether they belong to the railway or to British Telecom. The booster transformers are mounted on the masts at approximately 3-kilometre intervals, and each main running track has its own return conductor and transformers. Fibre-optic communication channels are not susceptible to electric interference, so no precautions have to be taken where British Telecom, Mercury or BR's own cables of that

Figure 18 *Diagram of BR standard arrangements of booster transformers for return traction current.* (BR)

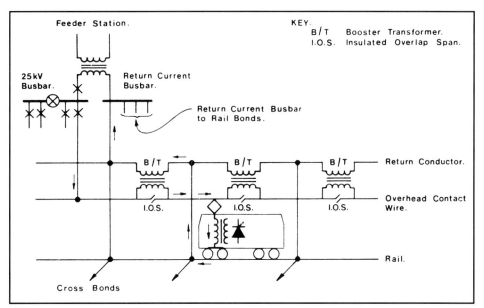

type run alongside the track. The passage of a large ac current can also easily induce a voltage in other nearby metal objects, so items such as masts, lighting standards and station awnings are all earthed. For the same reason, workers alongside the track, on a station perhaps, are not permitted to use metal ladders, which also cuts down the effect of any accidental contact with the live wires.

In a few places it is necessary to provide 25kV feeders for short distances alongside the line. These are also mounted on the masts, but have to be provided with insulators capable of taking full line voltage, which are thus larger than those used for the return conductors, whose potential only reaches a maximum of a few hundred volts. These 'Bare Wire Feeders' are sometimes required at a Feeder Station when the track geometry or signal locations may make it impossible to site the neutral sections exactly opposite places where land is available for the switch gear, and there are some other special conditions where they are also necessary. To differentiate these cables from the

A circular pile is vibrated into the ground at the lineside. Further piles can be seen stacked on the works train, ready to be installed further along the track. (BR)

return conductors, and so act as a warning, all Bare Wire Feeders have small triangular plates threaded on to them at intervals, which make them immediately obvious to anyone working on the lineside.

As already indicated, overhead electrification work necessitates the installation of large numbers of masts to support the overhead line equipment. In the case of the East Coast project some 33,000 were involved, and each had to be provided with a foundation of some sort alongside the line. Traditionally these have been constructed in situ from mass concrete, mixed in equipment mounted on one of the special electrification trains. After the hole has been dug, formers, reinforcing and a core are inserted and the concrete poured in. When this is set and cured, another train comes along with the masts, which are put into the holes using cranes. Aligning and grouting is then carried out, sometimes having to be completed on a third separate occasion. Two or three track occupations are thus required, which adds to the time and expense. In some cases a solid concrete foundation is constructed, and the mast attached by bolts.

A close-up view of a piled foundation, with the mast attached. (BR)

For much of the East Coast Electrification, however, a different foundation technique was adopted, which had been pioneered on the Southminster branch and the Romford–Upminster electrifications. Instead of digging holes and casting concrete foundations, cylindrical steel piles were vibrated into the ground, using hydraulic equipment clamped to the top of them. With no need to wait for concrete to set, the mast could then be bolted to the top edge of the pile immediately afterwards, without the need for a second track occupation. The technique is thus extremely rapid, and as many as eight piles and masts could be installed in a period of 25 minutes, although a more typical rate would be four to five per hour. This technique can only be used where the ground is consistently neither too soft, nor exceptionally hard or stony. In the course of my numerous journeys up and down the line while this part of the work was going on, it was amusing to see the occasional pile which had clearly hit an obstacle and was sticking up in the air, breaking the neat sequence of fully positioned masts. The system can also only be used for twin-track lines, as the length of the steel cylinders which would be needed for the taller masts supporting four-track headspans would make them too expensive and difficult to handle. However, the speed advantages are particularly useful when minimizing interruptions to services on twin-track sections, and the technique was used for most of the way from Newark to Leeds, and from Chathill to Tweedmouth. Although more expensive than concrete foundations, the piling system becomes more cost-effective when account is taken of the lack of disturbance caused to the travelling public. Nevertheless, every stretch of line was considered on its own merits, and it was determined that piled foundations would not have been economic between Newcastle and Chathill, even though the equipment was otherwise lying idle.

There were three major stretches of the East Coast Route where special arrangements had to be made to install the supports for the overhead wires. The first of these to be tackled was across Stilton Fen, between Yaxley and Holme, south of Peterborough. The track here is carried over the very fertile black soil of the area on a long straight embankment, where, in spite of the efforts of successive civil engineers, HSTs still have to restrict their speed over the 3 miles concerned because of the poor underlying soil conditions. Larger-than-normal concrete foundations were used here, on which were mounted portal structures with hinged bases, spanning the two tracks. The two other difficult locations were north of Newcastle, at Newham Bog and Grantshouse Bog, where the line had again been built on extremely soft foundations. The latter is situated just south of the Penmanshiel Diversion, and, when that was being constructed in 1979, a considerable depth of peat had to be dug out to reach the valley floor before the new formation could be constructed. To obtain the required stability for the masts, steel piles, made from universal-column sections, were driven into the bog until they reached bottom and obtained a 'set'. In places this was some 30 feet down, and successive lengths had to be welded on as the driving took place. Finally, the piles were capped with concrete, and, as at Stilton Fen, portal structures were used, crossing both tracks to give the required stability for the overhead wires. North of Doncaster on the Leeds and York lines, allowance was also made in places for the effects of possible colliery subsidence.

In a number of places special consideration had to be given to the visual effects of the overhead line equipment. The simplest cases were when a mast was due to be erected right outside the window of a lineside house, and the problem was solved by moving it a few feet along the track. In other places visually sympathetic arrangements were used by ensuring that a series of masts were of the same height. Perhaps the most unusual aspect of mast positioning concerned three of them at Abbeyhill Junction, just east of Waverley station in Edinburgh. Their tops would be visible from some of the upstairs windows at the back of Holyrood House, and permission had duly to be obtained beforehand from the Comptroller of the Royal Scottish Household.

There were more difficulties when it came to running out the wires past some of the railway's listed structures, notably the stations at York, Newcastle and Edinburgh, in addition to some of the major viaducts. It is rather ironic that, in spite of the fact that there were often outcries when the latter were built, there were similar protests that their appearance would be spoiled when BR wanted to put masts on top of them for the electrification. At Durham it was even suggested that a third-rail system should be used over the viaduct, with all the complications which that would have caused to the design of the locomotives. A special type of portal structure was eventually produced for use here, as well as on the Royal Border Bridge across the Tweed at Berwick. Designed by Ove Arup, these are very slender, and the cross-members are supported by 'knees' on their upper side. They are quite strong enough when in place, although they proved tricky to install, and were considerably more expensive to manufacture. Their low visual impact is very apparent when approaching the Tweed from the south, when they only become obvious from the train as it reaches the southern end of the structure, and the succession of masts can be seen end-on.

In the major stations the overhead wires have usually been suspended from headspans fixed to the roof structure, which makes them reltively unobtrusive against the dark background. This situation had already been met at St Pancras, where the designs used had been approved by the Royal Fine Arts Commission and other authorities. After that installation was complete, and it was being shown to the London Fire Brigade, they expressed some concern that the wiring was not sufficiently visible, so special markers had to be installed! It was often useful for those responsible for granting the necessary permission to be able to obtain an impression of final appearance, and photomontages were prepared for this purpose. At York a dummy headspan was put up a year in advance to enable people to see what these would look like. No publicity was given to this installation, and there was a complete absence of reaction from the public.

Formal consent is required for all alterations to listed buildings and structures, and this required considerable time and effort to obtain. In this connection it is worth recalling that during the five years between 1985 and 1990, BR's total of listed structures rose from 630 to 1,063. And it is not just listed structures that caused changes to the way in which the electrification was carried out. In Northumberland, where the railway passes through an area of 'outstanding natural beauty', a new design of booster transformer was used, cylindrical in shape, which was less visually obtrusive, although some 15 per cent more expensive. In some places, the cabins containing the lineside switch gear were painted green.

In most cases, the erection of the overhead line equipment could not start until much of the necessary civil engineering work and track changes were complete, although there were exceptional cases where some electrical work had to be done in advance. This was clearly possible if a mast was to be located clear of both present and future tracks, but in some cases conductors were run under bridges that not not yet been lifted. An outline of this civil engineering work will be described in the next chapter, but the new clearance standards for 25kV wires were an important consideration, as they avoided the need for much engineering effort on overbridges and tunnels. As a result of the experience gained with earlier electrification schemes, the former 'minimum' standards have become the 'normal' ones, with a new 'reduced' clearance being used where space is limited. The gap can now be as little as 200mm (7³/4 inches) when the conductor is in its static position, but it can lift by up to 50mm (2 inches) as the pantograph passes. Out in the open, the contact wire is well below the level of the catenary, but where the overhead clearance is tight a 'twin-contact wire' arrangement is used. Some distance on each side of the low-point, the catenary is cut and then joined to a second length of contact wire. This is brought down level with the ordinary one and the two run side by side underneath the obstruction, before reverting once more to the normal layout. This is always done where the pantograph might come into contact with both, and also where there is the possibility of roosting

Booster transformers in the storage compound at the Newcastle Electrification Depot. The standard type are on the right, and the others are the special cylindrical design used in parts of Northumberland.

birds causing a flash-over, which could damage the stranded catenary, but not the solid contact wire.

Under bridges or tunnels, the twin wires are supported resiliently from the overhead structure by a large-diameter glass-fibre rod, covered with poly-tetrafluoroethylene (PTFE) or silicone rubber. An important development in the successful use of this item was the redesign of the live metallic end-fitting which holds the wires. By replacing sharp corners with a domed top, there was less electrical stress, which reduced the likelihood of an arc being struck. Such a fitting can be allowed to rise to within 70mm (2³/₄ inches) of the underside of the overhead structure. The coatings on these rods are sensitive to excessive heat, and hot particles particularly. (This is why it was not possible to take *Mallard* through Stoke Tunnel to revisit the site of its exploit on the occasion of the 50th anniversary of its world speed record in 1988. Although the exhausts of a hard-working HST pump out a vast quantity of hot gases, these are not potentially laced with red-hot cinders like the blast from a steam locomotive.)

In 1978 British Rail's Director of Mechanical and Electrical Engineering took over the responsibility for the electrification work from the regions. This new section also adopted computer-aided design for overhead systems and compilation of materials lists for the work, which had previously been done manually by the contractors. The latter had not been able to start the work until a scheme had been authorized, and there were difficulties if, for example, the required track layout was changed. On the other hand, with the aid of the computer, BR's own staff could complete much of the specification before formal authorization, and could react much more quickly to changed requirements, both of which speeded up the completion of the work.

The overhead line equipment for the East Coast Electrification was put up by two firms, Balfour Beatty and Pirelli Construction. At the time that the project was authorized, the latter firm was working on the Ayrshire electrification, and negotiated contracts were let to Balfour Beatty for three sections, working northwards as follows:

Hitchin–Newark
Newark–Leeds and Northallerton
Northallerton–Cramlington

After Pirelli had completed its work in south-west Scotland, it was also awarded a £9m negotiated contract for the Chathill–Edinburgh stretch, and moved its construction teams over to the East Coast Route. That left the Chathill-Cramlington gap, and this was put out to competitive tender between the two companies. The £4 million contract was won by Pirelli which, in September 1989, on a similar basis, was also successful in obtaining the subsequent £4 million contract for the 'add-on' Edinburgh–Carstairs electrification.

BR has established a pool of works trains for use on electrification systems, and these are made available, free of charge, to the contractors. BR supply the motive power, the train crews and the lookouts on the same basis. For the East Coast scheme, four electrification depots were established, at Peterborough, Doncaster, Newcastle and Edinburgh. Experience had shown

Electrification work in the sidings at Skelton, just north of York. In the first illustration a works train pours concrete for mast foundations in July 1988, as an HST from the South West heads for Newcastle on the main line. Just beyond its leading power car can be seen Skelton signal box, which was demolished after its duties had been taken over by the new signalling centre at York. A short distance north of the site there is now one of the Feeder Stations for the East Coast Electrification.

In the second picture, taken a year later, the contractor's staff adjust the overhead wiring, their train temporarily blocking the exit from the yard for a Class '56' which has worked a coal train in from the north. The nearest vehicle on the electrification train is a half-deck one, fitted with a pantograph to check the alignment of the contact wire. In the intervening 12 months, the main lines have been completely wired.

that one of these could successfully deal with the electrification of more than 300 single-track kilometres, spread over a radius of 50-65 miles. At each of them there was office accommodation — in the same building — for BR and the contractor's staff, plus stores, workshops, and various sidings. Some of these had space alongside for stacking equipment, while other areas were used to handle and sort steelwork, conductors and foundation materials. An important part of each depot was the building where headspans and cantilever arms could be constructed to individual requirements, under cover. There was also provision for the maintenance of the various plant items, many of which were mounted on the works trains. On one visit I paid with a press party to the Peterborough depot when it was being inspected by Sir Robert Reid, I noted with amusement that the only concrete batching machines in the depot were those that had broken down. All the serviceable ones were out on the job! Table 12 gives a list of these depots, together with their approximate periods of operation.

The utilization of all this equipment out on the track had to be very carefully organized to minimize operating costs and avoid too many interruptions to the normal train services. The latter problem was particularly acute on some of the twin-track stretches, and ingenious operating patterns were adopted to minimize the disruption. Erecting the overhead line equipment could be done one track at a time, but even overnight it was not possible to handle all the normal traffic on the Stoke–Doncaster stretch using the other track. Accordingly, the night-time pattern saw the ordinary trains in one direction being diverted from Peterborough via Lincoln and Spalding, while

The jig for constructing cantilever arms in the Newcastle Electrification Depot.

the electrification work went on one track at a time. The overnight position on the other long twin-track stretch between Newcastle and Edinburgh was somewhat easier, as traffic was lighter, and had longer gaps between trains, particularly after the withdrawal of the East Coast sleeping-car services. It is rather ironic that much of the electrification work at York and Newcastle could not be carried out until after the layouts had been rationalized, which, in the process, removed the surplus tracks. The work had to be fitted in on Sundays or overnight, and in the summer of 1989 it was quite common, when one reached York on a late evening train, to find it had been diverted to an unusual platform, while an electrification train occupied the normal one.

On the East Coast Route, many of the final adjustments to the overhead line equipment were carried out from the track using ladders. Access to much of the lineside is now possible for BR road vehicles, and the contractors similarly used their own vehicles to reach these areas. BR again provided the look-outs and obtained the necessary clearances from the signal centres by telephone or radio. A considerable amount of work could be fitted in between trains in this way. When this stage had been reached on the Selby Diversion, on one occasion, as I travelled south in my HST, I was struck by how short the interval was between passing a group of men up the ladders on the other track and the next down HST using it.

Finally comes the task of commissioning each part of the new system,

Table 12: Electrification construction depots

Location	Operational period[1]	
	Start	Finish
Peterborough[2]	March 1985	September 1988
Doncaster (Hexthorpe)	August 1985	September 1990
Newcastle (Heaton)	March 1987[3]	May 1991
Edinburgh (Millerhill)[4]	March 1987	November 1989

[1] The dates are approximate, as the depot's activities did not start and finish like timetabled train services.

[2] Work on the East Coast electrification contract was carried out initially from Biggleswade, prior to the opening of the Peterborough depot. After completion of the work on the East Coast Main Line, the Peterborough depot continued in operation for the Cambridge–King's Lynn scheme.

[3] Although the Newcastle depot was formally opened in October 1986, work on the site did not begin until the date given.

[4] At the north end of the East Coast Route, the electrification work was initially carried out from Barrasie and Tweedmouth from October 1986, prior to the opening of Millerhill depot. After the completion of its East Coast activities, the depot was expected to remain open until December 1990 for the Edinburgh–Carstairs electrification.

which is carried out in several stages. First of all the alignment of the contact wires is checked with a pantograph on the roof of one of the construction trains, before they are energized. Experience has shown that if this inspection is satisfactory, there is usually no need for further tests at full line speed. Then comes the visit by the Department of Transport's inspecting officer, who is particularly concerned about the safety of the public and railway staff. He looks at items such as the provision of warning notices, guards to prevent people climbing the structures, and the raising of parapets on overbridges. When this is complete, the line is energized, but even then further tests have to be carried out before commercial services can start. After the static electrical tests have proved satisfactory, each line is then tested with a Mobile Load Bank, which has been converted from one of the early ac electric locomotives. It has no traction motors, but by opening the controller the 'driver' can allow it to take up to full power from the overhead line, dissipating the energy as heat in the resistances which have been installed. It is towed or propelled over every electrified line by a diesel locomotive, with technicians monitoring the currents and the behaviour of the system, while the signal engineers similarly keep an eye on the working of their equipment. It is rare, but not unknown, for some small but vital part of the overhead line equipment, such as bonds or jumpers, to be missing or misaligned, causing an electrical discontinuity or making the circuit-breakers operate. After the cause of any such problems has been identified, the circuit breakers are closed and the testing continues. When all this has been completed, the newly electrified stretch is handed over to the operators. It is then normal practice to keep the wires energized at all times until services start, not only to enable training and trial runs to be carried out, but also to discourage the activities of any light-fingered scrap-merchants.

In the case of the East Coast Route, the commissioning stages for the

'Spidermen' — in their distinctive orange overalls, contractor's workmen adjust the overhead wires where the East Coast Route crosses the Anglo-Scottish border. (BR)

On 17 September 1989, the Mobile Load Bank is hauled through Platform 5 at York by a Class '31' diesel locomotive in the course of the commissioning tests being carried out on the overhead electric wiring.

electrification up to the end of 1990 are given in Table 13. Full details of subsequent energization dates will be given in *The Railway Magazine* when the new services start. The rationale for the way in which this was done was very carefully worked out, taking into account the commercial demands as well as the engineering limitations. As far as InterCity was concerned, it was decided that the first long-distance public services would start on the line to Leeds. Although there was some inter-working of sets in HST days between the West Riding and the services to Newcastle and Edinburgh, from the short-term point of view most of the Leeds trains just operated over that stretch of line, so electric operation could be brought into use that much earlier. This would also enable the London–Leeds stretch to act as a proving ground for the first batch of the new Class '91' electrics, and enable any required changes in their design to be incorporated in the remaining 21 locomotives that would be built later. The major remodelling and resignalling needed at York and Newcastle would, of necessity, hold back these parts of the scheme, but, in any case, the Pirelli General wiring teams were not available to start work on the stretch between Chathill and Edinburgh until the Ayrline electrification had been completed in 1987.

On the other hand, with the foundations for the masts already in place over the 27 miles between Hitchin and Huntingdon, that section could be brought into operation comparatively quickly. The introduction of electric services over this stretch would enable the Huntingdon–Stevenage diesel railcar shuttle to be replaced, using existing — and proven — designs of EMU, which would be a big advantage for the booming commuter traffic developing over the route. From Huntingdon on to Peterborough was less than 18 miles, and the extension of electric Network SouthEast services to that point would relieve the loadings on the InterCity HSTs, some of which were working down light from Bounds Green every morning to handle the rising tide

Table 13: Energization dates for the East Coast Electrification up to the end of 1990

Section	Date
Hitchin–Huntingdon	13 October 1986
Huntingdon–Peterborough	16 March 1987
Peterborough–Grantham	7 March 1988
Grantham–Geldard Road (Leeds)	11 April 1988
Geldard Road–Leeds Central	4 July 1988
Doncaster–Copmanthorpe	4 July 1989
Copmanthorpe–York	4 September 1989
Leeds–Neville Hill	30 April 1990
York–Northallerton	25 June 1990
Belford–Edinburgh	3 September 1990*
Belford–Lucker	5 November 1990

* The official energization ceremony was carried out on 12 September 1990 by Malcolm Rifkind, Secretary of State for Scotland.

of commuters wanting to travel to London.

Accordingly, commercial electric services were introduced from Huntingdon on 3 November 1986, and on 13 April 1987 between London and Peterborough. The former inauguration had been two months earlier than originally planned, but when Princess Alice, Duchess of Gloucester waved EMU No 317 369 away from Peterborough to inaugurate the new Network SouthEast service between there and London, it was *five* months in advance of the date that had been given when the East Coast Electrification was authorized. Also in the spring of 1987, InterCity was able to announce that the electrification to Leeds was no less than a year ahead of schedule, and

On 3 November 1986, No 312 708 waits to leave Huntingdon with the first electric service to King's Cross. (BR)

electric trains would commence running between there and London some time in the summer of 1988. Delivery of the new Mark IV coaches would not have started by then, so special arrangements were made to enable the Class '91s' to haul modified rakes of 'InterCity 125' stock, as described in Chapter 8. For reasons that will be explained then, these 'Hybrid' sets included a working HST power car, which gave them a very high power/weight ratio, enabling them to achieve some remarkable performances over the route.

The energization of the line to York was pushed forward in the summer of 1989, partly to enable the delegates to the international conference on Main Line Electrification to be taken to York on 24 September using the first 'InterCity 225' set, which was specially chartered by GEC Alsthom, the builders of the Class '91s'. At the beginning of the winter timetables the following month, if one of the 'Hybrid' sets was available, it was used for the 06.00 service from York to King's Cross. There was no comparable down public working from London that finished in York, as the stock for the 06.00 came from Leeds via Doncaster just before midnight, and stood in the station overnight. It was not until the introduction of the special InterCity long-distance commuter trains on the East Coast in May 1990 that the new 20.45 from King's Cross formed the first regular down electric working to York. From the autumn of 1989 most of the London–Leeds services were being worked electrically, with the first 'InterCity 225' set being rostered for the prestige 'Yorkshire Pullman' workings, and the 'Hybrid' rakes were progressively displaced as the new Mark IV sets were delivered and commissioned during the following winter. In July and August 1990, it was decided to use 'InterCity 225' sets for three daily round trips between York and London on Saturdays, to provide welcome relief for the holiday crowds.

The major engineering and resignalling work taking place at Newcastle meant that it was not correspondingly possible to bring forward the extension of electric services further north, but energization of the electric system is due to take place during 1991 from Edinburgh through to the outskirts   of Newcastle. This will enable trial and training runs to be carried out with the new sets by the Scottish and Tyneside crews. The start of electric running through Newcastle and south to Northallerton requires the prior commissioning of the new Integrated Electronic Control Centre on Tyneside and the new signalling system for this section of the East Coast Route, as the old equipment was not immunized against the stray currents which can arise with ac electric traction.

Chapter Seven

OTHER ENGINEERING WORK

At the time that the East Coast Electrification was authorized, the cost of the civil engineering part of the scheme was given as £35 million, which represented a very modest 11 per cent of the total. To a large extent this reflected how much the East Coast Route had already benefited from major attention by the engineers, with some £100 million having been spent on improvements to the track and signalling in the 1970s. Even before the work that was done to prepare the line for the advent of the 'InterCity 125' in the late 1970s, it was being said that the line had been 'rebuilt by stealth' and, from the early days of the 'Deltics', passengers have benefited from the steadily-rising speed profile. This would not, however, have necessarily cut down on the civil work necessary for electrification, because much of it was concerned with overhead clearances; but even so, a number of significant improvements had been carried out in that direction too.

Back in the late 1950s, when the accelerated schedules for the 'Deltics' were being planned, major attention had to be given to the permanent way. North of Shaftholme Junction, the track inherited from the North Eastern Railway relied extensively on the use of ash ballast, and a relatively thin layer of it at that. As part of the speed-up required under the Modernisation Plan, the thickness of the ballast had to be increased, and the ash replaced with stone or slag. As already recounted in Chapter 2, at that time plans were also being developed for the electrification of the East Coast Route. As mentioned in my earlier book *Speed on the East Coast Main Line*, Maurice Barbey was then in the Bridge Section of the region's Civil Engineering Department, and personally examined every overhead structure between Shaftholme Junction and the Scottish boundary at Marshall Meadows, to determine what work would need doing to obtain the necessary clearance for the overhead wires. When it subsequently proved necessary to lift many of the overbridges to obtain the required thickness of ballast, it was frequently economic to obtain the additional clearance for the wires at the same time, even though electrification had not actually been authorized. In more recent years, all new overbridges have to be built high enough to take overhead wires, unless there is a very good reason for not so doing. Indeed, even the highway authority at Skipton had to get a special dispensation from the Department of Transport for the restricted clearances at Holywell Bridge when they were building it over the Embsay Steam Railway's eastward extension towards Bolton Abbey.

As a result of work of this sort, many of the overbridges north of York had already been lifted prior to 1984. The construction of the Selby Diversion in the early 1980s also meant that there were 13 miles of new railway between Shaftholme and York where overhead clearances were adequate. In spite of these bonuses, when the East Coast Electrification was announced there were still 127 overbridges that had to be raised or reconstructed, and this total eventually stretched to 157, although, as a partial compensation, the number of masts required fell from the initial estimate of 33,000 to 29,500. It is not possible to detail all this civil engineering work, but some of the more interesting examples are worth describing.

Dealing with bridges first, one of these overhead structures is particularly unusual, in that it is an aqueduct, situated just north of Abbots Ripton, where it carries Bury Brook across the line. While reprofiling a road surface across a bridge that has been raised does not normally cause much difficulty, the same clearly does not apply where water is involved. The railway at this point runs through quite a deep cutting, cut through London clay, which would have made it extremely difficult to provide adequate drainage if the track had been lowered. Fortunately it proved possible to redesign the aqueduct itself, which now crosses the four tracks in a single span. The trough was widened and a much thinner deck provided, which gave the necessary clearance for the overhead wires at this critical point. The new structure was put in place before the old one was taken out of use, and the stream was diverted once it was complete.

The new Bury Brook aqueduct near Abbots Ripton, viewed from the rear cab of the first 'Stansted Express' EMU on its record-breaking delivery run from York, travelling at 89 mph.

In many cases road overbridges were completely demolished and rebuilt to a different design. Many of those spanning multiple tracks were blown up with small explosive charges. At one of these, situated near Peterborough, the plunger was pressed by a 9-year-old boy who had won a BR-sponsored competition in the local paper. The explosive technique had been used extensively for many overbridges on the London Midland main line, as well as in the North Eastern Region, but demolition contractors had developed another way of dealing with brick arches that spanned only two lines. Using an air-operated pick mounted on the end of the arm on a hydraulic excavator, bricks could be 'chipped' away from either side of the centre of the arch until it collapsed. The clever part of the operation was the way in which the operator sensed the imminent collapse, and immediately lowered the arm so the excavator avoided tumbling into the cutting, remaining perched on the abutment with the end of the pick resting on what was left of the bridge.

As was the case with the Abbots Ripton aqueduct, many of the overbridges that needed reconstructing were rebuilt with a single span crossing all the tracks, rather than retaining the multiple arches of the original design. There were, however, two notable exceptions to this. The last bridge to be lifted south of York was No 9, situated on the very edge of the city, at Bonds Hill Ash Farm. Clearances under its twin skew arches, each carrying two tracks, were increased by using precast concrete units put in place by a crane operating between the two temporary Bailey bridges which had been constructed, one on each side. Only one of these was required to provide a temporary way past for road traffic, while the other supported no fewer than 14 ducts carrying telephone cables. To add to the difficulties of the bridge engineers, because the electrification to York had to come into operation very shortly after the bridge would be complete, the overhead wires had already been threaded through the structure before work commenced.

Immediately south of Doncaster station, the 140-year-old St James's bridge also required attention prior to electrification. It spanned the lines with no fewer than nine arches, each of which was used by at least one track, but only the three centre ones required to be raised to provide the extra clearance. The first idea was to build a completely new bridge, which would have been cheaper than reconstructing the existing one on the same site because in the latter case the road traffic and all the public utilities would have had to be diverted on to a temporary structure. However, Philip Payne, then the Eastern Region Project Manager for the whole electrification, came up with a much better solution. If only the three centre arches had been demolished, all the others would have collapsed like a set of dominoes, so the two outer piers of the affected spans were thickened to increase their lateral resistance. When this was complete, the centre arches could be safely demolished and replaced with a new single pre-stressed concrete span, 70 feet long. Only half of the bridge was dealt with at a time, so it remained open to road traffic throughout. The accompanying illustrations depict the 'before' and 'after' scenes.

The first overbridge south of York station is the steel truss example at Holgate; this was constructed in 1910 to enable the city's trams to run out to Acomb, and was too low for the overhead wires. Consisting of a single span

Bridge at Bonds Hill Ash Farm

In the middle of the night, demolition experts nibble their way through the brick arches of Bridge No 9, just south of York.

A few hours later the debris from one arch has been completely removed, and the overhead wires, which had already been strung through the bridge, are being fixed to the cantilever supports, getting them out of the way for the first Sunday train to pass.

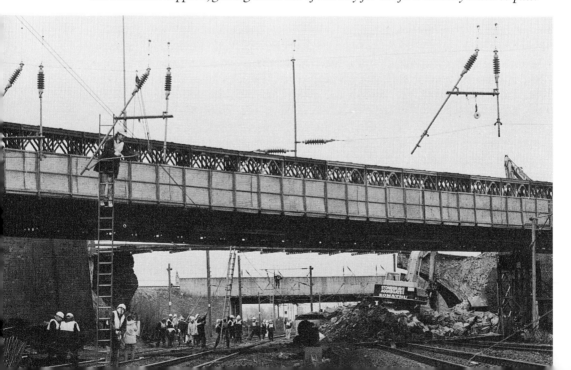

The new pre-cast skew arches are eased into place, under one of the temporary Bailey bridges. (all photos, BR)

across a number of tracks, on a very busy line, it was obviously a candidate to be lifted bodily, and plans were duly worked out to do this. Consultations were carried out with the highway authority, in this case North Yorkshire, and a plan of action agreed. However, when this was announced, howls went up from some of the York councillors, who claimed that as much as a quarter of the city would be cut off for up to six months. In fact, the proposal was for the jacking to take place in the middle of the night on two weekends, and, although road vehicles had to be diverted, pedestrians were still able to cross while the work went on. There were also other vehicle diversions while the road surfaces were relaid, but the actual degree of hardship was very small indeed, totally out of keeping with the fuss that was caused. One had much more sympathy with those living beside the line nearby during the long periods of overnight work on the track while the layout there was being remodelled.

The size of the bridge needing attention did not necessarily determine the amount of effort necessary to carry out the work. At Drem and Prestonpans, quite close to Edinburgh, the station foot bridges needed to be raised. However, they were both listed structures, and there was no way in which they could be altered to give the required clearances. With the agreement of the local planning authority, a totally new design was produced by a group of young engineers and architects, and the resulting structures, costing £80,000

St James's Bridge, Doncaster

Above *As it was with the nine original arches.*

Below *The bridge after the central spans had been rebuilt, as described in the text.* (both photos, BR)

Right *Lifting Holgate bridge, just south of York station, with a set of hydraulic jacks at each corner. Because the span is on the skew, temporary overhead bracing was required to maintain its stability during the operation.* (BR)

each, were highly commended by the Scottish Civic Trust. The redundant old bridges were offered to various heritage and preservation bodies.

Bridges are normally only a few yards wide, but there can also be difficulties with overhead clearances in tunnels, which, on the East Coast Route, are up to three-quarters of a mile long. Over the 32 miles from King's Cross to Hitchin, the 25kV wires had already been put up by 1977, when the Great Northern Suburban Electrification was completed, as described in Chapter 3. However, the 1984–91 East Coast Scheme inherited another bonus further north, where clearances had been improved through Stoke and Peascliffe Tunnels in 1978–9, when the track had been lowered to permit the passage of containers constructed to the new international dimensions. In Scotland, Penmanshiel Tunnel had tragically collapsed when it was receiving the same treatment, and, as a result, the line was diverted round it, in the open, once again eliminating any future problems there with clearances for overhead wires.

However, considerable work was still required on the tunnels in the Edinburgh area. Immediately outside Waverley are the two in the side of Calton Hill, bored through volcanic rock and boulder clay, where clearances were tight. As a result, both were singled and the track layout was altered so that they could be used in either direction. The 142-year-old south bore required strengthening over much of its length, at a cost of £600,000. This involved the use of 1,000 rock bolts, each nearly 15 feet long, while the eastern third was lined with pre-cast bolted sections, similar to those used on the London Underground. Complete closure to traffic lasted for four months. Clearances in St Margaret's Tunnel — just over a mile away — were dealt with differently, with the formation being lowered throughout. This also required complete closure of the two lines of track affected, but trains could be diverted along the Abbeyhill curve, round the north side of the Meadowbank international athletics stadium, to approach Waverley from the direction of Leith, using lines that were subsequently closed.

In addition to providing the necessary clearance for wires passing under a bridge, precautions must also be taken to prevent anyone from being able to touch them from the structure itself. Parapets had to be lifted in many places, and 'steeple' copings were frequently used to discourage people from climbing on to them. Following accidents where large road vehicles out of control have demolished whole sections of parapets and fallen on the track below, new bridges have to conform to higher construction standards to prevent such incidents happening in future. Open footbridges have to be protected by having panels fitting along the sides where they cross electrified tracks, and in places this has been done using sheets made of tough transparent plastics, which retains the lightness of the bridge's appearance. The most notable example of this is probably the footbridge in the middle of York station, dating from 1939–40. To obtain the required clearance for the wires beneath, part of the main cross-girder of this welded structure had to be cut out. By itself, this would have seriously weakened the bridge, but, with the removal of the two centre tracks through the curved trainshed, it was possible to provide an additional vertical support in the middle. To judge from the lack of vibration

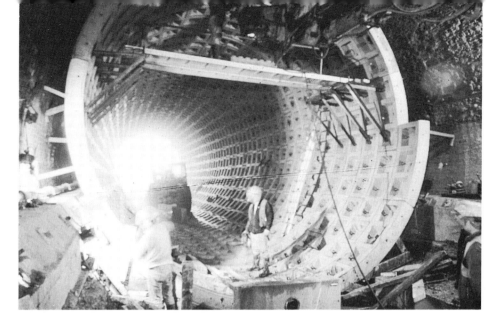

Relining Calton Hill tunnel at Edinburgh. (BR)

The station canopy at Morpeth after it had been moved 3½ feet away from the tracks. Some of the ornamental edging had been missing, but was replaced in the course of the work. (BR)

in mid-span as one crosses it these days, the structure is now appreciably 'stiffer'. Just north of Darlington station another solution was adopted for the long footbridge there, the sides and top of which form a transparent tube.

Increased clearances were also required in other places. As part of the East Coast Route electrification, a number of additional tracks and sidings in the London area had to be equipped with overhead wires, including the carriage-washing road between Hornsey and Alexandra Palace. Previously the mul-tiple-units had gone through their own washer in Hornsey Depot, but facilities were also needed to deal with the electric-hauled main-line stock without having to resort to diesel traction. This was fairly easily achieved by opening up the arch of the former washing plant, to give a clear passage for the pantograph on the locomotive.

Station awnings were not so easy to deal with, however, and in several places they were too near the proposed line of the overhead wires and passing pantographs. In many places these awnings formed part of listed structures, which complicated the task of the engineers. York was one such place, and there the width of the awnings was reduced slightly, the attractive edges being retained but set back a short distance. At Durham, the awning on the down side was also foul of the overhead wires, but, instead of cutting it back, the track was slewed slightly, and the platform extended forward, which addition-ally enabled the maximum speed through the platform road to be increased from 20 to 40 mph. Yet another solution was adopted at Morpeth, where the whole canopy was moved sideways away from the line by just over $3^1/_2$ feet. The five bays are supported on ornate cast-iron columns and trusses, the whole of which had to be jacked up and rolled into its new position. The actual move took place overnight, although the whole project, including the refurbishment and repainting, lasted for 15 weeks.

Major remodelling of the stations at York and Newcastle has taken place in connection with the East Coast Electrification, although these projects were separate from the original 1984 authorization. At both places a new power signalling scheme had been introduced in the 1950s, but very few changes had been made to the track layout at either station at that time. During the intervening years the whole way of railway working has altered drastically, and fewer facilities are needed to handle today's trains, particularly since so many of them are now capable of being operated in either direction. The track lay-outs were somewhat cramped, especially at Newcastle, and a number of awk-ward operating features would be able to be eliminated by the remodelling, which would give a useful bonus in reduced running times.

York was the first of the two areas to be completed, the work starting in March 1988 and finishing 15 months later. There were, at that time, nomi-nally 16 platforms, but a number of these had already either been closed or had virtually gone out of use. As shown in Figure 19, a drastic reduction in the number of tracks was possible, which also enabled the speed limits to be relaxed very considerably. There had been four tracks between the two main platform faces under the splendid curve of the 1877 train-shed. In the decade since the 'InterCity 125s' had been introduced, changed service require-ments had meant that every passenger train called at York but, from May

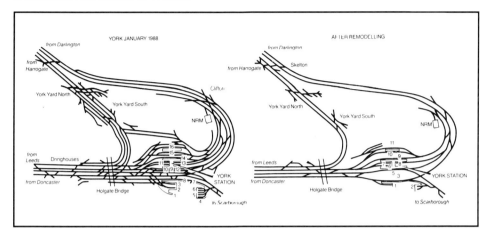

Figure 19 *Diagrams showing the old and new layouts of running lines in the York area.* (BR)

1990, some of the 'InterCity 225s' will pass through non-stop. There was, however, still no need for the pair of through tracks in the centre, and their elimination simplified the new layout, and also aided the task of wiring the tracks, since, as we have seen, the basic structure of the existing footbridge could be retained.

Although the great simplification in the track layout that took place is immediately apparent from Figure 19, it does not actually show the number of different and difficult routings that used to exist. A better idea of the complexities of the old set-up is given by Figure 20 (overleaf), but even in that the station curve has been eliminated, which removes some of the complexity of the old layout as seen by a driver of an approaching train. Coming into the main down platform (No 9) from the south used to involve a diversion to the left soon after Holgate Bridge, followed by a swing back to reach the south end of the platform, the whole operation having to be carried out at little over 15 mph. Similarly, an express leaving for the south from the main up platform (No 8), had to travel much of the distance to Holgate Bridge before its tail was clear of the speed-restricted turnout routing it on to the up fast.

After the alterations, from the south end of this platform, now renumbered 3, trains have a completely clear start along the up main for Doncaster and beyond. Through the station the speed limit has increased to 30 mph, which rises to 40 at the south end of the platform, and a few yards beyond Holgate Bridge the restriction is up to 90. This later rises to 100, and the full 125-mph line speed is permitted not long after the site of the one-time junction at Chaloners Whin, where Tesco has now built a supermarket partly on the formation of the old line to Selby. An HST leaving platform No 3 can now have full power applied from the moment the driver gets the starting bell from the senior conductor, and the controller only needs to be eased back when the full line speed is reached, somewhere south of Colton Junction. Compared with the former layout, the present diesel trains are a minute faster over the first 2 miles, and the 'InterCity 225s' should do even better with

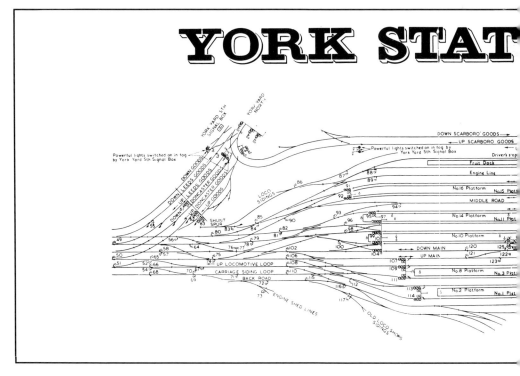

Figure 20 *Layout of tracks in York station in 1951, showing details of the new signalling.* (BR)

their higher power to weight ratio, once double manning is introduced on those serving York. Many East Coast trains in both directions also use platform No 5, and they additionally benefit from the altered layout, which, in this case, involves the forward extension of the platform face at the south end to match the realigned track at this point. The approach to the present platform No 9 from the south has also been improved, while the speed limits over the goods lines that avoid the station to the west have also been increased. This considerably assists the operation of freight trains, which can often be seen rounding the curve at Holgate, even during daylight hours, and the squeal of flanges is a thing of the past.

Carrying out all this work 'under traffic' was far from easy, and some interesting planning and operating procedures were employed. The first stage, in early 1988, involved the goods lines bypassing the station, and this was followed, in the autumn, by the removal of the through lines in the station itself, which enabled the remodelling of the north end to start. To give a better alignment on the main line round the sharp curve where there used to be a diamond crossing with the Scarborough line, the end of platforms Nos 9 and 12 was trimmed back. The track was removed from the latter, leaving the new No 8 for the Harrogate trains as the only one in that bay. Over on the far side of the old platform No 16, the track northwards was temporarily slewed to connect with the through line outside it, and trains had to stop somewhat

ION IN 1951

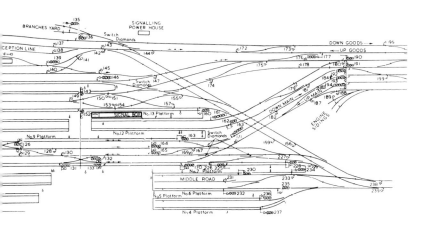

further south than usual, before a gap opened up between them and the platform face. When all this was complete, sweeping curves had replaced the former sharp turnouts, enabling the speed limit to go up to 30, and, over the winter period, there were 30 mph and 15 mph restriction signs back-to-back in the centre of the station.

As usual, much of the engineering work was carried out at weekends, but, with the limited number of tracks at the north end, the major remodelling inevitably blocked all of them at times. On these occasions, trains to and from the north used the freight lines west of the station, reversing into or out of the station between the platforms and Holgate Bridge. With an extra driver being provided to save those already on an HST having to walk the length of the train, the operation was quite slick. The work at the north end of the station was completed before the bad winter weather was expected, and during the following months stockpiles of materials were gathered for the onslaught on the southern end, which was being planned for early the following spring. In this case it was possible to split the work into two halves, so, even at its most disruptive, some of the tracks still remained in operation. Nevertheless, the scale of the work was much greater, with large panels of new track being pre-fabricated and moved bodily into place, while other lines were slewed sideways into their altered alignments. The final change-over of the platform numbers took place on 14 May 1989, and coincided with the commissioning of the new signal box.

At Newcastle the remodelling took a very different form, with a new island platform being constructed as part of the work. As at York, over the years the

Remodelling York station (I)

Above *In November 1988 work had just started on lifting the middle roads through York station as this up HST prepared to leave what was then Platform 8.*

Below *By the end of 1988, the platform awnings at York had been cut back and the necessary clearances obtained for the overhead wires under the footbridges. In March 1989, an up HST eases its way into Platform 14 past the back-to-back 15/30 mph speed restriction signs.*

Above right *New panels of track and pointwork were assembled in the former Dringhouses Yard, ready to be transported to the south end of York station.* (BR)

Below right *A named Class '47' in InterCity livery eases a southbound train out of Platform 9 at York as the engineers finish dismantling the old layout on the up side of the station.* (BR)

Remodelling York station (II)

Above *With the floodlit towers of York Minster in the distance, engineers move one of the new sets of pointwork into position south of the station, using the special transporters.* (BR)

Below *A few weeks later the new trackwork on the up side is in operation, and the engineers have moved across to deal with what remains of the old layout. The simplicity of the new track is striking. York signalling centre can be seen behind the block of the crane on the left.* (BR)

Right Figure 21 *Diagrams showing the old and new layouts of running lines in the Newcastle area.* (BR)

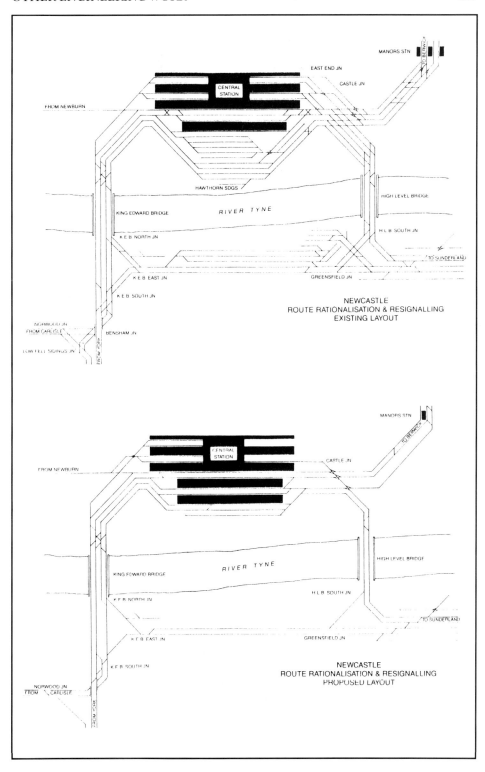

NEWCASTLE
ROUTE RATIONALISATION & RESIGNALLING
EXISTING LAYOUT

NEWCASTLE
ROUTE RATIONALISATION & RESIGNALLING
PROPOSED LAYOUT

train movements on Tyneside had altered very considerably. Not only had the Metro taken over the services to and from the coast on both sides of the river, but the Hexham and Sunderland workings had been integrated, to avoid the disadvantages of layovers in Newcastle station. After the demolition of the bridge across the river at Blaydon, the Tyne Valley services have run via Dunston rather than Scotswood, and the fly-under at Bensham means that they join and leave the main line on the east side.

The way was thus open for the Hexham–Sunderland shuttles to be kept completely clear of the East Coast Route, and to be given a new 'suburban' platform on the south side of the station, which, at the same time, would avoid the need for the celebrated diamond crossing at the north end of the High Level Bridge. Noteworthy though this layout was, it was costly to construct and maintain, and part of it had already disappeared when some of the bay platforms at the east end had been converted to car parks. Some of the trackwork has been saved by the National Railway Museum, however, and is expected to appear there in 'sculpture' form. As shown in Figure 21, more of the bays at Newcastle went out of use, leaving just No 7.

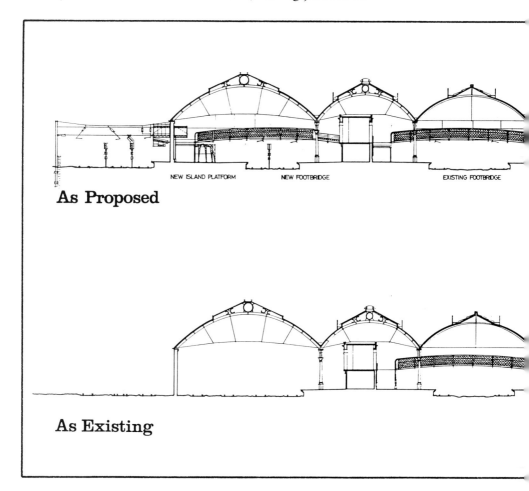

NEW ISLAND PLATFORM   NEW FOOTBRIDGE   EXISTING FOOTBRIDGE

As Proposed

As Existing

For the first 2 miles from Newcastle to Heaton, the East Coast Route used to be quadruple, but for almost the whole distance the four lines were squeezed on to viaducts or into cuttings. Lateral clearances were very tight, and this resulted in severe overall speed restrictions, the worst being at Manors, where the dc electrics at one time used to diverge to the left for Jesmond. To overcome this handicap, one of the four tracks was eliminated throughout. This has enabled a much better alignment to be adopted for the remaining ones, with consequent up-grading of the speed restrictions, while bidirectional signalling restores some of the lost flexibility. The work was complicated, however, by the fact that there were overbridges on this stretch where additional clearance had to be obtained for the overhead wires, so there was extensive track lowering.

Newcastle area remodelling (I)

A cross-section of the train sheds at Newcastle Central station as they were in August 1989, together with the proposed addition of the extra island platform on the river side. (BR)

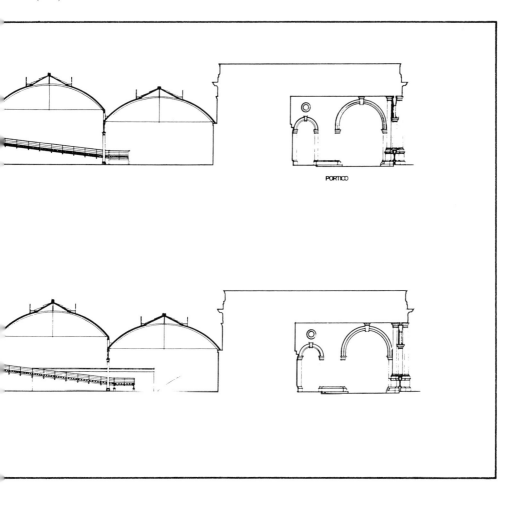

PORTICO

Newcastle area remodelling (II)

Left *A down HST leaves Newcastle Central over the famous diamond crossing.*

Below left *Diamonds are* not *for ever! The same scene after remodelling in 1990.*
(Neville Stead)

Above *The new Manors station begins to take shape in April 1988, but the better-aligned tracks on the left have not yet been connected.*

Below *A Class '47' works an up train through Redbarns 'Tunnel' in April 1988. The new concrete slab has been laid through the left-hand span, and the girders have been renewed. The arch just visible to the right of the locomotive used to take the electrified goods line down to the Quayside. The Metro's tracks are now situated immediately beyond the concrete wall on the far right.*

Going northwards along the line from Newcastle, Manors station has been renewed and placed somewhat nearer the Central, which has enabled a much better alignment to be adopted, with the previous 20 mph restriction at this point being doubled. A short way further east is bridge No 18, also known as Redbarns Tunnel, where the one-time electrified branch to the Quayside dived into a tunnel from the goods yard beside the main line. The main bridge is triangular in plan beneath a major road junction on New Bridge Street, which is an important traffic artery in the city, and raising it would have been impossible. The situation was complicated by the existence of a long retaining wall on the down side before the bridge, which had been given additional support by timber piles some 60 years ago. These had to be removed and replaced by a series of cross-girders which were cast into a concrete slab, 350mm (13^3/4 inches) in depth, which later supported the ballast and track. The southern parapet girder had to be replaced too, because of corrosion on the bottom flange; it had to support the ends of over 40 transoms on the skew.

Another structure to need major attention was bridge No 26, carrying Heaton Road across the line at the north end of the one-time Heaton station, with its two island platforms. In this case it was high enough for the overhead wires, but full use had to be made of the extra width in the cutting where the station had been for the new track layout at this point, and this necessitated the rebuilding. Because of the proximity of other bridges it was possible to close the road for three months, and the old structure was demolished, except for part of one of the intermediate piers. This was raised and used to support the new pre-stressed concrete beams, which formed the basis of the composite deck. Parapets to the latest Department of Transport design were required, capable of withstanding a blow by a large lorry out of control, and they were formed from blocks of 'reconstructed' stone, laid in random courses on either side of a reinforced concrete core. As is so often the case, the bridge carried a lot of services, which had to be maintained during the rebuilding. Getting the various utilities to move their mains and cables is an expensive business, and, only too often, they have to be moved back again at the end of the work. To avoid this here, a new small bridge, No 26A, of London Midland design, was constructed slightly to one side, and the services were diverted permanently on to it. Although the road closure was no great hardship to vehicular traffic, it was much less convenient for foot traffic, so a temporary deck was laid above the services, enabling pedestrians to continue to cross the line while the work was going on.

The extremely complex civil engineering work on these 2 route miles has formed part of the critical path for the completion of the East Coast Electrification, the position being made worse by the need of access for empty stock between Newcastle Central and Heaton Depot. At the time of my visit to the sites with the Railway Study Association, back in April 1988, bridge No 26 was already virtually complete, and the new ballast was being spread on the concrete slab under Redbarns Tunnel. Even so, over two years later trains threading their way along this stretch of the East Coast Main Line were still subject to major speed restrictions because of the continuing engineering work. In addition to the interruptions caused to road traffic, full or partial possessions of the railway tracks were required from time to time, and there have been occasions when Anglo-Scottish trains have been diverted via Carlise and Carstairs.

Diversions of East Coast trains off their normal routes are normally confined to weekends, but there was one blockage in connection with the Electrification Scheme which lasted for nine days. This was for major engineering work to take place on the viaduct at Durham, as a preliminary to the installation of the special portal frames for the overhead wires. At the start of the occupation, the old track was lifted, which enabled the spent ballast to be stripped off from the stone slabs which form the deck of the structure. It was dumped at the foot of the embankment in the south-west corner, where it could subsequently be landscaped and planted with trees. A two-foot thick layer of concrete was then cast on top of the stone slabs over the full length of the viaduct, leaving spaces for access to the voids in the tops of the piers. When the concrete was dry, a waterproof membrane was spread over it, sandwiched between two layers of geotextile, to ensure that all water falling on the structure would be diverted into the renewed drainage system. Finally the ballast and track were reinstated. Meanwhile, in the station the down platform face was being realigned, as recounted earlier, to provide the required clearances between the overhead wires and the canopy. Preliminary work was also started to extend the length of the platform at the north end by 60 metres, to accommodate longer trains. Some of the preliminary work for the new portal structures for the overhead wires was also carried out, but their installation took place somewhat later.

During this period trains were diverted between Tursdale and Pelaw, running via Leamside where special arrangements had to be made to overcome the chronic vandalism from which this line suffered. To serve Durham, a road service was introduced between there and Darlington, with an executive coach, complete with hostess, being provided for those using the 'Tees-Tyne Pullman'. For the first two days of the diversions there was also a road service between Durham and Newcastle, while work was carried out on several other viaducts and bridges on this stretch, but after that a rail shuttle was introduced between the two cities. In the main, trains maintained their normal schedules south of Durham, but the diversion added approximately 20 minutes to their running times. Northbound trains thus reached Newcastle 20 minutes later than shown in the timetable, and those continuing to Scotland were correspondingly retimed for the rest of their journey. In the opposite direction, departures were approximately 20 minutes earlier as far south as Newcastle, which enabled the trains to pick up their normal timings to London by the time they reached Darlington. All trains stopped at this latter station, for the bus connections to and from Durham, and a number of cross-country HSTs reversed here, as their turn-round time at Newcastle was less than 40 minutes. The whole operation was publicized extensively beforehand, and everything worked very well, both on and off the site.

The other large English city involved in the East Coast Electrification was Leeds. At the time of nationalization there were two major stations there,

Durham Viaduct repairs (I)

Concrete to waterproof the top of the viaduct is pumped up from road level.

The concrete is spread into position, covering the old tie-bars holding the parapets together.

After laying the geotextile covering, new ballast is spread by a bulldozer.

Finally the new track is laid. The up line appears to be complete, but the check rails still have to be put in place on the down one.

Durham Viaduct repairs (II)

Meanwhile, from the temporary walkways alongside the arches, holes have been bored to take the cross-members that will support the special portal structures for the overhead wires.

Durham station alterations

The track is relaid through the station after the down platform face has been realigned to give the necessary clearance between the canopy and the 25kV wires.

City and Central, and the idea of combining them was first mooted in 1959, the same year as the Newcastle colour-light signalling system was brought into operation. However, eight years were to pass before Central was closed, and all the passenger activities concentrated on the rebuilt City station. This resulted in a major reshuffling of the layout to the west of the station, and provided two routes for trains leaving in the direction of Wakefield Westgate and King's Cross. One of these was the realigned curve at Whitehall Junction, which enabled trains from the City station to climb up and join the lines which had previously served the terminus at Central. To supplement this, a major change was made to the one-time London & North Western viaduct line which crossed the south-western part of the city in the direction of Farnley on its way to Huddersfield and Lancashire. A new curve was constructed at its western end, severing its trans-Pennine connection, and linking it instead to the East Coast Route at Geldard Road Junction. The longest platforms in the new City station — used mainly by the London trains — were on the north side, nearest the passenger access, and to gain the Wakefield line by either of the new connections meant that these trains had to cross nearly the full width of the tracks at the west end of the layout, the 1959 option for a flyover in the Whitehall area having been abandoned. Although the viaduct was dead straight for much of its length, the sharp curves at both ends imposed severe speed restrictions in addition to those which resulted from the pointwork immediately outside the station.

When the East Coast Electrification was being planned, consideration was given to the possibility of remodelling the layout at Leeds in the same way as those at York and Newcastle, but any major changes were ruled out on grounds of both time and expense. As already mentioned, the strategy for the

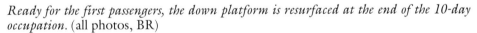

Ready for the first passengers, the down platform is resurfaced at the end of the 10-day occupation. (all photos, BR)

whole project involved introducing electric traction between London and Leeds 18 months ahead of the rest of the system. The whole station area is also a very difficult one from the engineering point of view, since it is built on a continuous viaduct. In recent years the area underneath the platforms has partly been developed as a shopping area, and those using it are able to see the two-dimensional array of arches which support the railway above. Some of these funnel the waters of the River Aire under the tracks, while the upper portion of another row was used for the new passenger subway in the station, which still leaves plenty of headroom for people to walk underneath it.

Unlike the situation in the late 1950s on the London Midland Region, when nearly all the existing tracks were electrified, the East Coast scheme was managed in a very different way. Under Sectorisation, the electrification of each track had to be justified on its own and InterCity was only prepared to pay for the wires through certain platforms, and over one pair of tracks from the Wakefield direction. As a result, the viaduct line was severed at its western end, and minor improvements were made to the approach via Whitehall, which gave a modest improvement in speeds. At the station end, the first section of the viaduct route was retained as a siding and electrified, providing a suitable stabling point for an 'InterCity 225' set, since at that time the £1.8 million extension of the wires to Neville Hill depot had not been authorized. The situation is altering again with the West Yorkshire Passenger Transport Authority's plans to electrify some of the routes it supports, and further tracks were wired in the City station to enable its first multiple-units to replace diesel railcars on the Doncaster line in the summer of 1990. The rapidly growing ridership in this rail-orientated PTA could well justify major changes in the layout at this end of the station in the not-too-distant future, particularly with major extensions of its electrified system. The need, in due course, to renew the power signalling system could also help the financial justification for such a scheme but for the East Coast Electrification the present original equipment was immunized against any stray ac currents in the usual way.

The civil engineers have also made many other contributions to the improved speed profile of the East Coast Route when the new electric schedules are introduced in 1991, but many of them involve techniques that are not solely applicable to this or any other electrification scheme. By far and away the most important of these was the development of the Dynamic Track Stabiliser, which compacts the ballast so that, when a relaid length of track is handed back to the operators, it is cleared for immediate 125-mph running. As recounted in *Speed on the East Coast Main Line*, these techniques, which also reduce the cost of the relaying work, were pioneered on the King's Cross–Edinburgh line, and enabled HST workings between London and Aberdeen to be speeded up by as much as 25 minutes. This not only provides a major business advantage, but there are additional savings in brake-pad wear and energy. By the summer of 1990, five non-stop HSTs a day were being booked to reach York in 111 minutes from King's Cross, which corresponds to an average of 101.8 mph. In July 1990, when I was official timekeeper for the high-speed delivery run of the first 'Stansted Express' unit from York to King's Cross, there was only one temporary speed restriction in the whole of the1188^1/$_2$ miles between these points.

Reference has been made earlier to the problems of putting up the electrification masts across Newham Bog in Northumberland. It was also possible to improve the stability of the track over this, by replacing the original raft of animal skins and brushwood with a layer of geotextile, on which were placed two layers of 'Geoweb', a three-dimensional plastic honeycomb approximately 8 inches deep. These were separated by a plastic net, and both layers were filled with stone chippings. On top of this complex structure a layer of ballast a foot deep was laid to support the track. Each line was dealt with separately during a full weekend track occupation when trains were diverted via Carlisle, but, once the track had stabilized, the speed limit over the bog was lifted from 80 to 100 mph.

We must now turn our attention to the work carried out by the signal and telecommunication engineers in connection with the East Coast Electrification. Their share of the original £306 million authorized on the project was £27 million, but this was increased by a further £49 million to cover the resignalling schemes at York and Newcastle, which, although associated with the electrification, were justified on their own account.

The 'basic' signalling work between Hitchin, York and Leeds involved alterations being made to some 1,500 track circuits, 1,000 signals and 600 point machines. Such work has always been an important part of any electrification scheme, even in dc days, since the large return currents flowing through the rails can easily energize a track circuit which had been occupied by a standing train, thus causing a 'wrong-side' failure. With ac electrifications the flow of power along the overhead wires can also induce voltages in the lineside signalling cables that could, potentially, move points or alter signal aspects, and all such possibilities have to be eliminated. For the East Coast project, even those track circuits which were already immunized had to be altered to cope with the return traction currents. Well-established ways of carrying this out have been developed, but they are expensive and require considerable time to complete. The operators may be able to dispense with the use of a particular track for a short period while the civil engineers remodel it, but doing without the signalling system is not possible, unless the line is also taken out of action, or speeds reduced in such a level that hand-signalling can be adopted. A lot of careful planning is thus necessary to carry out these aspects of any electrification scheme, and the East Coast Route was no exception.

The large power boxes controlling the station areas at York and Newcastle were installed in 1951 and 1959 respectively, and were notable examples of the signalling technology of their day. In each case large panels showed the tracks through the station, and these would be lit up with a line of white lights whenever a route had been set, while red ones indicated the presence of a train. Each signal, together with its aspect, was also shown by appropriately coloured lights. Trains were routed through the area by the signalmen turning route selection switches, a group of which on the control desk were associated with each signal. Any of these could be used to select a particular onward route from the signal, and, once a switch was turned, the interlocking system went into action in the adjoining relay room. Unlike a normal signal frame, where the signal levers themselves are locked, the switches were always free to move, and it was a series of electrical relays which prevented any conflicting movements. When the selected route had been proved clear, any points that required changing were then automatically operated. Once these had moved, and were locked and detected in their new position, the line of the route would light up on the panel and the controlling signal would clear. Applied to an area like York or Newcastle, the panel and its control desk were extremely impressive. However, they occupied a large area in the signal box; one of the Newcastle signals (No 47) had no fewer than 14 main routes radiating from it, plus a further four subsidiary ones, each of which required its own switch on the desk. The York panel was in four sections, with a total length of 43½ feet, and each section had its own signalman to work it.

Over the decades that followed, power signalling developed in several important ways. Relays were miniaturized, and an alternative way of operating the route-setting equipment was adopted. The display panel and the control desk were combined, and to set up any particular route the signalman just had to press two buttons on the panel, one at the entry point and the other at the exit. All this enabled the space required to be reduced, while another

Part of the old signal panel at Newcastle, with the track diagram beyond the route switches on the desk in the foreground. Some of the blanked-out portions of the diagram can be seen, where tracks had been lifted.

development brought about a vast extension of the operating area of the box. In the 1950s, boxes like York and Newcastle only controlled a relatively short stretch of track. The former interfaced with Naburn, Copmanthorpe, Burton Lane and Skelton Junction, the last two being only $1^1/_2$ miles away, while the area controlled from the box at Newcastle did not even extend to the junctions on the south bank of the Tyne. The reason for the relatively small area that could be controlled was largely the need for each item of equipment, be it a track circuit, or a signal or point machine, to have its own set of wires connecting it with the relay room. Although it had long been possible to use completely automatic signalling systems on lengths of plain track, as soon as any junctions intervened it was necessary to have a local signal box, as it was not feasible to wire each item to a power box many miles away.

This all changed with the development of the Time-Division Multiplex system (TDM), as mentioned in Chapter 5 in connection with the control of the electric supply system. Remote relay interlocking systems could now be built, at junctions for example, and each of these could be controlled from the main signalling panel by a single pair of wires. The high-speed scanning systems at each end are kept in step electronically, which enables each function to be compared at frequent intervals. If a track circuit becomes occupied, this is shown on the main panel, while the relays in the remote cabin clear and set up the necessary routes in the normal way whenever the signalman presses the appropriate pair of buttons. As a result, the latest York and Newcastle signalling systems, situated 80 miles apart, will actually interface with one another on the automatically signalled stretch between Northallerton and Darlington. The continuity of such a scheme also enables the identification number of each train to be passed automatically along the line. It is displayed in the appropriate position on the illuminated diagram, so the signalman is immediately aware of which trains are approaching.

The last few years have seen two other major step-changes in railway signalling systems, with the development of Solid State Interlocking (SSI) and the Integrated Electronic Control Centre (IECC). Both make use of extremely reliable high-power computers, the former system taking the place of the old relay room and the latter the display and control panels. Even though much of the vital equipment is installed in multiple, far less space is required to house it, and the cabling costs are also significantly reduced. A single SSI module can replace up to 3,000 relays, and can, furthermore, be tested in the factory before delivery, thus speeding up the installation process. These systems were developed by BR in conjunction with the signalling contractors GEC-General Signal Ltd and Westinghouse Signals Ltd, and both companies can now compete for installations put out to tender by the railway. They act as the main contractors, and many individual items of equipment, such as the microprocessors, are obtained from sub-contractors.

Because computers can fail from time to time, an appropriate degree of 'redundancy' is built into the system to provide the necessary safety levels. One way of doing this is known as Triple Modular Redundancy, where three identical machines operate in parallel. They constantly check their results, and, if one of them comes up with a different 'answer' from the others, it is

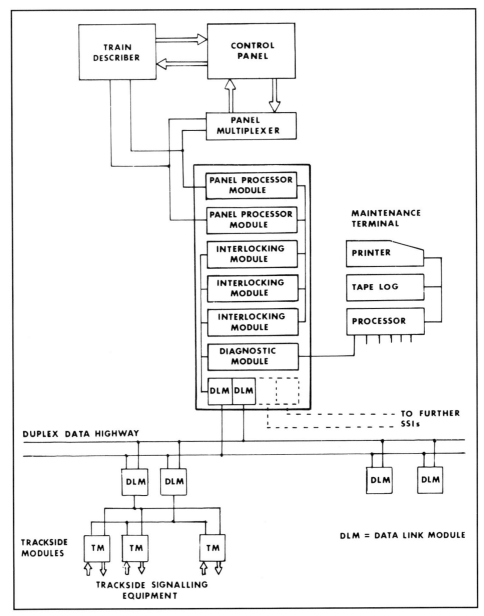

Figure 22 *Schematic diagram of a Solid State Interlocking signalling system.* (Westinghouse Signals Ltd)

automatically overridden, and a warning sounded. Even with items that are only duplicated, the reliability of the items ensures that the mean time between 'wrong-side' failures can be as long as 20 million years! With these SSI systems, electronic data highways are provided between the control centre and the lineside equipment, and these differ from the old TDM systems in that they allocate priorities to different types of electronic messages instead of simply scanning each function in turn. They are duplicated, but this may involve two totally different types of link, such as microwaves and fibre-optic cables.

To operate the railway, the signalman uses the IECC, which is in constant communication with the interlocking modules by means of a pair of panel processors, as shown in Figure 22. Instead of a panel with lights and buttons on it, a number of television screens and a keypad are provided. Some of the monitors provide overviews of a particular part of the system, together with the main signals. Information appears on these in much the same way as on the older type of control panel, showing the state of the points, signal aspects, and routes set, together with the position of trains and their identification numbers. Set into the desk by the signalman's right hand is a yellow ball which he can rotate to move a cursor about the screen. Placing the cursor over a signal and pressing one of the keys has exactly the same effect as pressing that particular button on the older type of panel, and routes are set up on the same 'Entrance-Exit' basis. In addition to these overview screens there are others which show the details in particular areas, and these can be used to operate the subsidiary, or shunting, signals in the same way. The system is much more versatile than a panel, and the cursor and keypad can, for example, also be used to put symbols on the screen to indicate stretches of line where the overhead power has been isolated, or the location of engineering possessions.

Because of the wide area covered by such a system, and the enormous computing capacity available, other functions can be built into it. For example, the timetable for all the trains due to pass through the area is fed into the control centre, and updated daily. If everything is running to schedule, this information is capable of controlling the signals and routes automatically. The signalman only has to step in to resolve problems caused by out-of-course running, such as the effects of holding a connection. The system is also capable of driving the arrival and departure indicators on the stations, but, again, if it is working in this mode it is necessary for the signalman to intervene if changes are being made. In the case of York, there may be a good reason for altering the priorities of trains on the fast and slow lines approaching the single southbound line from Skelton Bridge into the station. Intervention is then necessary to alter the public displays. The signalman is also provided with all the usual other communication equipment, such as the phones used by drivers when they are held unduly long at a signal, or need to report a breakdown. An example of the way in which they are used comes into the description of my footplate run on a Class '91' in Chapter 10.

As already mentioned, two major new signalling control centres of this sort have been built at York and Newcastle. The former, supplied by Westinghouse, was completed first, being announced in August 1986. It is situated on the north side of the tracks alongside the station, and the operations room first came into use in May 1989. That primarily covered the station area and the lines to the south, and control was progressively extended to include the Tollerton, Thirsk and Northallerton interlockings, the last of these being changed over at Easter 1990. By that time Northallerton signal

One of the Integrated Electronic Control Centres in the new York signalling centre. The first monitor to the right of the signalman's head shows the tracks out to the junctions at Hambledon. The other two display the layout at the south end of the station, at two different scales. The smaller work-station should be compared with the illustration of the interior of the King's Cross signal box on page 69.

box had provided over 50 years of service, having been commissioned on 3 September 1939, the day that the Second World War was declared. The distinctive brick building was subsequently demolished before the overhead wires through the station were energized, producing a train-load of rubble.

The York centre now controls trains on some 60 route miles, stretching from just beyond Northallerton, on both the East Coast Route and the line to Tees-side. In the south it interfaces with the Doncaster centre at Temple Hirst Junction, the southern end of the Selby Diversion, and also looks after the Leeds and Normanton lines as far as Church Fenton. In addition it controls the Harrogate branch as far as the start of the first single-track section at Poppleton, and the stretch between Gascoigne Wood and Selby on the line from Leeds to Hull.

On Tyneside a similar control centre is due to be completed in 1991, and the commissioning of its fully immunized equipment will permit the final stretches of the overhead wires on the East Coast Route to be energized, southwards towards Northallerton. There was no space for the centre to be located in the immediate vicinity of Central station, so it has been built on the south side of the river, adjacent to the motive power depot at Gateshead. The main contractor for that installation was GEC Alsthom Signalling Ltd, as the company is now styled. The Tyneside control centre's area only extends northwards for some 15 miles, as the existing boxes at Morpeth, Alnmouth and Tweedmouth have been retained. On the twin-track sections, bi-directional signalling enables trains to be diverted from one line to the other, either to permit engineering occupations, or to enable faster ones to overtake.

The completion of this Newcastle resignalling scheme was unfortunately delayed. In addition to the late delivery of equipment, BR were short of resources, particularly in view of the more stringent safety procedures introduced after the 1988 accident at Clapham. The 1990 Summer Timetable had made provision for diversions via Carlisle on two week-ends in September, but these had to be cancelled, and in November it was announced that there would be a delay in the introduction of the full electric services, originally planned for May 1991.

There is one further development in the signalling system which has an important bearing on the future electric operations on the East Coast Route. As will be described in the next chapter, it was decided to specify a 140-mph capability for the new trains. However, the existing four-aspect signals, spaced along the line at standard intervals, would not provide sufficient braking distances at the higher speed, since an increase of 25 per cent is required as the maximum speed rises from 125 to 140 mph. Accordingly a fifth signal aspect has been introduced — flashing green — which provides the driver with the authority to exceed the present maximum of 125 mph. This system has only been provided on the fast tracks over the traditional racing stretch of Stoke Bank, up hill as well as down, and its use is only authorized for trial running with the Class '91' locomotives and the Mark IV coaches.

Passenger services in excess of 125 mph will not be introduced without the Automatic Train Protection systems which British Rail is planning to install. The new signal aspect to provide the additional braking distance needed at such speeds is likely to be provided in the train's cab, rather than in the installations on the lineside. With the launch of the 'InterCity 250' project for the West Coast Route in the summer of 1990, which is designed to provide running speeds of up to 155 mph by the turn of the century, there is a strong case for the 140-mph capabilities of the existing 'InterCity 225s' to be utilized as soon as they can be economically justified. This provides a useful point at which to leave our consideration of the electrification infrastructure; we must now turn our attention to the developments in motive power and rolling-stock.

Chapter Eight

'INTERCITY 225'

The new electric locomotives and train-sets on the East Coast Route are being marketed under the brand name 'InterCity 225'. In the same way as aircraft and car manufacturers have exploited numerical series, BR has maintained a close connection with the highly successful 'InterCity 125' image which it has developed over the last decade and a half. While the figures in the latter case referred to the train's maximum speed in miles per hour, the new brand-name, 225, is metric, the Imperial equivalent of which is 140 mph, the design speed of the new trains. The 'InterCity 225' project on BR actually pre-dates the East Coast Electrification scheme, and a very different type of train was included in the submission to the Government which received the go-ahead in July 1984. We must therefore start this chapter by looking at the way in which the new BR 'flagship' trains were developed.

From the mid-1970s onwards, BR's strategic planning envisaged the Advanced Passenger Train (APT) coming into squadron service on the West Coast Route in the summer of 1984, but the project was dogged by problems of many sorts. Some were technical, but others were of a human nature, involving both the resources allocated to it and trade union attitudes to change. At the same time, the British media fastened on to the train as one of their targets for national denigration, adding further to the apparent poor image of our country. Over on the continent, France's *Train à Grande Vitesse* (TGV) was to remain in the development stage for broadly the same length of time, but was not constantly being decried by the French media. Had the APT been hailed by this country as a potential world-beater, successive governments and BR might well have been willing to back it to a far greater extent, with a very different final outcome. It must not be overlooked that, by the end of the 1980s, the speed of FIAT's tilting 'Pendolinos' was to be second only to the French TGVs, the trains routinely achieving 155 mph on the Italian '*Direttissima*'. Further west along the Mediterranean, many of the Spanish Talgo trains are 'passive' tilters, while the Swedish Railways have placed in service the first of their 125-mph 'X-2000' trains, which include power tilting.

One of the 140-mph speed restriction signs on Stoke Bank, seen from the cab of a Class '91'.

Here in Britain, the pre-production APT-P finally went into public service in December 1981 only to hit snags, in part due to the severe pre-Christmas weather that year. It did subsequently see limited public service, and three years later set up a Euston–Glasgow record of 3 hours 52 minutes 40 seconds, nominally non-stop, but actually suffering a dead stand at Stafford due to a points failure. A year before this, however, it had been announced that the P-train would not go into regular passenger service.

After sector management was introduced on BR, the whole approach to the provision of new rolling-stock became commercially led, and Cyril Bleasdale, Director, InterCity, was concerned about some of the features of the APT-P. During the first few years of the 1980s, numerous variants of the existing train were therefore proposed and evaluated, but time was already running out for squadron service on the West Coast Route by 1984, and alternative high-speed proposals were also being developed. Five electric HST power cars were ordered and then cancelled, but Brush was successful in obtaining an order for a prototype 125-mph Co-Co electric locomotive of nearly 6,000 hp — No 89 001 — which was subsequently to be named *Avocet*. It was argued by some that three-axle bogies were necessary for the haulage of heavy sleeping-car trains over Shap and Beattock, where the existing, less-powerful Bo-Bo electrics could, at times, have difficulties with adhesion. There were, however, a number of drivers who considered that the thyristor-fitted Class '87' *Stephenson* was somewhat better than the rest of the West Coast Bo-Bos in this respect.

One of the requirements for high rail speeds is a low unsprung weight on each axle. The design of the 'InterCity 125s' called for their power cars to exert no greater forces on the track at 125 mph than the 'Deltics' had imposed at 100, and the same criterion is applied as the speed is raised still further. On the APT-P, the twin power cars had performed well with their motors mounted in the body and driving the bogie axles by inclined shafts and right-angle gearboxes, which gave the low unsprung weight required (1.7 tons per axle). It was the cars' position in the middle of the train which presented problems, this configuration being dictated by two requirements. One was the need for the two of them to be coupled together so they could both take power from the same pantograph, and the second was that a 14-coach train was too long to be propelled from one end only. Experience with the APT-P had shown that a shorter train could be successfully handled by a single power car, and the drive to the axles could be further simplified if it did not have to tilt, regardless of whether this feature was retained for the passenger vehicles.

Accordingly, as the prospects for the APT waned, work started on the 'InterCity 225' project, which had a power car, complete with driving cab, at one end of the train, with the motors mounted in similar fashion to those on the APT-P. In the early versions, the presence of the cab made it impossible to fit four of them in, and its outer bogie would have had one powered and one carrying axle, but the basic concept of a new Class '91' locomotive had emerged.

At the time that the submission was being prepared for the East Coast Electrification, the 'InterCity 225' project was not sufficiently developed for inclusion, and the case was based on the use of the Class '89' Co-Cos. It was intended that these would haul rakes of improved Mark III coaches, with a Driving Van Trailer (DVT) at the other end, to avoid the need for the locomotive to run round its train at the end of each journey. After looking at the position carefully, InterCity decided that this combination did not provide the necessary step-change required to make the commercial impact with the public which they were seeking.

David Rollin was appointed Project Manager for the new East Coast trains, and when he walked into his new office one February morning in 1985, he found a note on his desk. As far as the speed on the East Coast Route is concerned, it ranks in importance with the celebrated comment by Sir Ralph Wedgwood to Nigel Gresley which led to the appearance of the 'A4' 'Pacifics' in 1935. The note came from Cyril Bleasdale, and, in typical fashion, was in a somewhat more flamboyant style:

> The Project Director's life is a lonely one. You have the difficult and important task of writing the conversion case from the Class '89' to the Class '91' for the ECML in three weeks. Good luck.
>
> Cyril Bleasdale.
>
> PS Perhaps you would like to use your initiative to find a telephone, a chair etc.

In company with the Project Engineer, Andrew Higton, a small team worked up the necessary case for the new trains by the deadline stipulated; it was subsequently accepted by the British Railways Board and agreed by the Department of Transport. Because of the higher cost of the new Mark IV coaches, the formation of the new trains had to be trimmed to eight vehicles plus the DVT, although, in the fullness of time, a supplementary authorization was given to build a further 31 coaches to handle the steadily rising passenger loads on the East Coast Route, stimulated by the journey-time reductions already brought about by the HSTs.

The arguments for the change revolved round the need for potential higher speeds and a further improvement in the ambience for the passengers. Although more powerful than a pair of HST power cars, the Class '89' would not, as it stood, be capable of higher maximum speeds than the diesel trains it replaced. It did not conform to the 1.7-ton unsprung axle-loading, and could not operate at the required cant-deficiency of 9 degrees. The reason for making a train tilt has nothing to do with the effect the train has on curved track, but is to make the ride more comfortable for passengers, by reducing the horizontal forces they experience. If curved track is canted so that the resulting forces are perpendicular to the coach floor, the passenger will not be aware of them, but a perfect balance like this can only be achieved at one particular speed. A slower train using the same track will experience too much cant, and this makes the inner flanges grind against the rail, producing unacceptable wear, particularly with high-axle-load freight wagons. As a result, the maximum true cant is fixed at around 6 degrees, which corresponds to a superelevation of almost exactly 6 inches on the outer rail of standard gauge track.

Provided that the track can withstand the lateral forces involved, it is thus customary to fix a maximum speed for each curve, which gives a limited cant-deficiency, which is usually measured in angular degrees, although the 1-to-1 correspondence noted above provides a useful way of relating the amount of superelevation to the cant in degrees. At the time the Mark IV coaches were designed, they were still required to be capable of being modified to provide tilting, were that to be called for in the future. This explains their different cross-section compared with their Mark III predecessors. Development work has, however, shown that seated passengers are prepared to accept a higher cant-deficiency than had previously been thought desirable. Coupled with this, InterCity did not consider that the provision of tilting on the Mark IVs for the East Coast Route would have been cost-effective, although it was expected at that time that a case could be made for a subsequent West Coast Main Line batch to be so equipped. The cant-deficiency experienced by the passengers has been limited to a maximum of 6 degrees, which takes into account the effect on those standing up when going round a curve. Those vehicles which do not carry passengers can curve at up to 9 degrees cant-deficiency, as the drivers do not have to move about, and this requirement has had a significant effect on the design of the motive power.

By the time the tenders went out for the Class '91s', BR was committed to the concept of competitive tendering — in an international market — based on a performance specification. The new class, by that time named 'Electra' by the image-makers, was also to be an asymmetrical design. One cab was to be streamlined, which would form the outer end when high-speed running took place, while the other would have a much 'blunter' profile. When coupled to a rake of Mark IV stock, there would thus be no 'V'-shaped gap between locomotive and train. This had advantages at high speeds: in both directions of travel there is far less energy-consuming drag, and the reduced turbulence also gives the pantograph a much smoother ride when the locomotive is propelling the train. On occasions when they are hauling earlier types of coaches, the locomotives are restricted to more modest speeds, so the lower maximum permitted should they be running with the 'blunt' end forward is no handicap.

Some people do not seem entirely happy about the idea of locomotives *propelling* trains at high speeds. I suspect that this concern may in some cases be a relic from the model railway days of our youth, when it was all too easy to get a train off the line under such circumstances. But railways at '12 inches to the foot' scale are very different, because main-line curvature is much less severe than that used in the confines of the average house. Before the introduction of the Bournemouth electrics in the 1960s, BR carried out many trials with instrumented locomotives and coaches on the Southern, and the largest sideways forces on the wheelsets were recorded at slow speeds while negotiating curves into sidings and the like. The use of high-power 4-REP sets on the Bournemouth line propelling eight unpowered coaches proved perfectly satisfactory for a couple of decades, and the 'ScotRail Expresses' followed in the 1970s. There was, it is true, the case of the cow at Polmont, but that was very exceptional, even confounding George Stephenson's famous remark on the subject. The fitting of a better 'cow-catcher' and the addition of further weight to the leading bogie provided a satisfactory cure.

Worldwide, the propulsion of trains is extremely common, and even in Britain is more widespread than one thinks. Virtually every two-car diesel and electric multiple-unit has only one power car, and so spends 50 per cent of its time propelling its trailer, few of which are provided with any special protection at the front end. Similarly, virtually none of the Southern four-car multiple-units have the power cars at the ends of the set, so are propelling at least one coach all the time. One comment sometimes made centres round the possibility of the locomotive continuing under power after the train it is propelling has derailed. In the case of the 'InterCity 225s', as soon as the air pressure in the train-pipe falls, power is automatically cut off. Regardless of this, the tractive effort exerted by the locomotive is small compared with the other forces that arise on the rare occasions when a train comes off the track. For those still not convinced, I would pose another question. 'In a derailment, is there any difference between the effect on the coach in front of a propelling locomotive and that on the third vehicle from the rear of a train being hauled? When working out the answer, take into account that the former has 82 tons behind it, while the latter would be pushed forward by the combined 88 tons of the last coach and the DVT.'

Initially, three firms bid for the contract: GEC Transportation Projects and Brush in this country, and ASEA from Sweden. Brush dropped out at a fairly early stage, but the resulting Anglo-Swedish battle was a hard-fought one. In the end, GEC came up with a winning bogie design by John Dowling, using a right-angle gearbox drive, but which moved the traction motors to the locomotive's underframe. As shown in Figure 23, they come within the space normally occupied by the usual bogie-mounted variety, so one of them does not compete with the space required for the cab. There was also room on the back of the motors' shafts for the disc brake, which avoided the complication of having to mount this on the axle in the normal way. The transformer was also located below the underframe, between the two bogies, and this enabled the overall length of the locomotive to be reduced, producing a stiffer design as well as economizing on weight and lowering the centre of gravity.

The letter of intent for the 31 locomotives at a cost of £35 million was signed in February 1986, which allowed only two years before the first of the initial batch of 10 would have to be rolled out in order to meet BR's timetable for adequate proving trials before entry into revenue-earning service in the autumn of 1989. An actual day — 14 February 1988 — was fixed for the hand-over of the first locomotive, and this was announced on the occasion of the formal signing of the contract in the 'InterCity 125' Executive Saloon between King's Cross and Huntingdon on 1 October 1986, by which time there were only $16\frac{1}{2}$ months to go to the deadline. BREL was the sub-contractor for the mechanical parts of the locomotives, which were assembled at Crewe, and the press was invited to the works there on Friday 12 February 1988. No 91 001 was duly handed over to Dr John Prideaux, Director, InterCity, in the bright winter sunshine by Brian McCann, Managing Director of GEC Transportation Projects. Away from the overhead wires there was no way in which the casual observer could be certain that it was actually in working order, but it made its first run over the West Coast Main Line on the Sunday morning, the actual day nominated two years previously.

Those attending the ceremony were able to see how much more impressive the new locomotive looked, even as a static exhibit, compared with any of the earlier artists' views showing its expected appearance. The visitors were able to inspect the rest of the batch under construction in the adjoining shops, and note various interesting features of the design before they were hidden behind panelling or other equipment. The Flexicoil secondary suspension is

A side-view of one of the bogies of a Class '91'. Some of the components can be identified by comparison with Figure 23.

Figure 23 *Diagram of the bogie of a Class '91'.* (GEC Alsthom)

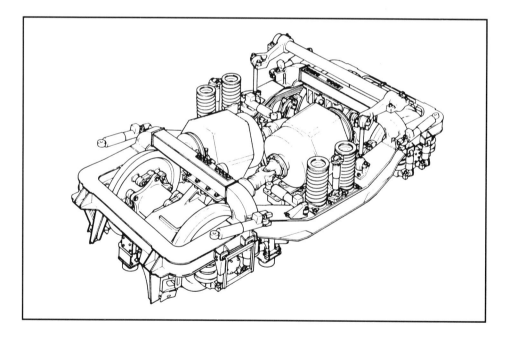

easily observed on a locomotive, but the traction link and pivot arrangements can only be seen from underneath or when the body has been lifted off the bogie, as they are set low down to minimize weight transfer. To handle heavy sleeping car trains on gradients like Shap, a maximum power rating of 6,300 hp was called for, and this has been achieved using motors which weigh the same as those on the Class '87s', which are 25 per cent less powerful. The

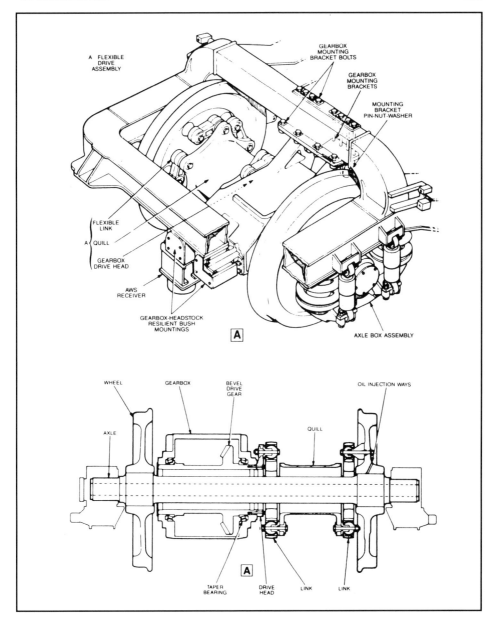

Figure 24 *Details of the final drive arrangements for the Class '91s'.* (GEC Alsthom)

development of inverter-driven three-phase motors came too late to be considered for the Class '91s', but the motors are of the separately-excited (Sepex) type, which have good anti-slip characteristics. Gate turn-off thyristors, cooled by oil, are used in both the field and armature circuits, and are controlled by a microprocessor. The latter can also be activated over the TDM link from the Driving Van Trailer when the locomotive is propelling

No 91 001 on the occasion of its hand-over at Crewe on 12 February 1988.

Don Heath, Project Director for the East Coast Electrification, is clearly relaxed as he inspects the locomotives on the Class '91' production line at Crewe Works on 12 February 1988.

the train, and, in both locomotive cabs and the DVT, speed-setting controls are provided for the driver's benefit.

It will be recalled that there was a school of thought which considered that a Co-Co design, with a weight of something like 120 tons, was necessary to give adequate adhesion for a locomotive capable of generating some 6,000 hp. A Class '91' weighs only two-thirds of this, but modern control systems make up for the lower adhesion weight by constantly comparing the currents in each traction motor armature. The microprocessor immediately notches back if any imbalance persists, since this indicates that more slipping is taking place than the Sepex arrangements can correct. There is also a doppler radar, which enables the degree of wheel-creep to be precisely controlled under poor adhesion conditions.

There are several interesting features about the braking systems. The brake lever is on the driver's left, and has seven notches, as on the HSTs, and activates the train-pipe pressure by means of a three-wire binary system. On the locomotive itself a rheostatic brake is used, which normally has priority over the discs and the small brakes on the wheel treads. These are normally blended into use as the speed falls below 30 mph, but will take over immediately if the rheostatic system stops working. Unlike all previous British designs, the electrical brake is not solely activated from the overhead line, but has its own battery system. The wheel brakes can also be applied hydraulically by the parking brake control. On a train of Mark IV stock, when a brake application is made, the pressure in the train pipe is reduced from the trailing and driving ends, to give the quickest possible response, in much the same way as with the HSTs.

From the driver's point of view, the programmes built into the microprocessors take care of the rate of build-up of current through the motors when power is applied, and there is no need for him to watch the ammeter when notching up, as was customary on the first generation of ac electric locomotives. Indeed, there is no ammeter, nor are there any notches on the power controller. This consists of a short lever, moving through approximately 90 degrees between 'Off' and 'Full', which applies whatever proportion of the maximum power output is required at that particular point on the journey. Translating the setting into the right number of amps is dealt with entirely by the microprocessor, which also controls the rate at which the power builds up to the set level. As already mentioned, any tendency to slip is constantly monitored, and appropriate action taken to check it, or, if this is not possible, to maintain the correct degree of wheel-creep.

The philosophy of the control system is very similar to that used on the Class '90' Bo-Bos, which were designed slightly earlier and built by BREL for British Railways, with GEC Transportation Projects providing the main electrical equipment. Because these less powerful locomotives are a mixed-traffic design, they are fitted with ammeters, and also an instrument which indicates to the driver how hot the traction motors are getting. With the Class '91s', the difference between the continuous and short-time ratings of the motors is remarkably small, being only 50 kilowatts, or 67 horsepower. As a result there is no need for the driver to be made aware of the internal temperatures of the motors, which can 'take anything thrown at them'. Some of the Class '90s' were originally due to make their appearance on East Coast Route freight trains after electrification, but it is not at present clear how the situation has been altered by the coming of the Channel Tunnel and the two-voltage Class '92s'.

On the Class '91s', each cab is fully air-conditioned, and the side windows, like the quarter-lights on an HST, do not open. Clearly there are times when the driver needs to put his head out to see what is happening during shunting movements, so to accommodate this, three auxiliary driving positions are provided, just inside the doors. At the No 1 end (the streamlined one) there is a set on each side, but at the other there is only one, positioned beside the left-hand door. Each is mounted at the back of the glass partition across the cab, where they cannot be reached from the seats. They consist of two levers, one for the horn and the other to control the locomotive's movements. The latter can be moved backwards through $47^1/2$ degrees to apply power, and forwards to give three different rates of braking. The Driver's Safety Device is activated by depressing the top of this lever, and a quick up-and-down move-ment will cancel the vigilance or AWS. When driving from one of these posi-tions, speed is limited. High up on the bulkhead at the back of the cab at the streamlined end is a switch to activate the train tilting equipment, but, in the absence of this on the East Coast sets, it is normally wired in the 'Off' position.

In addition to the completion date for the first of the Class '91s', the con-tract also contained a number of other important deadlines. The first batch of 10 locomotives had to be delivered by mid-June 1988, while BR had to con-firm the order for the remaining 21 by that September. The type-testing was not due to be completed until a couple of months later, while the endurance trials were programmed to last until the summer of 1989. By that time it was hoped that the locomotives would be filtering into revenue service on the Leeds line, ready for full electric operation on that route in October 1989. The following spring would see the completion of locomotive No 11, the first of the second batch, and the remainder would appear over the next 11 months. The last was scheduled to pass its acceptance tests by April 1991, ready for the beginning of the full electric services to Edinburgh, originally fixed for six weeks later.

Meanwhile, work was also in hand on the design and construction of the new Mark IV coaches, but the first rake was not programmed to be delivered until spring 1989. With the completion of the electric wiring to Leeds a year early, and the Class '91' progressing well, there was clearly an opportunity to introduce electric services over this route in advance of the originally planned date. This would enable more operating experience to be gained and also enable the travelling public to benefit. To make this possible, an ingenious solution was adopted: some of the existing 'InterCity 125' sets were used, with the diesel power car at the north end of each being replaced by a Class '91' locomotive. For reasons described in my earlier book, *Speed on the East Coast Main Line*, the HSTs, because they operated as unit trains, were pro-vided with a three-phase electric supply for internal use along the train. The Class '91s', like all the other locomotives on BR, can only power a single-phase train-line, and the cost of providing them with a three-phase inverter for a short period was not cost-effective. Accordingly it was necessary for the diesel alternator in the remaining HST power car on the 'Hybrid' HST sets to remain in operation to supply the lights, air-conditioning, and all the other 'on-board' services.

However, if a high-powered diesel motor, such as a 2,250-hp 'Valenta' on the HSTs, is allowed to run at low speeds for long periods, an appreciable carry-over of oil into the exhaust system can take place, and this constitutes a fire hazard. On the 'Hybrid' sets, therefore, the controls on the Class '91s' were arranged so that the HST's diesel alternator at the other end of the train was also utilized in the ordinary way for traction purposes. As we will see at a later stage in our story, the result was an exceedingly powerful combination: replacing a 2,250-hp diesel power car with a 6,300-hp electric locomotive provided an additional 4,000 hp compared with a normal 'InterCity 125' set.

It was also necessary for the HST power car to be provided with the means to control the electric locomotive when the latter was propelling the train. In the final 'InterCity 225' guise, this is carried out by the Time-Division Multiplex (TDM) system linking the Driving Van Trailer (DVT) with the locomotive, but for a short-term solution it was possible to provide a similar, but less comprehensive, system from the cab of the HST power car. Those which were modified for this purpose were also fitted with buffers and standard draw-gear, and a distinctive paint treatment — with more of the front painted yellow to make up for the removal of the skirt — was provided at the cab end of what became known as a 'Surrogate DVT'.

It would not have been economic to install a new TDM control line for the full length of the HST set, so use was made of the standard Railway Clearing House lighting control circuits, in the same way as on the ScotRail push-pull trains currently being worked by Class '47' diesel-electric locomotives. The Class '91s' have connectors for these behind the access doors on their ends, but where the circuits passed through the locomotives, it turned out that the TDM system could be upset by currents induced by the high-voltage supply from the overhead wires. The provision of a suitable electric 'filter' on the roof of the locomotive solved that particular problem. In the 'InterCity 225s', the TDM link between the locomotive and DVT is provided by a standard Union Internationale de Chemins de Fer (UIC) data highway, designed to be impervious to any outside electric disturbances. On the continent the connectors for this are normally mounted inside the top of the gangway connections at each end of the coaches. For our trains it was decided they had to be positioned externally, which necessitated the development of a waterproof version. The reason for this was the differing attitudes amongst certain elements of the travelling public in this country and abroad when it comes to meddling with equipment!

The introduction of a completely new form of motive power on an important trunk route such as the East Coast Main Line was also to involve the operators in a major training programme, for drivers as well as depot artisans. This could only be completed after the delivery of the hardware, although the arrival of the maintenance handbooks for the Class '91s' in advance of the locomotives was a big help (and very unusual!). Even before the hardware was due to arrive, it was desirable to start obtaining traction experience on the southern portion of the East Coast Route with electric locomotives as distinct from multiple-units. Some of the earlier classes from the London Midland Region were consequently based at Hornsey Depot in late 1987 (prior to the electrification of the tracks at Bounds Green, which was to become the London base for the Class '91s'). The unique Class '87/1', No 87 101 *Stephenson*, was lent to the Eastern Region for some time, as it was provided with thyristor control rather than the tap changers fitted to the remainder of the class. In December 1987 the solitary Brush Class '89' Co-Co locomotive was also transferred to Bounds Green, initially for driver training, but was subsequently introduced into public service. One of its early duties was to haul the 'Mallard '88' commemorative special from King's Cross on 3 July that year, which became the first electric working to Doncaster with passengers.

When the Friends of the National Railway Museum started planning the celebrations for the 50th anniversary of the world steam speed record in 1988, it was hoped that the train might be hauled out of London by one of the Class '91s', but, in the event, this was not possible. No 91 003 was, however, positioned on the down fast line at Doncaster, alongside the point where No 89 001 handed over to *Mallard*. It duly featured in the hundreds of photographs taken by the crowds who thronged the station on that occasion. Unfortunately, the other surprise planned by InterCity involving the Class '91s' did not come off. It was intended that, during its ascent of Stoke Bank, the special would have been passed by one of the Class '91s', doing 150 mph in the opposite direction. Unfortunately, the vital radio link with the test train had been 'lost', and the spectacular demonstration had to be abandoned. Nevertheless, as the passengers travelled south past milepost 90$\frac{1}{4}$ behind No 89 001 that evening, two toasts were drunk. The first was to *Mallard*'s world record, and the other to InterCity's new electrics, one of which had already reached a speed of 144 mph.

Within a week a more demanding duty was found for No 89 001 on the commuter run between Peterborough and King's Cross. A non-standard set of HST coaches was made up at Bounds Green (Set No BN29) with one of the 'Surrogate DVTs' at the south end, which could be used either with another HST power car or an electric locomotive. This resulted in the 17.36 down service from King's Cross being switched to the InterCity section of the departure indicator, rather than the Network SouthEast part, as was the case when the train was worked by a pair of Class '317s'. At the country end of the new rake, the 'TGS' (Trailer Guard Standard) was fitted with buffers and a normal coupling to attach the locomotive in the down direction. At that time the Class '89' was not equipped to operate with a Time-Division Multiplex system, so it could not be controlled from the opposite end of the train like a Class '91'. As a consequence the locomotive had to run round at each end of the journey, although it could come into King's Cross at the north end of the empty stock in the evening, ready for the down run, with drivers at both ends, one to apply the brake and the other the power. While the locomotive and stock were capable of 125 mph, the train was restricted to

No 89 001 waits to leave King's Cross on 3 July 1988 with the special train commemorating the fiftieth anniversary of Mallard's world record. The locomotive's buffers had been burnished in best 'Top Shed' traditions.

The 'Mallard '88' special comes to a stand at Doncaster beside No 91 003.

115 because of braking considerations. The through control wires on an ordinary HST set ensure that brake applications are propagated from both ends of the train, which was not possible with the special set used with the Class '89'. The performance was nevertheless impressive, as will be described in Chapter 10, and with the start of the winter timetable the working was extended to Grantham.

The set additionally formed a suitable stand-by during the day if there were any major upsets in the rostered HST workings. On 12 August 1988 it was called on to form the 08.20 from King's Cross to Leeds, which made it the first electric passenger train to reach that city, 14 months ahead of the original date given for the start of electric services over this part of the East Coast Route. It was only on the previous day that the first electric locomotive had covered the same stretch, this being a Class '91' on a test train. It was at about this stage of the development programme for the new motive power that various rumours started to circulate about their frequent failure to appear on rostered test or training workings. In July, for instance, observers at Newark were reporting anything between two and eight daily Class '91' workings. The truth was that the whole test and training programme was an immense operation, and the maximum number of paths was included in the working timetables, which had to be compiled nearly a year in advance. However, in steam days these would all have been 'Conditional' or 'Q' workings, the significance being 'Runs as Required'. The decision to operate any particular one depended on many different things, including the availability of instructors and trainees as well as the rolling-stock. In addition, a series of trial workings might be arranged to sort out a particular problem, and the quicker the solution was found, the more days there would be when the train did not have to run!

In June 1988 the extensive 'IVA88' international transport exhibition was held in Hamburg, and three electric locomotives formed part of the exhibits in the very impressive contribution from this country, entitled 'Britain's New Railways'. No 89 001 was joined by a representative of each of the Class '90s' and '91s'. The last two were parked nose-to-nose, and I was struck by the 'King'/'Castle' visual analogy between these two similarly styled locomotives. The rumour machine was even active while these British exhibits were abroad, word getting back to England that they had been derailed *en route* to Germany. This was not true, in spite of the difficulties of getting them across the link-span of the train ferry at Dunkirk. On the other hand, while I was in Hamburg I saw the German prototype Inter-City experimental high-speed electric train, which had just set up a new world rail speed record, running through the city with Sir Robert Reid and the heads of many other European railways aboard. It was minus the rear power car, which had developed a fault on one axle!

The Class '91s' went into revenue-earning service on 3 March 1989, when No 91 001 worked the 17.36 commuter service from King's Cross to Peterborough. One of the 'Hybrid' Bounds Green sets was used, and the performance was impressive. The train even had to wait outside Huntingdon, the first stop, because the train which had left the terminus 23 minutes earlier was

No 90 008 and No 91 003 on exhibition at Hamburg in June 1988.

still in the station! (It had made six intermediate stops, but was nevertheless due out 6 minutes before the 'InterCity' train was booked to arrive.) A few weeks later I was able to travel on this working, which had reverted to the usual BN29 set, and the performance will be described in more detail in Chapter 10. These InterCity outer commuter services have continued to be popular, and some new workings of this sort were introduced in May 1990, using two rakes of refurbished air-conditioned Mark II stock. In the mornings they ran up from Grantham and Peterborough, but in the evening three separate workings were provided from the two sets. The 17.36 from King's Cross returned empty from Peterborough and then formed the 20.45 to York, filling the two-hour gap between the last HSTs for Yorkshire and the North East. Although the Mark II stock is limited to a maximum of 100 mph, thanks to the acceleration of the Class '91s' the train only took 2 hours 25 minutes to York, inclusive of stops at Peterborough, Retford and Doncaster.

On 11 March 1989 the first passenger run to Leeds was made by one of the 'Hybrid' sets with a Class '91', the combination working up to two round trips a day. On the second northbound journey, Mr W. E. Long, a member of the Railway Performance Society, was on the train, and recorded an average of no less than 114.3 mph, start-to-stop, between Stevenage and Grantham, the ascent of Stoke Bank included. Other similar examples of very fast running have also been recorded, and in the summer timetable that year one of the up workings was scheduled to take only 29$^{1}/_{2}$ minutes for the 48.8 miles from Peterborough to Stevenage. This corresponded to an average of 110.5 mph — the first 110-plus-mph booking to appear in a British timetable. A log of such a run is included in Chapter 10.

The next step forward with electric traction on the East Coast Route was to come in the autumn of 1989 when the Mark IV coaches came into service, but before describing the changes that resulted from this, we must go back to the beginning of 1987 to discuss the philosophy of this new generation of high-speed passenger vehicles.

★   ★   ★

The average member of the travelling public is not concerned with the motive power on the train, except in so far as it may affect punctuality or atmospheric pollution. On the other hand, the comfort and ambience of the coaches, and the ease of getting in and out, are all-important. As already mentioned, InterCity wished to improve both these aspects of travel on the East Coast Route after electrification, and it was considered that the basic design of the Mark III coach would not accommodate the required step-change that was being sought. It had been a very successful and popular design, and plans were already in progress to refurbish the vehicles internally, which moved them appreciably up-market as far as the 'finishes' were concerned. A new batch was also built for the West Coast Pullman services, and these first class vehicles had yet better interior appointments. Britain was also well out of step with the type of exterior doors used on its fastest expresses, and fitting power-operated ones to a 15-year-old design would also have been difficult. However, the overwhelming reason to give up the idea of using a develop-ment of the Mark III design for the East Coast electrics was the need to pro-vide 'stretch' with future maximum speeds. There was also the requirement for the design to cater for tilt, should that be required later on other routes, so plans were accordingly drawn up for the Mark IV coaches.

For the whole of the 'InterCity 225' project, BR adopted the 'keep it simple, build it fast' approach, and only looked to new technology when the already proven variety would not do the job, as with the final-drive arrange-ments for the locomotives. With the coaches there was very little technologi-cal risk, but tests were to show that the initial design of bogie which had been chosen for the Mark IVs did not give the required ride at high speeds. This was the BREL 'T4' type, and, after the evaluation of the test data, it was decided to specify the Swiss SIG design instead. Ironically, the high-speed test runs with both types, carried out between York and Darlington, resulted in two new world record speeds for *diesel* traction being set up, references to which will be found in Chapter 10.

There was also an important early debate about another basic feature of the coaches — their length. Understandably there is a strong economic case to make railway vehicles as long as possible, as this maximizes the seating capac-ity relative to the number of major and expensive components, like bogies, and the amount of 'wasted' floor areas, such as the end vestibules and gang-ways. The process was already well-established on BR, with the Mark IIIs being longer than their predecessors, while the 'Super Sprinters' were also deliberately stretched from the earlier Class '150s'. Other constraints have to be taken into account, however, such as the effect of swing-over on curves, in addition to structural considerations. It was originally proposed that the Mark IVs would be 23.5 metres (77 feet) long, and there were discussions concerning lengthening them to 26 metres. This would have given three more rows of seats in the second class coaches (as they then were before the 'Standard' nomenclature was adopted). In the end it was decided to stick to the original figure, and the final Mark IV body length worked out at 76 feet

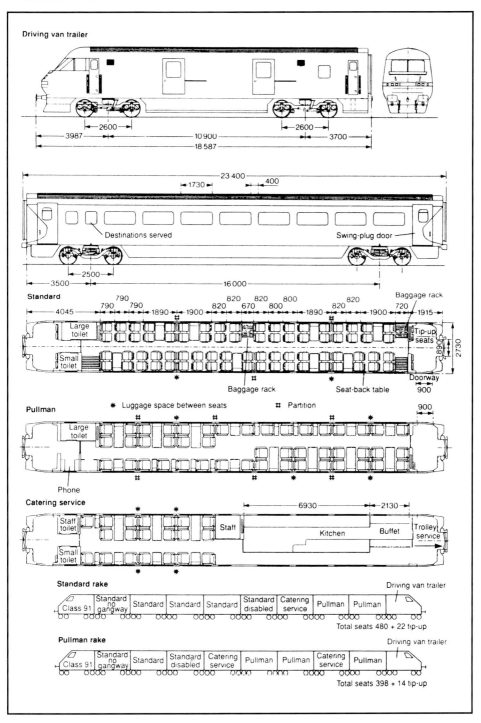

Diagram of Driving Van Trailer and Mark IV coaches for the 'InterCity 225' trains.
(Railway Gazette International)

9 inches, which should be compared with the corresponding figure of 72 feet 2 inches for a Mark III.

As with the locomotives, BR went out to competitive tender for the Mark IVs, and the £80 million contract for the initial 283 vehicles, including the DVTs, was awarded to Metro-Cammell. The company had already secured the order for the Class '156' 'Super Sprinters', which were to precede the Mark IVs on the production line in its Washwood Heath factory in Birmingham. Although the company used to build railway rolling-stock there from scratch, its new manufacturing philosophy was to make it an assembly plant, with components coming in from external sources, but constructed to its design. The 'Super Sprinter' contract was to show how well this system worked from both the design and manufacturing aspects, which was a good augury for the Mark IVs. The largest components for the latter, the bodyshells, were, in the main, sub-contracted to BREL, although a batch was ordered from Breda, a public-sector rolling-stock constructor in Italy. Metro-Cammell was also awarded the contract for the additional 31 Mark IV vehicles to strengthen the sets to nine cars. In 1989 the ownership of the company changed, and it is now part of the GEC Alsthom Transport Division. The contract was let at the beginning of 1987, with the first rake being due for hand-over in the spring of 1989. Type tests would last six months, with service evaluation beginning of the May. The first 10 rakes were due for completion by February 1990, after which there was a 2½-month gap in the delivery schedule before the remaining vehicles started to arrive, with the order being completed by the middle of 1991.

One of the important successes of the whole 'InterCity 225' project was the way the contracts were managed by BR and its contractors, particularly with regard to subsequent changes in the specification, which form one of the classic ways of losing control of cost and delivery. Much of the present-day InterCity image has resulted from the upgrading of the passenger accommodation in recent years, and the vital question is not 'Is it good enough?' but 'Could it be better?' The application of this principle resulted in two important changes being made in the Mark IVs, the first involving the design of the first class seats, and the other the vestibules. It was relatively easy to get a firm to 'productionize' an existing seat that BR already had in the development stage, but the vestibule problem, could not be solved from existing components. Power-operated exterior doors were planned for the Mark IV coaches from the beginning, which would eliminate the need for opening windows, and so reduce the perennial problems of cold draughts in winter and loss of air-conditioning capacity in hot weather. In spite of these drawbacks, in recent years a type of passenger has appeared who prefers to travel sitting — or lying — on the vestibule floor. This is not particularly welcoming as passengers get on, nor is it conducive to easy access along the train during its journey. It was therefore decided to carpet the vestibule floors and walls, improve the lighting and heating, and provide a number of tip-up seats for use at peak times. These changes started to show up the existing inter-vehicle gangways as being inadequate, so BREL produced a new, fully-sealed design, which has proved very satisfactory. So pleasant is the new vestibule ambience that I have even seen a mother playing with her toddlers on the floor there in one of the new sets. In several coaches in each rake there is also a card-phone in one of the vestibules.

In pre-nationalizations days, it used to be said that the colours used for the interior or coaches were chosen by the Chief Mechanical Engineer's wife, or, if it was a particularly important vehicle, by the wife of the Chairman. Nowadays the whole business of interior design and decoration has become a lot more sophisticated, and, to some extent, 'a game for *n* players'. In their presentation on the trains to the International Conference on Railway Electrification, held at York in September 1989, David Rollin and Andrew Higton referred to this aspect of the vehicles.

> Despite building fast, the interior styling of the Mark IV coach was radically revised several times, each change reflecting a new set of perceptions as Sector Management, BR design management and InterCity design consultants changed. As a result, the interior finishes schedule was signed-off six months later than scheduled.

The first opportunity for us to see the results of all this work was on 20 September 1989, when British Rail launched the new trains with a press trip from King's Cross to Leeds and back. Alongside the new train at King's Cross was a full set of earlier BR standard vehicles, going back to the first all-steel Mark Is of 1951. Visually the rake of Mark IVs made an immediate impact, the locomotive and DVT at the ends blending well with the coaches, thanks to the use of the same cross-section. In designing its latest livery, InterCity was very anxious to make the train seem to be an entity, and this has also been achieved with the 'InterCity 225s'. The overall image is, however, a lot 'chunkier' and more purposeful when compared with the HSTs which we have got to know so well over the last decade and a half.

The power-operated doors on the Mark IVs are an innovation on British main-line stock, although they have been standard on continental 'InterCity' trains for many years now. There is, however, a very different philosophy from the way in which the doors work in other countries. The swing-out plug type on the Mark IVs automatically lock when they close, and each door is provided with a sealed emergency release handle on the inside and outside. The continental standard, on the other hand, is for rams to push the doors shut when the guard activates his button, but the locking only takes place when the train reaches 5 km/h. I have, before now, quite inadvertently opened a door — even on the side away from the platform — after the guard had carried out the closing sequence, but before the train has moved off! In Britain, the doors are also provided with controls so that the passengers can open them once they have been released by the guard, and closure buttons are also provided on the inside so they can be shut in cold weather. As on the 'Sprinters' and other modern multiple-unit stock, the surrounds of the passenger buttons light up when they have been activated, and audible warning is given before the doors are closed by the guard.

On the first rakes, a new method of operating the internal vestibule doors was adopted. This involved the passenger pressing an illuminated button at waist height, which caused the single or split double-door to slide back quickly. On the 'InterCity 225s' the doors are worked by a pressure pad in the floor, which requires no deliberate action by the passenger, and the Mark IVs also had a similar pad to hold the door open while a procession of passengers passes through. The buttons are much better situated than the operating handles on the West German *IC* trains, which are at chest height and extremely inconvenient when carrying luggage. However, the button idea on our Mark IVs did not prove satisfactory and the system has been altered so that the doors are automatically opened by pressure on the treadles.

To meet the stringent performance requirements, the Mark IVs have worked out appreciably heavier than earlier designs, an ordinary open coach weighing just over 41 tons, which should be compared with 33 tons for a similar Mark III. However, the 'Large Pullman' nine-car rake used for the special train tared 369 tons, including the DVT, so that if one added in the 82 tons of the Class '91' locomotive, the whole train weighed 451 tons. This represents an 11 per cent increase on the 410 tons of an East Coast HST, which has a lower seating capacity than a comparable Mark IV set. Metro-Cammell was clearly weighing each vehicle as it was completed, as there are differences of up to a few hundred kilogrammes between the painted signs of their ends. One has only to look at the variation in the tare weights of a rake of 'merry-go-round' hoppers to realize that the standardized stickers applied to the Mark III coaches cannot be identical to the claimed accuracy of two decimal places of a ton. Successive coats of paint applied over the years would, for one thing, appreciably alter the weight anyway!

There are five different types of passenger-carrying Mark IV coaches, as follows:

TOE   Standard class vehicles, one end of which is equipped with full buffing and draw-gear, but does not have a gangway connection.

TO   Ordinary Standard class vehicles.

TOD   Standard class vehicles with special facilities, including those for the disabled.

SV   Catering vehicles, with seating, kitchen and buffet.

PO   First class vehicles, the 'P' referring to 'Pullman'.

Our train on 20 September consisted of four Pullman Opens, two Standard Opens and a pair of Service Vehicles, and there was also the 41½-ton Driving Van Trailer No 82 201 at the south end of the train, its profile matching that of No 91 001 *Swallow*. I was travelling in the rear Pullman Open, and found it very comfortable indeed. The new type of seat provides a greater range of adjustment than those provided in the first class Mark IIIs. One has to ease one's weight off them to let them rise up as one lifts the control lever, but that is not too much of a hardship. Each of the comparable seats on one of the French TGV-A trains has its own power-operated system to do this, which must all add to the cost. I personally found the new seats very comfortable, but know that some women consider that they are not so accommodating for their shorter height, a criticism my wife also makes about those in the TGVs.

As already mentioned, the cross-section of the Mk IVs was designed so that subsequent builds for the West Coast Route could be made to tilt. The maximum tilt angle specified was a lot less than that for the APT, and the resulting appearance of the coach interiors is nothing like so constricting as it was on the latter. Their exterior lines are reminiscent of the SNCF's *Grand Confort* coaches, which were also originally designed to be capable of taking tilt. Much thought has been given to the whole of the interior design, and my own feeling is that the visual effect of the taper contributes to the overall snug impression. Smoked-glass partitions have been used to break up the long tube, the lower seating density in the Pullman vehicles enabling this to be done extremely effectively. The big problem for first class passengers will now be to decide which of the many different types of location to choose! Each coach has seven tables for four people, and five pairs, with the rest of the 46 seats at single tables. The central aisle along the vehicle crosses over between two of the smoked-glass partitions in the centre, on each of which is mounted an intriguing 'feature' of four differently-profiled and textured horizontal rods, reminiscent of field-marshals' batons.

The Standard class vehicles have straight rows of 2+2 seating throughout, some in 'airline' style and others in sets of four around tables; 32 of the 74 seats in a normal coach are of the facing-pairs variety. There are several well-designed luggage spaces at seat level along the vehicle, in addition to the continuous overhead racks, and the asymmetric smoked-glass partitions again help to break up the tube effect. The seats have swing-up arm rests to facilitate getting in and out, although these are made from a single plastic moulding and are thus appreciably harder on the elbows than the immoveable fabrication design used in the Mark IIIs. The fold-down trays on the backs of the airline-type seats have springs to secure them in the 'up' position.

When the 'InterCity 125s' were first introduced in the 1970s, their internal decor was best described as 'bright and cheerful', with orange or turquoise loose covers that could easily be removed for cleaning. When the sets were refurbished the upholstery was changed to patterned moquette, with a warm red in Standard class and purple in first. In the Mark IVs much more subtle colours are used, first class being in shades of grey, while those in Standard class have a 'tweed' finish in two versions, one predominantly rust-coloured, and the other light grey. One of the Standard coaches in each rake is specifically designed for wheelchair passengers. The space allocated for them, next to the vestibule, is provided with a special call button, and a similar feature is provided in the adjoining disabled toilet. Attention has also been given to the other toilet facilities, each vehicle having one large and one small one. The former has enough space for an adult to change quite comfortably, and also has a fold-down shelf which can be used for dealing with a baby. A hot-air drier is provided to supplement the usual paper towels. It is always difficult to spot the absence of a particular feature in a new design of vehicle, and the Mark IV toilets provide an example of this. Missing is the time-honoured notice telling passengers not to use the toilets in stations, the change resulting from the fact that they are of the retention variety, which do not discharge on to the track.

The interior of one of the first class Mark IV coaches. (BR)

Lighting in both classes is much less brash than that of the 'InterCity 125s', with the overhead illumination being indirect from behind slotted grilles along the length of the ceiling, continuing a trend which started with the Mark IIIb vehicles. In the firsts, high-powered spotlights in the luggage racks are provided for each seat, and are extremely effective Even on a sunny day, one does not have to readjust one's vision as the train dives into and out of the many tunnels on the exit from London, the intensity of the lighting at table level enabling one to continue reading normally while all goes dark outside.

The press launch of the new train began with the naming ceremony for the first of the Class '91s', the *Swallow* nameplate on which was duly unveiled by Sir Robert Reid, in the company of Lord Prior, Chairman of GEC. Guests

Passengers relax in one of Standard class Mark IV coaches. (BR)

Dr John Prideaux, Director, InterCity, alongside No 91 001 Swallow *after its naming ceremony at King's Cross on 20 September 1989.*

were then taken to Leeds, and in both directions the speed capabilities of the new train were very effectively demonstrated. It was not until after Peterborough that we had the first example of what the Clas '91s' could achieve, as it is only on Stoke Bank that the signalling has been modified to permit running at over 125 mph, and we promptly had a chance to see what could be done. Up the bank we had reached 132 by milepost $91^1/4$, which was precisely where *Mallard* had managed its 126-mph record in 1938 after the benefit of over 10 miles of down grades. Speed fluctuated slightly up the rest of the bank, with a minimum of 128 at milepost $95^1/2$, and a final 132 through Corby Glen, before the brakes went on for the restriction through the tunnel. We were allowed 10 minutes for the 15.3 miles from Tallington to Stoke, and cut this 91.8-mph booking to just 7 minutes 17 seconds, corresponding to a flying average of 121.6 *uphill*.

After lunch on the way to Leeds, guests were transferred to the city's Town Hall for the press conference which involved an extremely impressive presentation, complementing the splendours of the Victorian building in which it was staged. One of the questions that cropped up concerned the recently achieved speed record by No 91 010, when the press report had referred to a maximum of 162 mph. It was actually 161.7, which conveniently rounded up to the figure quoted, and apparently put it ahead of the best the APT had achieved ten years earlier. David Rollin had investigated the earlier record and had to admit that the true maximum had been 162.2 mph, making it slightly higher than had been claimed, which still left the East Coast Route in second place — for the moment. More detailed information about these two records is given in Chapter 10.

On the way back to London, the press special was able to give another demonstration of the speed capabilities of the Class '91s', this time descending Stoke Bank. We ran closely to the 96-mph schedule as far as this, with speeds well under those normally achieved with HSTs. In view of the previous

The 'InterCity 225' press launch special waits to depart from Leeds on 20 September 1989 with the Driving Van Trailer at the south end.

On 17 September 1989, after setting up a new East Coast speed record of 161.7 mph, No 91 010 was hauled to York to take part in the commissioning tests for the overhead wires through the station. It is seen after if had been moved into Platform 3, and was waiting for approval from the Doncaster Electrical Control Centre to raise its pantograph. The special wiring, used between the locomotive and the train during the high-speed runs earlier in the day, can be seen draped on the end of the locomotive.

Carrying its special headboard, No 91 001 Swallow waits to leave King's Cross on Sunday 24 September 1989 with the GEC Alsthom charter train conveying the delegates to the International Conference on Railway Electrification being held at York.

Sunday's record on this stretch, we were hoping for something faster than usual, and were not disappointed. After only 90 through the tunnel, we were up to 126 by milepost 96^1/$_2$. Two and a half miles later we were running at 136, and held this speed to milepost 90. Both *Mallard* in 1938 and the 'Tees-Tyne Pullman' launch in 1985 had reached their maxima before Essendine. However, it was not until we were passing the site of the former double junction that our Senior Conductor announced over the public address system: 'From my privileged position at the front of the train I can tell you we are now cruising at 140 mph, and will continue to do so for the next 6 miles.' My stopwatch timings showed two brief peaks at 141, and over the 7 miles between mileposts 89 and 82 we averaged exactly 140. So the speed profile with electric traction turned out to be very different from those with diesel and steam power, but provided a clear indication of the capabilities of the Class '91s'. The more powerful electrics do not need any help from gravity, and have achieved their fastest speeds *propelling* their trains. Although the 'Tees-Tyne Pullman' launch involved a lightweight 2+5 set, and we reached a maximum of 144 mph, the 1989 run was actually 4 seconds faster between Little Bytham and Werrington Junction, and the standard of the ride left that of the HSTs in the shade.

Three days before, on 17 September, the day of the record, No 91 010 had later been hauled to York with its rake of coaches to help with the commissioning of the overhead equipment as far north as Skelton Junction. The Mobile Load Bank was also in evidence, trundling through each of the electrified tracks, and in the early afternoon the Class '91' was positioned at the south end of No 3 platform. After clearance had been obtained, the pantograph went up and the first electric locomotive to run at York was in business. Numerous tests were carried out to confirm the reliability of the power and signalling systems, ready for the following weekend, when GEC Alsthom had hired a train from BR to convey delegates from London to York for the International Conference on Railway Electrification.

No 91 001 *Swallow* was rostered for the train, and, as it was a charter special, GEC applied its own headboard, which took the place of the InterCity swallow on the grille covering the horns at the front of the locomotive. It was not the first electric passenger working at York, as there had been a BR special from that city to London on the previous day, as a 'thank you' to those of the staff involved in the electrification project. It used Mark I charter stock, so, although No 91 003 had, exceptionally, been turned to head south from York with the streamlined end leading, the train was unable to exceed 100 mph. The GEC Alsthom special on the Sunday used a rake of Mark IV stock, but we were rostered for only one driver, so did not exceed 110 by any significant margin. The overseas guests were nevertheless extremely impressed with the new train, making its first revenue-earning run, and the 'InterCity 225' and the East Coast Electrification project both featured heavily during the conference that followed.

Business travel to and from West Yorkshire has shown a steady growth in recent years. Leeds has become an important provincial legal and financial centre, with government offices such as the National Health Service head-

quarters and part of the Tax Offices relocating there. This has boosted the
morning InterCity peak, and the popularity of the 'Yorkshire Pullman' in particular. In the past, some of the East Coast 'InterCity 125' Pullman sets had
a 2+9 formation, but the increased load meant that these trains had a lower
power to weight ratio. Their timings were stretched slightly, but these longer
sets were later abandoned. On the other hand, the 'InterCity 225' is not a
unit-train concept, and the 6,300 hp available from the Class '91s' enables
them to work heavier trains at 'normal' schedules. As we have seen, the rating
was fixed by the demands of working a heavy sleeping-car train up Shap, and
the Class '91s' may still have enough power available for longer trains, when
140 mph running is introduced. From an early stage, therefore, it was proposed to deploy some special Pullman rakes, and it was decided to introduce
the new rolling-stock on the up morning/down evening 'Yorkshire Pullman'
service at the start of the winter services on 2 October 1989. For the business
fraternity in Yorkshire at large, this was a double bonus, as the cascade process
enabled one of the Neville Hill HST sets to be redeployed on to the Midland
line between Sheffield and St Pancras.

The new 'Yorkshire Pullman' settled down to regular operation, normally
working two round trips per day from Leeds to King's Cross, although, in the
busy pre-Christmas period, it actually managed three for a period, clocking
up just over 1,130 miles per day in revenue service. During the validity of
these timetables, the final down working of the 'Yorkshire Pullman' continued on from Leeds to Harrogate, with a Class '47' diesel locomotive coming
on the back of the DVT for the final leg. There are no facilities to run round
at Harrogate, so the empty stock continued back to Neville Hill for overnight
servicing via Knaresborough and York. During the winter the commissioning
of further rakes of Mark IV stock continued and was coupled with a pro-

*With its streamlined end facing south, No 91 003 leaves York on train 1G50 on 23
September 1989, taking BR staff involved with the electrification on a day out to
London. The use of Mark I charter stock limited the speed of this first electric passenger
working between York and Doncaster to 100 mph.* (Neville Stead)

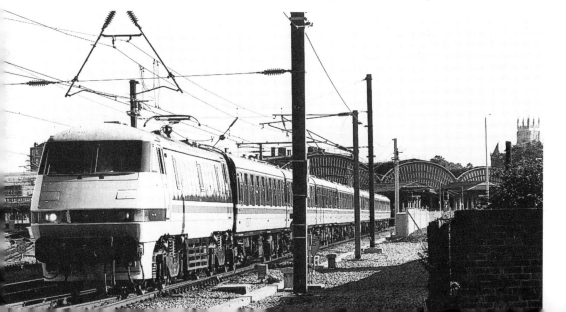

gramme of training for the train crews. Further sets were phased into service, replacing the 'Hybrid' ones, until, by the start of the 1990 summer timetable, they were virtually monopolizing the Leeds–King's Cross workings.

York also got a solitary electric working, on the 06.00 service to King's Cross. Initially a 'Hybrid', it changed over to 'InterCity 225' stock during the winter, but was single-manned as far as Doncaster; the stock reached York from Leeds via Doncaster just before midnight. There were occasionally other workings, one that came to my notice being on the Fridays-only 18.30

No 91 001 Swallow *in Platform 3 at York after arrival from London with the GEC Alsthom special on 24 September 1989.*

The DVT on the rear end of the GEC Alsthom special.

LONDON KING'S CROSS
Wakefield—Doncaster—Grantham— Peterborough

One of the carriage destination labels for the 'Yorkshire Pullman', the first train on which the 'InterCity 225' sets went into regular service.

from London to Newcastle. One day in October, Gordon Wiseman of *Railway Gazette International* was aiming to catch it as far as Darlington, but when he reached King's Cross from Sutton by Thameslink he found it consisted of a 'Hybrid' set, which, not surprisingly, was announced as 'Tonight terminating at York'. They left 15 minutes late behind No 91 004, but had recovered 7 minutes by the time they left Peterborough, and were only 4 minutes down when they stopped at Newark. This implied that they had averaged 116 mph from King's Cross, inclusive of the Peterborough stop. York was reached a minute early, and a quick change into the 'Devonian' got Mr Wiseman into Darlington in only 3 hours 27 minutes from Surrey. During July and August 1990 the availability of the new trains enabled them to be used to provide extra services between York and London on Saturdays, with four up and three down passenger workings.

To conclude this chapter it is worth looking at the 'InterCity 225' alongside the French and German high-speed trains. At the International Electrification Conference in York in September 1989, comparative figures were given for these, and I have quoted them in Table 14, together with the corresponding percentages in brackets, taking those for the 'IC225' as 100 per cent in each case. For a speed increase of only 11 per cent, the seat cost of the 'ICE' is over twice that of the 'IC225', and it took well over twice as long to develop and build. The TGV is less costly than the German design, although still two-thirds as expensive again as 'IC225', but the development time — for the first units on the Lyon line — was over three times as long. On both counts the British train thus shows up well. It was therefore gratifying when the Worshipful Company of Carmen presented the train with the Sir Henry Royce Foundation Memorial Award for excellence in engineering. This covered not only the train's design, but the way in which it had met the tight budget and delivery targets, underlining the highly commercial way in which BR's engineering resources are organized.

At the time of writing, the rakes of 'InterCity 225s' are rolling out of the manufacturers, and are being commissioned on BR by being 'rotated' through the West Yorkshire services. Only a limited number can be used commercially at present, so the surplus sets are being 'mothballed' and stored ready for 1991. Some fine tuning is still being carried out with two general

No 91 008 speeds northwards near Tallington with a train for Leeds in the summer of 1990. (Peter Kelly)

When the second batch of Class '91s' started to be delivered in 1990, the first of them, No 91 011, was named Terence Cuneo, *after the artist who had produced so many splendid railway paintings over the years, many of which had been used in railway posters. Before the naming ceremony, Mr Cuneo had painted one of his well-known mice on the side of the locomotive, using railway-approved paints, and poses here with this unique example of his trademark.* (Colin J. Marsden)

Table 14: Cost and development time comparisons for British, French and German high-speed trains

Train	Design speed (mph)	Cost per seat (£)	Procurement schedule (months)
BR 'InterCity 225'	140 (100%)	9,000 (100%)	45 (100%)
DB 'ICE'	155 (111%)	21,000 (233%)	102 (227%)
SNCF 'TGV'	186 (133%)	15,000 (167%)	145 (322%)

aspects of the design — the riding of the vehicles, and the comfort of the Standard class seats. But with more than six months still to go, both are confidently predicted to have been fully optimized before the new services start, details of which will be given in Chapter 11.

Dr John Prideaux, Managing Director, InterCity, holds the Sir Henry Royce Foundation Memorial Award for Engineering Excellence after being presented with it in 1990 for the 'InterCity 225' project. With him are (left) Andrew Higton, the Project Engineer, and (right) David Rollin, Project Director. (BR)

A portent of the future: a line-up of four Class '91s' at King's Cross in February 1990 — and not an 'InterCity 125' in sight. (Colin J. Marsden)

Chapter Nine

INFORMING THE PUBLIC

The marketing and publicity for any new services on BR are the responsibility of the business sectors concerned, which, in the case of the East Coast Electrification, involves InterCity and Network SouthEast. With any major project like this, however, particularly one scheduled to occupy seven years, there is also the need to keep the public generally informed about its objectives and progress. This is where the BR Public Affairs people have an important role to play, both with the media as well as the public direct. During the time it has taken to electrify the East Coast Route, considerable changes have taken place within the managerial organization of British Rail, and it is necessary for us to touch briefly on these to see how the task of informing the public about the project has been tackled.

Back in 1984 the sectors were just two years old, and their responsibilities and methods of working have changed considerably since that time; Network SouthEast, for example, only came into existence in 1986. Prior to 1982 the Regions were all-powerful, with their General Managers, in Sir Robert Reid's words, being 'railway barons exercising great power in the geographical territories they commanded'. This steadily changed during the 1980s, and in the summer of 1990 the Regions started to be disbanded. Under the new arrangements, John Nelson, the former Eastern Region General Manager, has become the InterCity Route Director for the whole of the East Coast Main Line, thus taking over ScotRail's involvement for the route north of the Border and answering to Dr John Prideaux, who is now Managing Director, InterCity. Even before this, the two Regions involved had worked very closely together from the publicity point of view, and, because of the greater length of track being electrified in England, the Eastern Region's Public Affairs Department has been largely in the forefront of the public awareness work.

During recent years there has been a boom in the provision of news services — particularly on a local scale, with newspapers fighting back against the local radio stations and additional television channels — and public transport features prominently among the topics covered. While major national events are dealt with by the BR Press Department, coming under the Director of Public

As part of the publicity build-up for the electrification, the Eastern Region Public Affairs Department organized a very large 'Paint by Numbers' picture of a Class 91 locomotive in the concourse at Leeds station, with local schools doing the colouring. Here the art master and a pupil get down to work, watched by the then Area Manager at Leeds, Mike Hodgson. (BR)

Affairs in London, who has overall responsibility for the coverage of Board projects such as electrification, a constant stream of local press releases and other media events has to be handled by each of the regional offices for their own areas. For instance, before the line over Durham viaduct was closed for nine days in March 1989, the Eastern Region's Department organized a press conference in Newcastle, where representatives of the civil engineer and InterCity were able to explain to the media the reasons for the work and the implications for travellers. This also touched on the new Ove Arup design for the electrification masts, and the progress of the electrification project in general. In addition to the sending out of invitations to the conference, press releases and photographs had to be provided for those attending, with other versions to be sent out to more distant media, whose reading, listening or viewing public was likely to be affected by the diversions.

It is sometimes possible for media representatives to be allowed to photograph or film, on site, in the course of major engineering work. A press officer has to be present on such occasions to provide the answers to any background queries, and this again is often dealt with more easily by the regional offices. Such visits inevitably have to be limited, not least on safety grounds, but there are other occasions when the public affairs people are able to arrange major photo-calls, when the more media who attend the better. Typical of such occasions as the hand-over of the £19.5 million from the European Regional

HRH The Duchess of Gloucester waves away the first electric passenger service from Peterborough on 8 May 1987. The then General Manager of the Eastern Region, David Rayner, stands behind her. (BR) **Inset** *The plaque recording the event, which was unveiled by HRH The Duchess of Gloucester inside No 317 369* (BR)

Development Fund as a contribution towards the Newcastle area resignalling scheme. This took place there in July 1989, and the cheque was presented by the Rt Hon Bruce Millan to John Nelson, General Manager of Eastern Region. Such an event has to be very carefully staged to make maximum impact, and particularly to provide suitable photographic opportunities. In this case the cheque hand-over was combined with the Lord Mayor of Newcastle opening an on-going exhibition outlining BR's plans for the reconstruction of the station, both parts of the event being organized by the Eastern Region's Public Affairs Department at York, under W. A. (Bert) Porter.

In the early 1980s I was given a gradient profile of one of Amtrak's routes in the eastern seaboard of the United States, and was amused to see that it also showed the names of the various politicians whose constituencies bordered the line. While I do not think that the BR Public Affairs Departments have quite gone that far, they are certainly aware of all those elected representatives who are affected by the railways, and it has often been possible to involve them in events connected with the electrification of the East Coast Route. Some of the Electrification Depots were formally opened by local or national politicians, while the ceremonial planting of certain of the electrification masts has also provided an opportunity for publicity. What was nominally the first of the 33,000 was put up at Peterborough in February 1985, that particular ceremony being carried out by Frank Paterson, the Eastern Region

General Manager at that time, although the Mayor of Peterborough was asked to assist.

North of the Border, the ScotRail Public Affairs Department, under John Boyle, organized the placing of the first mast at that end of the project, in Waverley station, Edinburgh. This was done by Michael Anchram, the Scottish Office Minister for Home Affairs and the Environment, with the assistance of Chris Green, then the BR Regional General Manager in Scotland. Most of these events were planned well in advance, but there was one occasion when the arrangements were carried out at very short notice. In

The then Prime Minister, Mrs Margaret Thatcher, unveils the plaque (inset) on the '12,000th' mast she had just placed in position on York station on 7 February 1987. Behind her are David Kirby (Vice-Chairman BRB), Don Heath (Project Director for the East Coast Electrification), and David Rayner (General Manager, Eastern Region). (BR)

THE FIRST MAST TO CARRY OVERHEAD WIRES FOR ELECTRIFICATION OF THE EAST COAST MAIN LINE WAS PLANTED AT PETERBOROUGH ON 7TH FEBRUARY, 1985. EXACTLY 2 YEARS LATER, ON 7TH FEBRUARY, 1987, THIS 12,000TH MAST WAS PUT IN PLACE BY
THE PRIME MINISTER
THE RT. HON. MARGARET THATCHER M.P.
TO MARK THE COMPLETION OF ONE THIRD OF THE TOTAL PROJECT AND THE START OF WORK IN THE YORK AREA.

February 1987, the Prime Minister, Mrs Margaret Thatcher, made one of her rare journeys by train, travelling by HST in the 'InterCity 125' Executive Saloon from London to York and back, to attend a political meeting at Scarborough. The opportunity was taken to ask her to plant what was nominally the 12,000th mast at York, where the commemorative plaque she also unveiled can be seen behind the buffer-stops of what is now No 1 platform.

As well as reaching the public via the media, there are ways in which the BR Public Affairs organization provides information to them direct. For the East Coast electrification project, the Eastern Region people were put in charge of producing a periodical newsheet, as well as a series of four videos. The latter was a new venture for a public audience, although they had commissioned many such items for internal or media use. In my earlier book, *Speed on the East Coast Main Line*, I referred to the BBC TV film *Race to the North*, which featured several of the National Railway Museum's exhibits. Michael Marshall, the producer of that feature, now has his own company — Cinécosse Film and Video Productions, based near Aberdeen — and they were responsible for the production work for the East Coast electrification videos. They were all presented by Martin Young, whose family, as it grew up over the seven-year period, provided a link for the 'growing project' itself. The series was called *The High Road North*, with the individual videos having the following sub-titles:

1985	*Going Electric*
1987	*Miles of Progress*
1989	*The Future now Arriving . . .*
1990	*Up and Running*

With a viewing time of approximately 20 minutes each, they were intended for any local organizations who were interested in — or concerned about — the electrification project, and combined a number of specific messages with visual images of the action going on along the line. Copies could be borrowed free from the regional Public Affairs offices. Don Heath, the Project Director, spoke to camera in each, and in the first he outlined BR's prime objectives for the scheme, as follows:

1   To complete the project with the absolute minimum of interruption to existing customers, passenger as well as freight.

2   To deliver the electrification to plan, to budget and within the agreed time-scale.

3   To produce a more reliable, and much more effective, economic railway.

4   To ensure that BR is in the best possible position to obtain an increased share of the market, and, having done so, to hang on to it.

After Dr John Prideaux had taken over as Director of InterCity, he also appeared in the videos, giving the public an idea of what the new trains would mean to them. Looking back at the series when I was writing this chapter, it was very interesting to see how the early ones had constructed images of the new trains from nothing more concrete than artists' impressions and models. The latest example of a signalling centre that could be filmed in 1985 also bore no resemblance to what has since appeared at York and Newcastle, so

ELECTRA

ELECTRIFYING INTERCITY   East Coast Main Line   No. 8

'UP AND RUNNING'

...the Trailblazers are here!

InterCity 225 – your train for the 21st century – is up and running.

The first of InterCity's new generation of high-speed trains – nine new Mark 4 coaches hauled by a Class 91 electric locomotive – is now zipping between London and Leeds. More trailblazers will appear soon and the whole London-Leeds service will go electric by next May.

The new coaches are among the best passenger vehicles in the world. In business terms, the 225 is the most cost-effective high-speed train in the world, built at the lowest cost per seat, developed and constructed to the fastest timescale and with the lowest development cost anywhere.

This flagship reflects everything InterCity is aiming for in efficiency and improved quality. It is now running on the 0715 Yorkshire Pullman from Leeds, the 1010 from Kings Cross to Leeds, the 1410 from Leeds and the 1750 from Kings Cross.

The Mark 4 coaches create a new style in passenger comfort and the train marks the same kind of significant advance achieved by the diesel-powered InterCity 125 some 13 years ago.

Introduction of the 225 on the East Coast will also benefit InterCity travellers elsewhere. For, as the 225s appear, the ever-popular 125s they replace will be transferred to other routes like the Midland and Great Western Main Lines, providing extra services and extra capacity.

The Mark 4 Coaches on acceptance trials.

MAY 1991 EDINBURGH
MAY 1991 NEWCASTLE
MAY 1991 DARLINGTON
YORK MAY 1991
LEEDS
DONCASTER
PETERBOROUGH
HUNTINGDON
LONDON KINGS CROSS

The front page of issue No 8 of the BR news-sheet Electra, *produced by the Eastern Region's Public Affairs Department.*

rapid has been the rate of technological progress. On the other hand, the work of running out the wires could be depicted in some detail, even in the first video, and there were some extremely informative shots showing the speed at which the circular pile foundations were vibrated into the ground.

The second way in which the public was made aware of the progress of the electrification was by the publication of the coloured news-sheet *Electra* at intervals of about nine months. The first of these was produced for the Board by an outside agency, but the subsequent issues have all been edited by Alan Moorby of the Eastern Region office at York, with the ninth coming out in the autumn of 1990. All of them use the same distinctive masthead, with a diagram of the route down the right-hand side of the front page. This has enabled the progress of introducing the new electric services to be marked by changing the colour of the line from black to red. This publication carried on the Eastern Region's tradition in this field, as a similar series of *Live Wire* news-sheets had been produced for the King's Cross suburban electrification in the 1970s, although, with standards of presentation moving on, these now look far less imposing, in retrospect, than does *Electra*. In addition to the news items, and interviews with many of those directly concerned with the implementation of the electrification, several of the issues have included competitions for readers, the prizes being a free train trip or rail-related holiday.

There have been many other ways in which the Eastern Region Public Affairs team has been able to exploit local news stories about the electrification. One that comes to mind was about a lineside resident who discovered the site for one of the electrification masts was in line with her house window, thereby obscuring the view of the passing trains. A day or two after this had appeared in the local paper came the BR announcement that they were pleased to move it a few feet along the track. The householder's initial reaction was, incidentally, somewhat of a contrast to that of many people in Kent, who not only object to the potential noise of trains on the future Channel Tunnel Link, but also to the disturbing visual effect of their movement!

Another aspect of all electrification shemes concerns the safety implications when the supply system is energized, and this must be extensively publicized throughout the area concerned. Much of this work is carried out in advance by the British Transport Police, who, by the time the wires are live all the way to Leeds, Edinburgh and Glasgow, will have talked to some 2 million children in 5,000 different schools located near the line. This has to be supplemented by press release from the regional Public Affairs offices to the local press and media, giving the date of the switch-on and again stressing the dangers of the high voltage. Typically, the press release includes a message such as:

'The overhead wires and structures are perfectly safe but, if tampered with, they kill or maim,' said an Eastern Region spokesman. 'Railway electrical installations must always be regarded as being live at all times and we strongly urge all parents to warn their children to keep well clear of railway tracks and electrification wires and structures.'

From my observation of the local papers they are very good at passing this

A redundant electric multiple-unit from East Anglia was adapted as a class-room for safety instruction purposes, and worked northwards along the East Coast Route in advance of the wires being energized. While train crews were given lectures on safety as part of their other training, the mobile classroom was used for staff from many other departments, such as those working on the permanent way, signalling and in stations. By the time it was photographed in one of the station platforms at Leeds in 1989, it had been painted in InterCity livery.

warning on to their readers, and the effectiveness of the campaign has been extremely good, with no fatality having arisen from such a cause up to the time of writing.

All public relations and press work also involves the people and departments directly concerned with the story, equally as much as the Public Affairs people. It is the latter who have to put the ideas together in a form that they know will appeal to the press or the public, and then carry out the organization necessary for it to happen, using their expertise and experience in this field, but they are the first to acknowledge the vital role played by those 'on the ground' who are actually doing what is being highlighted for the public. Indeed, one of the ongoing responsibilities of the Public Affairs departments is to provide training for managers on how to handle press and television interviews.

Chapter Ten

ELECTRIC PERFORMANCE

In the course of the earlier narrative, references have been made to a number of journeys with electric traction on the East Coast Route. Many of these were noteworthy because of the novelty of the type of traction, while others provided a record of the standards of running we hope to experience over a wider canvas in the years to come. For those interested in the details of train performance, I have concentrated the logs of the running in this particulr chapter, together with a brief commentary, before concuding with an account of a footplate run I was able to make on a Class '91' locomotive in the summer of 1990.

The first new electric workings along the East Coast Route after 1984 were with the multiple-unit services as they extended towards Peterborough, initially with the Class '312s'. However, the four suburban sets included in the East Coast Electrification Project were Class '317s', and they were joined by others displaced from the Midland by the dual-voltage Thameslink units, taking over completely as the Class '312s' were cascaded to East Anglia. I will therefore begin this chapter by recounting two runs with the '317s'. Table 15 gives details of a fast King's Cross–St Neots journey in May 1988, with an evening commuter service. A year earlier there had been an 80.9-mph booking from Finsbury Park to the St Neots stop with one of these Peterborough trains, but during the currency of the 1987/8 winter timetable it ran non-stop from the terminus.

We had a pair of Class '317s', and left from Platform 8, which was a last-minute change, possibly as a result of a three-hour signal failure at New Barnet earlier in the day. This gave us a fairly direct exit from the station, and our speed through Copenhagen Tunnel averaged 57, before reaching 78 through Finsbury Park. Then 81 was touched briefly before Alexandra Palace, and, from 79 at the bottom of the bank, we accelerated to 89 by Hadley Wood. Even time had been attained at milepost $6^1/2$. We reached 103 through Hatfield, finally clearing the climb to Woolmer Green at 92 mph. A speed of 105 had just been reached at Stevenage when we got a brief check, probably from signals protecting a movement at Hitchin on to the

Table 15: Class '317' non-stop King's Cross–St Neots

Date: May 1988
Formation: 2 x 4-car Class '317' EMU
Unit Nos: 317 353 and 317 346
Load: No/empty/full (tons)   8/270/290

Dist *miles*		Actual *min sec*	Speeds *mph*
0.0	KING'S CROSS	0 00	—
2.4	Finsbury Park	3 29	78
4.9	ALEXANDRA PALACE	5 18	81/79
6.4	New Southgate	6 25	81
9.1	New Barnet	8 19	88
12.7	Potters Bar	10 45	89/88
15.5	Welham Green	12 34	101
17.6	Hatfield	13 49	103
20.2	WELWYN GARDEN CITY	15 29	98
21.9	Welwyn North	16 27	94
23.8	*Woolmer Green*	17 38	92
25.0	Knebworth	18 25	101
27.5	STEVENAGE	19 56	105
—		sigs	74*
31.8	Hitchin	22 46	103
41.1	Biggleswade	28 13	105/101
44.1	Sandy	29 55	103/106
47.5	*Tempsford*	31 53	102
51.7	St Neots	35 09	—

* Speed restriction

Cambridge line, which brought us down to 74. We quickly recovered, and were doing 95 by the junction, passing another down Class '317' in the platform.

Then we reeled off the next 16 miles from milepost 34 in only 9 minutes 20 seconds, at a flying average of 102.9 mph, while the homeward-bound commuters finished their drinks and refreshments from the trolley which had come round earlier on the trip. Finally we came to a fairly gentle halt in the fast-line platform at St Neots in 35 minutes 9 seconds from King's Cross, giving a start-to-stop average of 88.3 mph. I estimated that the check after Stevenage cost us 22 seconds, so our net time was 34³/4 minutes, corresponding to an average of 89.3. With this sort of day-to-day performance, it was easy to see the practical advantages of the 'Sparks Effect' for commuters and their life-style, which was currently bringing so much new business to the railways.

The conclusion of the next journey to be considered takes us off the East Coast Route, but the fastest running on the express services between King's Cross and Cambridge takes place on the main line as far as Hitchin. The one-stop trains run every hour in each direction, and in March 1990 had public

Table 16: Class '317', King's Cross–Cambridge

Date:	7 March 1990
Formation:	4-car Class '317' EMU
Set No:	317 360
Load: No/empty/full (tons)	4/135/140

Dist *miles*		Actual *min sec*	Speeds *mph*
0.0	KING'S CROSS	0 00	—
2.4	Finsbury Park	3 19	81
4.9	ALEXANDRA PALACE	4 59	94
6.4	New Southgate	5 59	90
8.3	Oakleigh Park	7 15	90
9.1	New Barnet	7 47	89
10.6	Hadley Wood	8 44	90
12.7	Potters Bar	10 11	90/93
14.4	Brookman's Park	11 18	97
15.5	Welham Green	11 58	99
17.6	Hatfield	13 16	95
20.2	WELWYN GARDEN CITY	14 56	91*
21.9	Welwyn North	16 11	88*
—		sigs	70*
23.8	*Woolmer Green*	17 40	83
25.0	Knebworth	18 31	93
27.5	STEVENAGE	20 44	—
4.3	Hitchin	4 05	87/40*
7.1	Letchworth	6 50	73
9.0	Baldock	8 19	86
13.4	Ashwell & Morden	11 27	83
17.3	Royston	15 02	50*
20.4	Meldreth	17 54	63*
22.3	Shepreth	19 59	48*
23.4	Foxton	21 08	60*
25.0	*Harston*	22 42	68
27.8	*Shepreth Branch Junc*	25 34	30*
29.3	*Trumpington*	27 08	69
30.7	CAMBRIDGE	28 46	—

* Speed restrictions

bookings of 57 minutes down and 58 up, inclusive of the stop at Stevenage. The overall speed thus worked out at just over 60 mph for the 58.2 miles, and some smart running was needed on the main line to achieve it. These trains were not introduced immediately after the line was electrified, although there was an hourly fast Saturdays-only service during the summer of 1988. With one intermediate call at Finsbury Park, this was booked to take a minute less than the present trains, which first appeared in May 1989. Table 16 gives the details of a journey I made on 7 March 1990.

From a standing start, a Class '317' can beat an HST over short distances,

and, when I returned to York the same evening, it was not until Welwyn
Garden City, 20 miles out of the terminus, that the 'InterCity 125' on which
I was travelling managed to draw ahead of the suburban EMU. Shortly after
that point my Cambridge train was checked to 70, and I assumed that this
was a preliminary to being turned slow-line at Woolmer Green. However, it
was actually due to a sister unit which was slightly tardy getting itself clear of
the twin-track bottleneck over Welwyn viaduct and through the two tunnels.
Even so, we managed a final maximum of 93 before the stop at Stevenage, the
27.5 miles from King's Cross being covered at a start-to-stop average of 79.6
mph. On the branch from Hitchin there are many slowings to contend with,
starting with the 40 restriction over the junction off the main line, and concluding with an even more severe one to 30 as we joined the Great Eastern
main line at Shepreth Branch Junction. Our average over these 30.7 miles
worked out at a more modest 64.0 mph because of the slacks.

There was a catering trolley on the train, which reminded me that, when
the LNER introduced some fast buffet-car trains over this route in the 1930s,
the Cambridge undergraduates promptly christened them 'Beer Trains'. Col
Michael Cobb recorded a number of fine runs on these during his time at the
light-blue university, and kindly sent me some details of the running he
recorded. On the best run, a Class 'C1' 'Atlantic', No 4402, with seven
bogies, achieved a maximum of 78 at Hatfield, and the minimum up the 1 in
200 to Potters Bar was, for the time, a very respectable 56.

While BR's multiple-units normally only work as far north as Peterborough
in passenger service, other trains of this type can frequently be seen between
that point and York. These are the new units built by BREL in the latter city,
and, since the electrifiction moved north, the 25kV variety have regularly
been tested on the line, as well as being delivered under their own power to
the south of England. In July 1990 the builders handed over the first Class

*EMU No 317 360 at Cambridge on the occasion of the March 1990 run described in
the text.*

Class '317' No 317 370 approaches Alexandra Palace with the 14.35 from King's Cross to Peterborough on 17 February 1989. It is in almost the same place as the GN 'Single' shown in the photograph on page 13, which was taken 82 years earlier. (Colin J. Marsden)

'322' 'Stansted Express' set to the Managing Director of Network Southeast, and it made a non-stop delivery run to King's Cross, with representatives of the press aboard. The 188.2 miles from Holgate Junction were covered in an actual time of 144 minutes 47 seconds, at an average of 78.0 mph, but we had lost 18¼ minutes through checks, many of them from an up Leeds electric, which called at all stations from Doncaster to Peterborough. Our net time was 123½ minutes, corresponding to an average of 91.4 mph. There had been a special dispensation to exceed the unit's normal maximum of 100, and we achieved 112 descending Stoke Bank.

In Chapter 8 I referred to the 'Mallard '88' commemorative special on 3 July 1988, which was worked from King's Cross to Doncaster and back by the Brush Class '89' Co-Co, this being the first passenger-carrying electric working to reach *Mallard*'s birthplace. In view of the historic nature of this journey, I have included the log of the down run in Table 17, but only from Stevenage onwards, as the earlier stretch had involved some slow-line running because of Sunday engineering work. To be compatible with the vacuum brake of the new 'A4', the train had to be made up from the pool of Mark I InterCity charter stock and was thus limited to a maximum of 100 mph, which meant that we were not going to be able to experience the full capabilities of the 125-mph locomotive. Like all the new generation of electric locomotives, No 89 001 is fitted with 'dial-a-speed' or 'cruise control', and this appeared to have been used to good effect. Once we were up to speed just after Tempsford, I recorded nothing outside the 98-101 range until the brakes went on for Peterborough, and our flying average between mileposts 47 and 73 was 99.3 mph. Over the remaining stretch to Doncaster, No 89 001 was limited to a lower maximum of 90, the reason given being that more tests were needed to match the pantograph's behaviour with the catenary. Again the start was gentle, but we had reached our 90-mph limited by Werrington Junction, 3.1 miles out. From that point to milepost 143, where power was cut off for a track slowing, the speed remained in the range 88-92, uphill and down.

Table 17: Inaugural electric passenger run to Doncaster, Stevenage–Doncaster

Date: 3 July 1988
Locomotive:
  Wheel arrangement   Co-Co
  No   89 001
Load: No/empty/full (tons)   11/399/415

Dist *miles*		Schedule *mins*	Actual *min sec*	Speeds *mph*
0.0	STEVENAGE	0	0 00	—
—			SL †	85/70
4.3	Hitchin	5	4 23	81
—			sig stop	—
13.6	Biggleswade		17.55	—
—			sig stop	—
16.6	Sandy	13	23 12	—
—			FL†	—
20.0	*Tempsford*		26 33	94
24.2	St Neots		29 08	100
28.4	*Offord*		30 39	99
31.3	HUNTINGDON	23	33 25	99
34.4	*Milepost 62*		35 21	98
41.8	*Holme*		39 45	101
45.0	*Yaxley*		41 48	99
47.4	*Fletton Junc*		43 21	—
48.8	PETERBOROUGH	38	46 30	—
3.1	*Werrington Junc*		3 57	73/90
8.4	*Tallington*	9	7 24	90
12.3	*Essendine*		9 59	90
15.8	*Little Bytham*		12 22	88
20.7	*Corby Glen*		15 40	90
23.7	*Stoke*	24	17 44	88
28.8	GRANTHAM	31	21 13	90
33.3	*Barkston S*	37	24 00	92
43.8	Newark	44	30 55	89
50.0	*Carlton*		35 05	90
55.6	*Tuxford*		38 50	89
62.3	RETFORD	57	43 16	92/89
67.6	*Ranskill*		46 49	91/88
—			trs	28*
71.4	*Bawtry*		50 01	—
75.0	*Rossington*		55 23	91
79.6	DONCASTER	75	60 39	—

* Speed restrictions
† SL = Slow Line, FL = Fast Line

Within a couple of months I was able to record a much better performance from No 89 001 after it had gone into regular use on the commuter run

Table 18: Class '89', 17.36 King's Cross–Huntingdon

Date:	31 August 1988
Locomotive:	
Wheel arrangement	Co-Co
No	89 001
Load: No/empty/full (tons)	9†/336/360

Dist _miles_		Actual _min sec_	Speeds _mph_
0.0	KING'S CROSS	0 00	—
2.4	Finsbury Park	4 00	80
4.9	ALEXANDRA PALACE	5 50	81
—		sigs	75*
6.4	New Southgate	6 59	87
9.1	New Barnet	8 41	98/105
12.7	Potters Bar	10 46	104
17.6	Hatfield	13 37	106
20.2	WELWYN GARDEN CITY	15 08	101
21.9	Welwyn North	16 06	101
23.8	_Woolmer Green_	17 10	101
25.0	Knebworth	17 50	101
27.5	STEVENAGE	19 11	100
31.8	Hitchin	21 42	117
37.0	Arlesey	24 30	106
41.1	Biggleswade	26 45	110
44.1	Sandy	28 22	109
51.7	St Neots	32 29	112/101
55.9	_Offord_	35 04	94
—		sig stop	—
58.8	HUNTINGDON	40 42	—

* Speed restrictions
† Includes DVT (adapted HST power car)

between Peterborough and King's Cross, as described earlier. On the occasion of my journey there were eight Mark III passenger-carrying vehicles in the train, made up from one First, five Standard-class saloons, the TGS and a W-prefix buffet car, but on a subsequent occasion it appeared to have acquired a further TS vehicle, which would have provided some useful additional seats in the peaks. The details of our run, on the 17.36 from King's Cross, are given in Table 18. I was travelling in the rear FO, next to the DVT, and it was unusual for the train to get going without the customary surge of noise from the diesel motor in the power car behind us as the driver opened the controller. At this time the Class '89' had not been fitted with TDM equipment, so the spare power capacity of the Surrogate DVT could not be used for traction. We were past Finsbury Park at 80 mph in 4 minutes exactly, but speed then fell back to 75 through Alexandra Palace, presumably because of signals, rather than the neutral section just beyond the station. We had left

No 89 001 waits to leave King's Cross on 31 August 1988 with a commuter train for Peterborough, as described in the text. From the visual point of view, the appearance of this electric locomotive is nothing like as impressive as that of the more familiar HSTs.

only 6 minutes behind the 'Tees-Tyne Pullman', with the 'Hull-Executive' sandwiched between us, and I suspect the electric's performance throughout might well have been hampered by signals from the two longer-distance expresses ahead.

After this check, we accelerated to 105 up the bank to Potters Bar, which was rather faster than an average HST, and maintained much the same speed down the other side as far as Hatfield. We then eased off to 101 all the way to Knebworth, and this was followed by a brief drop through Stevenage. Then came the fastest speed of the whole trip, 117 at Hitchin, but this was quickly eased, and we were down to 106 by the time we passed the new station at Arlesey, currently under construction. It was interesting to see the reappearance of this traditional East Coast landmark, but the new station, with its platforms on the slow lines, is not quite in the same position as the previous one, and the distances used by recorders need altering slightly.

Beyond this we got a chance to run at 109/110 as far as Sandy, where it would appear that the train ahead began to pull clear, as we were treated to a maximum of 114. However, this did not last, and before St Neots the speed started to tail off, so that we snaked over the Offord curves at a mere 91. We had probably caught up the 17.13 from King's Cross, which was booked to stop at Huntingdon from 18.12 to 18.13, so we were halted for a minute at milepost 58 before taking the turnout on to the slow lane to make our own stop in the station. We ran the 57.9 miles to the first pause on the main line in 37 minutes 41 seconds, which corresponds to a start-to-stop average of 92.2 mph, appreciably better than the Class '317' run to St Neots referred to earlier. To the Huntingdon stop the actual average came down to 86.7.

A few weeks after the first revenue-earning operation by the Class '91' electric locomotives, I was able to arrange my homeward journey from London to use the same Peterborough commuter train, the haulage of which they had taken over from the Brush Class '89'. When I reached the terminus at about 17.15 on the Friday evening, I was somewhat disconcerted to see a large electronic notice warning passengers that there would be no Pullman facilities

Surrogate Driving Van Trailer No 43123 at Peterborough on 31 August 1988, after arriving on the rear of the 17.36 commuter train from King's Cross. When working with No 89 001 at that time, it could not provide power for traction purposes.

that evening on the 17.30 departure. The loudspeakers were also apologizing for the $1^1/_4$-hour late arrival of the 'Highland Chieftain', these two trains being only two of the many affected by a major signalling failure earlier in the day at Doncaster. Joining the crowds of homeward-bound commuters already lining the edge of Platform 1, I waited to see what would appear when our empty stock emerged from Gas Works Tunnel, feeling fairly confident that the electric set would not be directly involved in the delays, since its normal roster only included the corresponding up journey in the morning. One of the adapted HST power cars, No 43083 *County of Derbyshire,* duly headed the set into the station, and even from where I stood, quite close to the buffer-stops, the squat and purposeful shape of a Class '91' could be identified following the seven Mk III coaches into the platform. In spite of being barred to railcard and Saver ticket holders, the train rapidly filled with passengers, and, three-quarters of a minute late, we were on our way.

To gain the down fast line, trains leaving No 1 platform at King's Cross have to foul the majority of incoming movements, and, on a Friday afternoon when most of the long-distance services were topsy-turvy, we did not get a good start. The train crawled into Gas Works Tunnel and almost came to a halt before an up HST passed us, clearing the junctions ahead to give access to the down fast. I was travelling up in the rear coach, and as the train started to accelerate there came the unmistakable sound of the 'Valenta' in the DVT power car behind us running up, accompanied by the usual mild bumping and boring that goes on in the last coach of an HST departing from King's Cross. This was the first indication I had received that the East Coast Route had joined the Southern Region in providing Mixed Technology traction in the rush hours, the reasons for which have already been described. So for the first time I was able to experience travel over the East Coast Route with a train that had in excess of 8,000 hp available for traction purposes. Inclusive of both power units, the train weighed only 380 tons empty, which gave us a power to weight ratio of 21 hp/ton, putting us in the TGV class. So, as soon as the up HST had cleared the junctions between the King's Cross tunnels,

Table 19: Class '91', 17.36 King's Cross–Peterborough

Date:	14 April 1989
Formation:	Class '91' + 7 + HST power car
Loco/power car Nos:	91 007/43084
HST power car name:	*County of Derbyshire*
Load: No/empty/full (tons)	7/380/410

Dist *miles*		Actual *min sec*	Speeds *mph*
0.0	KING'S CROSS	0 00	—
—		sigs	5*
2.4	Finsbury Park	4 46	82
4.9	ALEXANDRA PALACE	6 33	89
6.4	New Southgate	7 31	95
8.3	Oakleigh Park	8 40	105
9.1	New Barnet	9 07	105
12.7	Potters Bar	11 09	105/107
17.6	Hatfield	13 58	97
20.2	WELWYN GARDEN CITY	15 27	105
21.9	Welwyn North	16 24	103
23.8	*Woolmer Green*	17 24	109
26.6	*Langley Junc*	18 47	127
27.5	STEVENAGE	19 13	129/122
—		sigs	40*
31.8	Hitchin	23 28	73
37.0	Arlesey	26 17	127
—		slow	—
—		line	43*
41.1	Biggleswade	29 51	—
44.1	Sandy	32 14	77
—		trs	69*
51.7	St Neots	38 13	82
55.9	*Offord*	41 25	76/81
<u>58.8</u>	HUNTINGDON	<u>44 09</u>	—
4.6	*Abbots Ripton*	4 32	81/64
10.5	*Holme*	9 26	74/87
13.7	*Yaxley*	11 23	117/114
16.2	*Fletton Junc*	12 38	82
		trs	—*
<u>17.5</u>	PETERBOROUGH	<u>14 46</u>	—

* Out-of-course speed restrictions

we were able to get motoring in no uncertain fashion.

The log of the journey to Peterborough is given in Table 19, but some further aspects of the running are worth mentioning. Because of the initial check we only averaged 51 mph through Copenhagen Tunnel, but were up to 82 before Finsbury Park; 90 was reached by Alexandra Palace, and by Oakleigh Park we were doing 105 up the 1 in 200. Even time was reached at milepost

9¹/₄. A brief 107 at Brookmans Park was trimmed to 97 through Hatfield, and we then accelerated to 109 by Woolmer Green, the summit of the climb out of London, by which time we had averaged 82.1 mph from the start, inclusive of the bad initial signal check. We touched 127 mph at Langley junction and 129 just before Stevenage, but then experienced a severe signal check, our speed being reduced to what felt like a crawl, but was probably nearer 40 mph. After Hitchin, with the road clear again, we accelerated from 73 to 125 in less than 4 miles, and were doing a comfortable 127 at Arlesey. That was the end of the really high-speed running, however, as we were slowed to 43 and turned on to the slow line at Biggleswade to permit an unidentified HST to overtake us. In spite of the nominal 80-mph maximum on this track, and the various other checks, we stopped in Huntingdon in 44 minutes 9 seconds, having averaged 79.9 mph overall.

After many of the passengers had alighted we set off again, and the acceleration up the 1 in 200 to Leys summit was extremely brisk. The line limit is 80, and we reached 81 mph by milepost 60¹/₄ in just 1³/₄ minutes from the start. With a maximum of 117 across the Fen between Holme and Yaxley, we stopped in Peterborough in 14 minutes 46 seconds from Huntingdon, which gave us a section average of just over 71. Our overall speed worked out as 76.1 mph from King's Cross, inclusive of the stop at Huntingdon and all the checks.

Shortly after the 'Hybrid' sets started running to Leeds, a pair of remarkable runs was recorded between Stevenage and Grantham on the 13.20 from King's Cross on different Saturdays. In Chapter 8 I referred to the faster of the two, recorded by Mr W. E. Long, but in Table 20 I am listing the other one, which lost about 20 seconds on the Offord slowing. The driver later regained nearly all of them with a very smart stop at Grantham, where the

On 14 April 1989, No 91 007 propels the empty stock of the 17.36 commuter train from King's Cross out of Peterborough on its way back to London. At that time the numbers on the Class '91s', like other newly repainted locomotives, were ridiculously small, as well as being positioned where they got very dirty, and thus became virtually unreadable.

Table 20: 'Hybrid' set, King's Cross–Grantham

Date:	1 April 1989	
Formation:	Class '91' + 8 Mk IIIs + DVT	
Loco/power car Nos:	91 008/43068	
Load: No/empty/full (tons)	8†/287/440	

Dist miles		Actual min sec	Speeds mph
0.0	KING'S CROSS	0 00	—
2.4	Finsbury Park	3 49	81
4.9	ALEXANDRA PALACE	5 37	90
6.4	New Southgate	6 34	99
8.3	Oakleigh Park	7 42	105
10.6	Hadley Wood	8 56	106
12.7	Potters Bar	10 11	106
15.5	Welham Green	11 47	106
17.6	Hatfield	12 59	107/105
20.2	WELWYN GARDEN CITY	14 28	112
21.9	Welwyn North	15 20	-/101*
23.8	*Woolmer Green*	15 27	108
25.0	Knebworth	17 01	120
<u>27.5</u>	STEVENAGE	<u>18 53</u>	—
4.4	Hitchin	3 21	129/123
9.4	Arlesey	5 46	127/125
13.6	Biggleswade	7 46	127/125
16.5	Sandy	9 09	127
24.1	St Neots	12 50	113/104*
28.3	*Offord*	15 10	108
31.3	HUNTINGDON	16 42	126
35.9	*Abbots Ripton*	18 56	127/126
41.8	*Holme*	21 46	111/103*
45.2	*Yaxley*	23 42	117
47.4	*Fletton Junc*	24 54	110
48.8	PETERBOROUGH	25 40	103*
50.4	*New England North*	26 36	114
54.3	*Helpston*	28 30	125
57.2	*Tallington*	29 53	125
84.7	*Little Bytham*	33 27	124/125
69.5	*Corby Glen*	35 48	126
72.4	*Stoke*	37 13	115*
73.9	*High Dyke*	38 02	103*
76.9	*Milepost 104½*	39 52	90
<u>77.9</u>	GRANTHAM	<u>40 56</u>	—

* Speed restrictions
† Including DVT

overall time was just 4 seconds longer. This second run was timed by Frank
Collins, the editor of the Railway Performance Society's journal *Milepost*, and

he estimated the power production at the rail at several stages of the run. Nothing more than 4,400 hp was required before Potters Bar, but a burst of 6,850 was used to accelerate from Woolmer Green to Knebworth. The Stevenage start was very smart, with an output of 7,100 hp being sustained for 2 minutes, with a peak of 8,000. Even time was achieved in 2¼ miles from the start, and it only took 170 seconds to accelerate from rest to 120 mph. It must be remembered that the widely available gradient profiles show the old location for Stevenage station, which used to be a mile further north than the present one. Then the gradient used to fall northwards at 1 in 200 from the platform end, but today's trains have a mile on the level to traverse before reaching the downhill stretch. Remarkable though the uphill running was, even the ascent of Stoke Bank required no more than 4,500 hp out of the 6,300 available from the Class '91' alone.

In the 1989 summer timetable, most of the up Leeds trains that called at Peterborough and Stevenage were given start-to-stop bookings of 29½ minutes, inclusive of a 3-minute recovery margin. The 13.10 from Leeds, however, had its allowance moved south of the Stevenage stop, which raised the booked average from Peterborough to no less than 110.5 mph. While the performance of the 'Hybrid' sets had been outstanding, there had been fast HST schedules over the same stretch in the opposite direction which had never been kept. Back in 1979, two down HSTs were booked to cover the 48.8 miles in 27½ minutes. This corresponded to an average of 106.5 mph, but I never saw any runs that came anywhere near this, and it quietly disappeared from subsequent editions of the timetable. Even ten years later, the Railway Performance Society's 'Fastest HST Time' for this stretch was only 1 second over 28 minutes. In the light of this I wondered whether the new schedule was feasible in practice, so was very pleased to get details of a run with one of the 'Hybrid' sets over this stretch, timed by Peter Barlow.

The details are given in Table 21. Mr Barlow was travelling on the 18.10 from Leeds, rather than the 13.10, and the schedule was the more usual one

Table 21: 'Hybrid' set on 110 mph working, Peterborough–Stevenage

Date: August 1989
Formation: PC + 8 + Class '91'
Load: No/empty/full (tons) 8/411/430

Dist miles		Schedule mins	Actual min sec	Speeds mph
0.0	PETERBOROUGH	0	0 00	—
1.3	Fletton Junc		2 04	39.2
3.3	Milepost 73		3 20	94.7
7.0	Holme		5 23	106.8
17.5	HUNTINGDON	10	10 31	122.7
24.7	St Neots		14 09	118.1
35.2	Biggleswade	[3]	19 01	126.0
44.5	Hitchin		23 30	127.6
48.8	STEVENAGE	29½	26 30	87.0

of 29^1/$_2$ minutes for Class '91'-powered trains, inclusive of the recovery time. However, they left Peterborough 2 minutes late, which inspired those at the front end to see what they could do. As a result they stopped in Stevenage in exactly 26^1/$_2$ minutes, demonstrating that the record-breaking schedule was possible. The log only gives the average speeds over the various sections, but the train seems to have been running at slightly over the official line speed in places. The arrival at Stevenage was a full minute early, and they then left 1^1/$_2$ minutes before time, this being a 'set-down only' stop. King's Cross was finally reached 5 minutes early.

In Chapter 8 I described the 'InterCity 225' press launch on 20 September 1989, and I am now including the logs of the interesting sections of the down and up runs, given in Tables 22 and 23. The former features the fast climb of Stoke Bank, which followed an additional stop at Peterborough to set down a television crew, and the day's 141-mph maximum is included in the second log. These provided us with an exciting glimpse into the future, but the high-speed trials on the previous Sunday had done better still. Nowadays

Table 22: 'InterCity 225' launch, Peterborough–Doncaster

Date: 20 September 1989
Locomotive:
  Wheel arrangement   Bo-Bo
  No   *91 001*
  Name   *Swallow*
Load: No/empty/full (tons)   9/369/385

Dist *miles*		Schedule† *mins*	Actual *min sec*	Speeds *mph*
0.0	PETERBOROUGH	0	0 00	—
3.1	*Werrington Junc*		3 44	97
8.4	*Tallington*	4	6 33	126
12.3	*Essendine*		8 23	129
15.8	*Little Bytham*		10 00	132/130
20.7	*Corby Glen*		12 16	129/132
23.7	*Stoke*	14	13 50	93
28.8	GRANTHAM	17	16 55	92
33.3	*Barkston South*	20	17 27	—
39.0	*Claypole*		22 07	126
—			trs	60*
43.8	Newark	26	25 00	–*
			trs	60*
55.6	*Tuxford*		32 55	118
62.3	RETFORD	38	36 36	121/115
67.6	*Ranskill*		39 12	126
71.4	*Bawtry*		41 06	105/110
79.6	DONCASTER	56	47 06	—

* Out-of-course speeds restrictions
† Schedule from passing Peterborough

Table 23: 'InterCity 225' launch, Doncaster–King's Cross

Date: 20 September 1989
Locomotive:
  Wheel arrangement   Bo-Bo
  No   91 001
  Name   *Swallow*
Load: No/empty/full (tons)   9/369/385

Dist *miles*		Schedule *mins*	Actual *min sec*	Speeds *mph*
0.0	DONCASTER	0	0 00	—
4.6	*Rossington*		4 40	111
8.2	*Bawtry*		6 35	110
12.0	*Ranskill*		8 37	105
17.3	RETFORD	13	11 45	101
24.0	*Tuxford*		15 46	87*/107
35.8	Newark	23	22 38	96
40.6	*Claypole*		25 23	105/109
46.3	*Barkston South*	28	28 35	105
50.8	GRANTHAM	30	31 20	86*
55.9	*Stoke*	35	34 26	106/90
58.9	*Corby Glen*		36 05	129
63.7	*Little Bytham*		38 19	136
67.3	*Essendine*		39 49	140
71.1	*Tallington*	43	41 32	141
76.4	*Werrington Junc*		43 49	—
79.6	PETERBOROUGH		45 33	105
80.9	*Fletton Junc*		46 29	105
83.3	*Yaxley*		47 34	113
97.1	HUNTINGDON	56	54 53	122/118*
100.0	*Offord*		56 26	110
104.2	St Neots		58 39	121
111.8	Sandy	63	62 20	126
114.8	Biggleswade		63 45	126
118.9	Arlesey		65 43	125
124.0	Hitchin	72	68 11	122
128.4	STEVENAGE		70 28	108/102*
130.9	Knebworth		71 57	106
132.0	*Woolmer Green*	76	72 39	104
135.7	WELWYN GARDEN CITY	79	74 59	100
138.3	Hatfield		76 28	105
140.4	Welham Green		77 41	105
143.2	Potters Bar	82	79 17	101
146.7	New Barnet		81 50	87*
151.0	ALEXANDRA PALACE	89	85 23	—
153.4	Finsbury Park	91	87 08	—
155.9	KING'S CROSS	96	91 18	—

*   Out-of-course speed restrictions

achievements of this sort are normally recorded on magnetic tape, and almost certainly in metric units! However, Mr D. J. Harland, the Brecknell Willis project engineer, was on the special, keeping an eye on the performance of his firm's pantograph, and he has kindly provided me with a log of the record-breaking run. This is given in Table 24, which shows the performance down Stoke Bank on the third high-speed run that morning. The train left from the *down* platform at Grantham, so had to cross over on to the up line before full power could be selected. The rain earlier in the day had cleared, but some wheelslip on the climb to the summit meant that they were only doing 99 over the top, which was appreciably lower than on the second run. The speed through Little Bytham was still only 146, and 150 was not reached until mile-post $90^1/_2$. The next quarter-mile was where *Mallard* had reached its maximum, but these days the peak speeds are attained appreciably further down the bank, as the contribution made by gravity is no longer so important. There are also the curves higher up that have to be taken into account, where the normal maximum speed allowed is only 135 mph.

On the second round trip, after the locomotive had briefly cut out, they had managed 146 just after Tallington, but on the final run the speedometer recorded 161 slightly earlier, near milepost 87, three miles on from where the 1938 record was established. The test instruments subsequently confirmed a maximum of 161.7 mph, which was just half a mile per hour below the 162.2 achieved by the APT-P. The start-to-stop average from Grantham to Peterborough was 91.5, but the previous northbound run had been completed in considerably less time, in spite of the steady rain. Full power was used as far as milepost 88, by which time the speed was up to 144. Then the locomotive was eased to 130, before being given the 'stick' on the final part of the climb. A maximum of 136 was attained at milepost 96 before the power was cut off for the speed restriction through the tunnel. Their time to the Grantham stop on that run was 16 minutes 16 seconds, corresponding to an average of 106.2.

In view of the various incorrect figures that appeared in the popular press following the runs by No 91 010, I have prepared Table 25 (page 204), which lists all the 100-plus-mph speed records achieved on the East Coast Route by different types of motive power, the achievements of the steam and diesel eras being listed separately. Although Dynamometer Cars were used on several of the steam runs, it is still not wise to quote the speeds with any greater accuracy than 1 mph. The same applies to my own stopwatch figure of 144 mph for the 'Tees-Tyne Pullman' run in 1985, but the others have had the benefit of modern electronic instrumentation, and are thus quoted to one decimal place. According to the previously published figures, No 91 010's 161.7 mph should have been a British record, but more information about the 10-year-old APT record came to light at the 20 September press conference. I have therefore included all four speed records achieved by the APTs in Table 26.

To enable me to obtain first-hand experience of the way in which the Class '91s' are handled, I was privileged to be able to ride in the cab of one of them working a London–Leeds service on 13 August 1990, three months after the

Table 24: Record run with No 91 010, Grantham–Peterborough

Date:	17 September 1990
Locomotive:	
Wheel arrangement	Bo-Bo
No	91 010
Load: No/empty/full (tons)	7†/244/250

Dist *miles*		Actual *min sec*	Speeds *mph*
0.0	GRANTHAM	0 00	—
1.3	*Mp 103½*	3 54	58
3.1	*Mp 102*	5 21	80
4.1	*Stoke Tunnel entrance*	6 06	85
4.6	*Stoke Tunnel exit*	6 27	92
5.1	*Stoke Box*	6 46	99
6.1	*Mp 99*	7 21	113
7.1	*Mp 98*	7 51	123
9.1	*Mp 96*	8 45	136
11.1	*Mp 94*	9 36	145/146
12.1	*Mp 93*	10 00	145
12.8	*Little Bytham*	10 17	146
14.1	*Mp 91*	10 49	146
14.6	*Mp 90½*	11 01	150
15.1	*Mp 90*	11 13	152
15.6	*Mp 89½*	11 25	154
16.1	*Mp 89*	11 37	155
16.6	*Mp 88½*	11 48	157
17.1	*Mp 88*	11 59	158
17.6	*Mp 87½*	12 10	160/161
19.1	*Mp 86*	12 45	155
19.6	*Mp 85½*	12 57	—
20.3	*Tallington*	13 15	141
22.1	*Mp 83*	14 02	130
22.6	*Maxey Crossing*	14 18	132
23.2	*Helpston Crossing*	14 34	135
25.1	*Mp 80*	15 25	—
28.8	PETERBOROUGH	18 53	—

† Including DVT

beginning of the 1990 summer timetables. The train concerned was the 12.10 down, and I found that the locomotive was none other than No 91 010, the record-breaker of 7 September 1989. Our train in Platform 5 at King's Cross consisted of seven Mark IVs and a DVT, and in the middle of the holiday period the Standard class coaches were well filled, so the coach weights, including the DVT, came to 328 tons tare and 350 full. After I had climbed into the cab, Chief Traction Inspector Geoff Mansell introduced me to the two drivers — F. Johnson from Leeds, at the controls, and F. Elliott from Doncaster, who would alight when we passed through his home town. This

Table 25: 100-mph-plus speed records on East Coast Route

Date	Speed (mph)	Location	Locomotive	Comments
Steam				
30 Nov 1934	100	Stoke Bank	4–6–2 'A1' *Flying Scotsman*	—
5 March 1935	108	Stoke Bank	4–6–2 'A3' *Papyrus*	British record
27 Sept 1937	112	Hitchin–Huntingdon	4–6–2 'A4' *Silver Link*	British record
3 July 1938	126	Stoke Bank	4–6–2 'A4' *Mallard*	World steam record
Diesel				
6 June 1973	131.0	York–Darlington	Prototype HST	British record
12 June 1973	143.2	York–Darlington	Prototype HST	World diesel record
27 Sept 1985	144	Stoke Bank	HST 'Tees-Tyne Pullman'	British passenger-carrying record
9 Nov 1986	144.7	York–Darlington	HST BREL T4 bogie trial	World diesel record
1 Nov 1987	148.5	Darlington–York	HST SIG bogie trial	World diesel record
Electric				
17 Sept 1989	161.7	Stoke Bank	Class '91' No 91 010	—

was because the maximum permitted speeds between there and Leeds are less than 110 mph, which did not require the services of a second driver. There is a tip-up seat on the rear bulkhead on the left-hand side, and I was invited to take that, while Inspector Mansell had brought a folding camp stool wth him, so all four of us could travel sitting down — a big difference from the days of steam.

The sub-tropical spell of weather was over, which had prompted a slow-down throughout BR in case long-welded track should become unstable in the 90-plus temperatures, but it was still a warm day, and I was grateful for the air-conditioning, the effect of which we began to appreciate after the cab door had been closed. A full minute before our booked departure time, the signal at the end of the platform cleared to green, and at 12.10 and 55 seconds a double, high-pitched trill from the senior conductor's buzzer gave us the authority to start.

We could be quite precise about the time, as the radio phone in the cab had been used to contact the talking clock a few minutes earlier, and we had all checked our watches. As soon as he got the 'Right away', Driver Johnson pushed the master switch into the 'Forward' position, and then acknowledged the starting signal. The previous quiet throb from the air-conditioning equipment behind us rose in intensity as the cooling fans for the transformers and thyristors came into action, and then the main controller was pulled back to 'Full'. When I made my first cab journey in one of the East Coast's diesel-

Table 26: APT speed records

Date	Speed (mph)	Location	Locomotive	Comments
3 Aug 1975	151.3	Uffington–Goring	APT-E	British record
10 Aug 1975	152.3	Uffington–Goring	APT-E	British record
12 Dec 1979	155.0	Beattock–Lockerbie	APT-P	British record
20 Dec 1979	162.2	Beattock–Lockerbie	APT-P	British record

The driver's controls in the cab of a Class '91' locomotive. (Colin J. Marsden)

1	Parking brake 'on' button	28	Electric train supply (ETS) warning light
2	Parking brake indicator	29	Line indicator
3	Parking brake 'off button	30	Pantograph auto-drop light
4	Brake overcharge switch	31	High-speed brake indicator light
5	Instrument light switch	32	Pre-set speed control
6	Cab light switch	33	Drivers Aid System (digital display of maximum permitted speed, not yet in use)
7	Clipboard light switch		
8	Cab air treatment switch, heat/ventilate/cool		
9	Cab air treatment switch, high/low	34	Speedometer
		35	Noticeboard
10	Sand button	36	Driver/guard call button
11	Foot warmer switch	37	ETS 'on' button
12	De-mister switch	38	Passenger communication override button
13	Tail light switch		
14	Marker light switch	39	Pantograph up or reset button
15	Emergency brake plunger	40	Fire alarm test button
16	Brake controller	41	ETS 'off' button
17	Bogie brake cylinder gauge	42	Fire extinguisher delay button
18	Clock	43	Pantograph down button
19	Main reservoir gauge	44	Loco/shore radio system
20	AWS alarm	45	Headlight switch
21	AWS indicator	46	Tractive effort boost button
22	Brake pipe gauge	47	Ashtray
23	AWS isolate warning light	48	Power controller
24	Headlight warning light	49	Windscreen wiper controller
25	Wheelslip warning light	50	Master switch key socket
26	General fault light	51	Master switch
27	Tilt warning light	52	AWS re-set button
		53	Horn valve

electrics, over 30 years earlier, the driver had had to juggle with the power controller of the Class '40' to keep the amps below the limit as we worked our way out on to the main line from the platform. It was not until our speed had worked up to 30 mph that he had been able to pull the lever round to 'Full', whereupon he turned to me and said 'That's it'. There was nothing more he needed to do with that lever until he shut off for the next stop. Thanks to the thyristors and microprocessors of the Class '91s', the build-up of tractive effort is controlled automatically, and the rate at which it happens is determined by how far back the driver pulls the lever, but is always within the limits imposed by the equipment.

Speeds out of the terminus at King's Cross are, however, restricted initially, and Driver Johnson had set the dial of the speed controller at 15 mph, which meant that the microprocessor would automatically stop our acceleration when the speed reached that figure. As our eyes became adapted to the darkness of Gas Works Tunnel, we could see the illuminated '45' sign part-way through, and after we had cleared this the speed setting on the dial was moved up to conform. The whine of the gears on the axles below us started to increase in pitch as we accelerated, but neither that nor the other travel noises were to be oppressive throughout the journey, GEC having successfully quietened them down from their original condition. As we reached Copenhagen Tunnel, the driver leaned forward again to move the speed setting to 65, before giving a blast on the chime hooter as we dived into the darkness. Emerging at 52, as we completed the 1 in 107 of Holloway Bank, we were already beginning to overtake the Class '317' multiple-unit on the slow line to our left. The speed limit now starts to ease quite rapidly: to 90 before Finsbury Park, 95 just north of Harringay, and then the full 100 a train-length beyond the far end of Wood Green Tunnel. As we passed each of

Table 27: Class '91', King's Cross–Leeds

Date: 13 August 1990
Locomotive:
  Wheel arrangement   Bo-Bo
  No   91 010
Load: No/empty/full (tons)   8†/328/350

Dist *miles*		Schedule *mins*	Actual *min sec*	Speeds *mph*
0.0	KINGS'S CROSS	0	0 00	—
2.4	Finsbury Park	4½	3 51	80
4.9	ALEXANDRA PALACE	6½	5 35	95
6.4	New Southgate		6 31	99
8.3	Oakleigh Park		7 39	105
10.6	Hadley Wood		8 52	100
—			trs	96*
12.7	Potters Bar	11	10 08	105
15.5	Welham Green		11 35	116
17.6	Hatfield		12 46	116
20.2	WELWYN GARDEN CITY	15½	14 08	114

Dist *miles*		Schedule *mins*	Actual *min sec*	Speeds *mph*
21.9	Welwyn North		15 00	115
23.8	*Woolmer Green*	17¹/₂	15 58	117
25.0	Knebworth		16 35	123
27.5	STEVENAGE	19¹/₂	17 40	126
31.8	Hitchin	21¹/₂	19 54	127
37.0	Arlesey		21 19	126
41.1	Biggleswade		24 17	126
44.1	Sandy	27¹/₂	25 42	126
51.7	St Neots		29 19	125
55.9	*Offord*		31 28	106
—			trs	100*
58.8	HUNTINGDON	34¹/₂	33 11	106
69.3	*Holme*	39¹/₂	38 27	126/104
72.6	*Yaxley*		40 20	110
75.0	*Fletton Junc*		41 41	83
<u>76.3</u>	PETERBOROUGH	<u>45¹/₂</u>	<u>43 54</u>	—
3.1	*Werrington Junc*		3 35	100
8.4	*Tallington*	7¹/₂	6 13	126
15.8	*Little Bytham*	[2]	9 36	126
20.7	*Corby Glen*		12 09	120/125
23.7	*Stoke*	17	13 39	112
<u>28.8</u>	GRANTHAM	<u>20</u>	<u>17 50</u>	—
4.5	*Barkston South*	4	3 51	115
—			sigs	24*
<u>15.0</u>	Newark	<u>10</u>	<u>12 25</u>	—
6.2	*Carlton*		4 48	120
11.8	*Tuxford*		7 28	125
18.5	RETFORD	11¹/₂	10 51	120
27.6	*Bawtry*	[3]	15 21	110
32.1	*Loversal Carr*	21	17 40	126
—			sig stop	—
<u>35.8</u>	DONCASTER	<u>25</u>	<u>24 14</u>	—
4.1	*Carcroft*		4 13	100
4.8	*Adwick Junc*	4¹/₂	4 37	100
—			sigs	—*
8.7	South Elmsall		7 00	85*
10.1	*South Kirkby Junc*	8	8 07	70*
13.2	Fitzwilliam		11 03	86
16.0	*Hare Park Junc*	12	12 45	100
18.2	Sandal & Agbrigg		14 10	60*
<u>19.9</u>	WAKEFIELD WESTGATE	<u>16¹/₂</u>	<u>17 27</u>	—
2.5	Outwood		3 18	83
—		<u>[3]</u>	—	—
8.6	*Wortley South Junc*		8 18	43*
9.5	*Whitehall Junc*		—	23*
<u>10.0</u>	LEEDS	<u>16</u>	<u>12 34</u>	—

* Out-of-course speed restrictions

† Including DVT

these landmarks, the 'cruise control' was moved upwards accordingly, to enable us to utilize more of our 6,300 hp, and the acceleration was rapid, keeping our speed close to the various limis. Speed increased from 78 to 90 up the three-quarters of a mile of 1 in 445 through Finsbury Park, where we were already a good half-minute ahead of schedule, and had stretched this lead to virtually a full minute as we passed Alexandra Palace at the full 95. For those interested in the details of train performance, there is a full log of the speeds and times in Table 27.

By now the single 'All clear' 'ping' from the AWS at each signal was starting to alternate with the 'peep-peep-peep' of the vigilance, which Driver Johnson silenced by releasing and depressing the pedal of the Driver's Safety Device. In the dip to Alexandra Palace we touched 96 before the controller was eased shut for the first of the neutral sections we were to encounter. The automatic controls on the Class '91s', like those on multiple-units, permit the controller to remain open as a neutral section is passed, but drivers have adopted the practice of closing the controller briefly before the lineside magnets trip the circuit-breaker. This avoids cutting off the power suddenly, which can cause a little bump as the train's inertia starts to push the locomotive along. The position was worse with the Surrogate DVTs, whose diesel-alternators took some time to run back.

The process is a much quicker operation than it is with locomotives like the Class '86s' and '87s' on the West Coast Route and the Norwich line, where the tap-changer has to be notched back and up again, a process requiring as much as a minute. As a result, on our journey the Alexandra Palace neutral section only lost us 1 mph, while 5-6 is quite common with the earlier loco-motives, and this gave us a good start up the long 1 in 200 climb to Potters Bar. We had attained 100 mph just after New Southgate, but could not take

With the author in the cab, No 91 010 speeds northwards near Abbots Ripton on 13 August 1990. The streamlined 'skirt' at the front of the locomotive had been removed for modifications to its attachments. (E. H. Sawford)

full advantage of the next rise in the limit to 115, as we had actually slowed to 96 just after Hadley Wood because of a temporary track restriction to 100. To negotiate this stretch, Driver Johnson shut power off and reduced the speed with the brake. If the speed selector is moved to a lower figure under power, it activates the rheostatic brake on the locomotive, rather than those on the whole train, and the comfort of passengers in the leading coaches will again suffer. We were nevertheless back to 105 by Potters Bar, which we passed in just over 10 minutes from the start, still virtually a minute up on schedule, having fully recoverd the fractionally late start.

Down the other side we accelerated to 116, but the neutral section after Hatfield lost us a couple of miles per hour as we started to climb again to the next summit at Woolmer Green. We cleared the end of the twin-track Welwyn bottleneck, at 117, 1½ minutes up on schedule. Just before this point the first 125-mph racing stretch starts, spanning 30 miles to the Offord curves. Over the 26.7 miles from Knebworth to St Neots, our flying average was 125.8 mph, with the speedometer reading an almost constant 126, regardless of the changes in gradient. Just beyond St Neots, Driver Johnson shut off and braked for the 105 limit around the curves beside the Great Ouse, but was in no hurry to re-apply power as we got back on to the straight towards Huntingdon. This was because there was another 100-mph temporary restriction ahead, and speed was allowed to tail off for this without any further braking. At Sandy we had been 1¾ minutes up on schedule, and this second out-of-course slowing cost us only a few seconds, but the power lever came fully back as we accelerated up the 1 in 200 bank towards the summit at Leys. Whereas an HST has a balancing speed of less than 120 on such a gradient, the Class '91s' pick up speed quite quickly, and we were doing 120 by the time we reached the summit level.

Once over the top, we shot under the Bury Brook aqueduct after a brief maximum of 127, and then, as we passed the civil engineer's tip at Conington, Driver Johnson shut off for the restriction over Stilton Fen,. which begins at Holme, and then started to brake. As we ran on to the twin-track length, the speed controller was set to 105 and the power lever pulled back. Halfway across, where the portal structures supporting the overhead lines across the boggy ground finish, the restriction goes up to 115, but we only managed to reach 110 as we climbed off the Fen and past the first of the brickworks that crowd in on the line for the rest of the way to Peterborough, where we were scheduled to stop.

Shortly after Yaxley, a flashing double yellow followed by a flashing yellow signal indicated that we were being routed over the turnout ahead. This particular indication informs the driver of the need to slow over the approaching junction, and replaces the older 'Approach Control' system, where the signal would only clear from red when the train was quite close to it, a procedure which results in much more restricted speeds. Easing our way over the hump of the Nene Bridge, we slowed to 30 for the turnouts into Platform 4, where we stopped in 43 minutes 54 seconds from London, which represented a start-to-stop average of 104.3 mph. We were just over 1½ minutes up on schedule, and had arrived just over half a minute early.

Although the public timetable showed a departure time of 13.56 from Peterborough, the booked time was actually 13.57$\frac{1}{2}$ but, because of the crowds, we were actually a full minute late leaving on the 20-minute run to Grantham. This was a relatively modest 86.3-mph booking, but did include a 2-minute recovery margin between Tallington and Stoke. In spite of the initial 25-mph restriction over the turnout on to the down main, we reached 60 mph in 117 seconds from the start. Another 56 seconds saw speed up to 80 as we approached the next neutral section. Immediately beyond came the first indication of the future capabilities of the Class '91s' in the shape of a 140-mph speed restriction sign, while the flashing green colour-lights over the next 20 miles would have enabled us to exceed 125 mph, had we been authorized to do so. The 140-mph limit does not apply unbroken all the way to near the top of the bank, as there are restrictions to 135 round the curves on this stretch of line. For us, with the control lever in full power again, it only took 25 seconds to accelerate from 90 to 100, the 'ton' being reached as we passed Werrington Junction.

The 125 mph mark was reached just before Tallington, after less than 2 further minutes, and we began the long climb to Stoke Tunnel, the summit of the East Coast Route in England. We ran at a steady 126 on the 'clock' as far as the Bytham neutral section, which, as is usual because of the gradients, knocked us back a full 5 mph, confirming my explanation for the dip in speed here on the day of the 'InterCity 225' press launch. With an HST on the same stretch, although one can continue at full power, speed normally falls off to about 118 mph because of the gradients. After the neutral section slowing, however, we accelerated to 126 again up the steepest portion of the bank.

The recovery margin was thus not needed, other than to compensate for the late start, but we only just held our own on the running schedule from Tallington to Stoke, which calls for an average of 96.5, increasing to no less than 122.2 if the recovery margin is ignored. We actually averaged 123.3 *up* Stoke Bank, which was a remarkable demonstration of the capabilities of a Class '91'. In the early days of the HSTs, trains were limited to 90 through Stoke Tunnel for aerodynamic reasons, and this used to be very carefully observed. However, some time ago the restriction was lifted to 105 and has now gone up to 115, so it would appear that the problems of pressure pulses were not as severe as first calculated. We eased to 112 as we entered the bore, and, with power off, we drifted down the other side, and I was able to catch sight of the board alongside the line giving drivers notice that it was 2 miles to Grantham. We stopped there in 17 minutes 50 seconds from Peterborough, which represents a saving of only 10 seconds on the schedule, excluding the recovery margin — trains on the East Coast Route are tightly times these days. The cab radio telephone was also reset to the new frequency here, as indicated by the sign on the lineside.

Our next booked stop after Grantham was at Newark, just 15 miles away. With favourable gradients, the booked time was only 10 minutes, corresponding to an average of exactly 90. Full power could be used right from the start, except for the passage of the neutral section in the cutting before Peascliffe Tunnel, and we reached 125 mph after 4 minutes 25 seconds, just

Driver Johnson in the cab of No 91 010. As he glances down at his instruments, his right hand rests on the power controller, which is fully open, while his left hand is not far from the brake lever, situated in front of the bank of switches.

as an adverse signal was sighted ahead. Power was cut off immediately, and the brake lever moved forward, well before we passed the AWS magnet in the track and Driver Johnson had to cancel the warning 'squawk'. Speed was down to 24 mph as the red signal cleared to 'yellow', and then, as speed picked up again, the next signal in the distance flicked to 'green' and we were away. As we shot past Claypole crossing box at 76, we could see the cause of the delay in the down loop, a Class '47' on a Total oil train. We were only able to reach 110 by the time we passed the sign showing 2 miles to Newark, and, by the time we had stopped in the station, the check had cost us 2 minutes 25 seconds.

Still 3 minutes late when we restarted, I was able to compare the rate of acceleration on the level with that on the downhill start from Grantham, the existence of a neutral section on both stretches making them comparable, except for the gradient. This time it took us only 25 seconds more to reach 120 mph. The climb out of the Trent Valley to Askham Tunnel was taken at a minimum of 113, the water-level in my bottle of mineral water showing an appreciable amount of cant-deficiency as we took the reverse curves below Tuxford. Down the other side we accelerated to 120, and shot through Retford at that speed, more than double the 55 that used at one time to apply over the flat crossing that once existed just south of that station. We had saved just over half a minute from Newark, and the 3-minute recovery margin between there and Loversal Carr was enough to put us back comfortably on time. Unfortunately there had been a minor derailment in the north bays at Doncaster, and this made platform availability there rather critical. In sight of the station we were brought to a stand, and stood for nearly 2 minutes. By the time the red light had cleared and we had stopped on the Works side of the down island platform, we were slightly late again, although still within the overall running time allowed, inclusive of the recovery margin.

Here we said goodbye to Driver Elliott, which prompted a seating change, as I moved up into the right-hand seat to get a better idea of the view ahead as experienced by the second driver. The large split windscreen had provided quite adequate visibility even from the 'jump-seat' I had used previously, and was quite excellent from further forward, in spite of all the squashed insects we had collected. (The partridge that had been too slow in getting out of the way on the ascent of Stoke had been hit by the bogie, so that had not added to the accumulation on the windscreen!) When the train was ready to leave again, the platform inspector signed to Driver Johnson through the window that the signal box wanted a call from him. The derailment had caused one of the track circuits to hold the starting signal at danger, and we had to get per-mission to pass it at 'red'. The drill for this is for the driver to use the tele-phone on the signal post, as this identifies his position to the signalman; only if this intrument is out of order does the driver use the radio phone in the cab, although, with Driver Only Operation, different rules apply, as the radio phones on those trains provide identification of the caller and have a more secure speech channel.

As a result of all these delays, we were nearly $4^3/4$ minutes late in leaving, but Driver Johnson pointed out a bonus ahead, as the line speed for most of the way to Wakefield had gone up from 90 to 100 only two weeks previously. The modern road-type speed signs have not yet replaced all those along the Leeds line, and, as we took the curve away from the main East Coast Route, it was one of the traditional LNER 'cut-out' type that gave us the authority to run up to 100. We quickly reached this limit, which seemed very tame after the running we had experienced for most of the previous $1^1/2$ hours. There was a slight signal check before South Elmsall which brought speed down to 85, and shortly after South Kirkby Junction comes the 50-mph slowing for a colliery subsidence. This serves as a reminder of what the main line to York would have suffered had the Selby Diversio not been built to avoid the coalfield. Clear of the restriction, we touched 100 again at Hare Park Junction, but then came the easing over the viaduct into Wakefield, where we stopped alongside the very effective blue wooden 'feature' on the left-hand side, $1^1/2$ minutes down on the running time.

The start from Wakefield is on a rising gradient of 1 in 100, but this was no problem for the Class '91' as we got going on the concluding stretch to Leeds. Clear of the curve beyond the station, 85 is allowed as far as the tunnel just after the summit, where the limit comes down to 75, and we reached a maximum of 83 through the new West Yorkshire PTA station at Outwood. This is located virtually on the same spot as the former Lofthouse, closed in 1960 (which had originally been called Lofthouse & Outwood, but lost the second half of its name as long ago as 1865). Just before the summit, Driver Johnson shut off the power and speed drifted down to the new limit, which was easily maintained on the descent without the use of brakes. The complex entry to Leeds was not far ahead, and, as we passed the Leeds football ground away to our right, the brakes went on for the first restriction — to 60. Signals were also threatening as we passed the former junction at Wortley South and that at Holbeck with speeds of 43 and 36 respectively, before creeping round the Whitehall curve at a mere 25. In spite of the succession of 'yellows', we did not get stopped and drew to a stand at the east end of the station at 14.34 exactly, 3 minutes early by the public timetable, but a couple late by the working one.

I said my farewells to Driver Johnson, who was off home, while Inspector Mansell was returning to Doncaster on the next working of our set, due out of Leeds at 15.10. Meanwhile the up afternoon 'Yorkshire Pullman' had left the platform on our right as we came to a halt, and would later return from King's Cross with the busy 17.50 down. In the course of my journey at the front end, I was struck by the number of other Class '91s' to be seen. Had they only been working the hourly Leeds services, we should have passed an 'InterCity 225' train in the opposite direction every 30 minutes or so, but we saw many more than this. The variety of different duties was also marked, ranging from light-engine to one hauling a Mark IV set 'blunt-end first', while a group of new traction recruits was being shown over No 91 005 alongside Doncaster Works. A couple of days later I saw No 91 019 leaving King's Cross, so by the middle of August 1990 nearly two-thirds of the class were in service.

In the course of my $2^1/2$-hour journey, on two of the six stages of our trip we had set up times which were better than those in the latest list of 'Fastest Electric Times' published by the Railway Performance Society (RPS), and I was to chalk up another the following day going south on the 'Yorkshire Pullman'. It is interesting to compare the RPS's 'Fastest Times' for the three latest types of high-speed train to run over the East Coast Route, and they are given in Table 28 for the Peterborough–Grantham stretch.

One must bear in mind that the figures were published in June 1990, and thus included a far shorter period of running for the 'InterCity 225s' than for the HSTs. Even so, the electrics have a minute's margin over the diesels on the northbound journey, and three-quarters of a minute in the up direction,

Table 28: RPS 'Fastest Times', Peterborough–Grantham

Type of traction	Up direction (min sec)	Down direction (min sec)
HST	18 35	18 22
'Hybrid' set	16 54	17 06
'InterCity 225'	17 53	17 24

while the 'Hybrids' were faster still. All these trains were running to a *nominal* maximum of 125 mph, although those who study East Coast performance in detail will know that speeds often creep up above this limit. Within a couple of days of my footplate journey on the Class '91', I travelled north on an HST working one of the 111-minute, non-stop schedules to York. We had covered appreciable distances at 129 mph, but were still a minute slower than No 91 010 to Yaxley. From 1991, therefore, East Coast running will be appreciably faster south of Darlington compared with what is achieved at present, while further north the extensive track improvements, currently being completed, will also read through to faster speeds.

Against this background we can look at the electrics' chances of achieving 4-hour timings (3 hours 59 minutes is the aim) between London and Edinburgh. Although BR will have done detailed simulations, our best starting point for this is the RPS's 'Fastest HST Times'. With the two intermediate stops at York and Newcastle, the figures are as shown in Table 29.

Table 29: RPS 'Fastest HST Times'

Stretch of line		Down direction min sec	Up direction (min sec)
King's Cross–York		103 46	104 31
York–Newcastle		49 12	49 27
Newcastle–Edinburgh		85 25	87 58
	Overall times	238 13	241 56

The actual requirements are given in the next chapter, but in the light of the track improvements still to come, and the superior performance of the electrics, the omens are favourable, even with today's 125-mph maximum. Some time in the 1990s, 140-mph running is expected to begin, which will give a further lift to East Coast performance, and match the rising speeds expected from the 'InterCity 250' project on the West Coast Main Line. The travelling public, as well as the student of train performance, has a lot to look forward to in the remainder of this century.

Chapter Eleven

SCHEDULING THE FUTURE

When the East Coast Route introduced its first 'InterCity 125' trains in 1978, only eight sets were phased into operation on the Anglo-Scottish services at the start of the summer timetable. The build-up continued progressively over the next 12 months, until squadron service began in May 1979, which also included the West Yorkshire routes. The new motive power had, furthermore, already been in service on the Western Region for two years prior to its introduction on the East Coast Route. On the other hand, with the new 'InterCity 225s', while some have been operating between London and Leeds since 1989, the big change-over is scheduled for 1991, when virtually the full complement of sets will come into operation to provide an all-electric service on the Anglo-Scottish and West Yorkshire routes.

The original intention had been to introduce the new electric service at the start of the 1991 Summer Timetable on 13 May. The phasing in of new trains like this is not something which can be done overnight, particularly since the displaced HSTs have also to be cascaded to other routes at the same time. To ensure a carefully phased and controlled build-up of the electric workings, BR decided that only two 'InterCity 225' sets would be introduced every week, taking over existing workings from the diesel HSTs. On this basis, with the delayed completion of the Newcastle signalling system and consequent late energization of the overhead wires in that area, it would no longer be possible to bring the full electric timetable into operation then, and the date was accordingly put back.

At the time of writing, this momentous change still lies more than half a year into the future, but timetable planning is always started well in advance, which enabled Laurie Holland, the then InterCity Marketing Manager for the East Coast Route, to give me a privileged insight into the ambitious plans for the future. The business had produced a commercial specification for the services required to meet their specific marketing needs, and, by the beginning of September 1990, the Regional Operators Manager's Department had turned this into the second draft of a timetable which also took into account the physical constraints of the route and stock, as well as the deployment of other resources, such as train-crews.

Before going into the details of the schedules and the philosophy behind them, we need to discuss a number of important considerations which underlie present-day InterCity timetabling. Right across British Rail, as part of the current 'Quality Through People' drive, there is a major campaign to improve reliability, which is always an important factor in the mind of travellers. High on the list comes punctuality, for which there are two publicly-stated targets for InterCity: more than 70 per cent of trains should be on time, and 90 per cent should arrive within 10 minutes of the schedule. Statistics are continuously collected and rigorously analysed to determine the reasons for any lost time, and are then allocated to that part of the organization responsible for causing the delay. Departments even have a 'delay budget', against which the achieved timekeeping performance is constantly being compared, and any adverse deviations are subjected to an appropriate inquiry. There is, of course, nothing new in management chasing up delays: back in the 1920s my father was told by one of the signalmen at Saltash about a 'Please Explain' letter he had received after causing the 'Cornish Riviera' to lose a minute. What is different is the rigour of the present system, with timekeeping figures now being collected automatically from the new signalling centre by the TRUST computer system, while the engineers' 'delay budgets' are being split between the separate areas to facilitate management action being taken to avoid lost time.

The timetables being introduced in 1991 incorporate far more of the above philosophy than any previous ones for the East Coast Route, and are thus expected to be far better from the timekeeping point of view. The longer the journey for a particular train, however, the greater is the chance of some unexpected delay occurring, which means that the Anglo-Scottish services need more allowances for out-of-course checks than those to and from West Yorkshire. As a result, some of the time-savings after electrification are not quite as large as might have been expected, but the East Coast Route is very anxious to avoid a repetition of the 'Electric Scots' story. When the West Coast electrification through to Glasgow was inaugurated in 1974, the fastest 5-hour schedules could not be maintained all the year round, and soon slipped back. It is only in recent years that we have seen them restored, and, in May 1990, with the benefits of 110-mph running and the assistance of the dynamic track stabilizers, the schedule of the down 'Royal Scot' was reduced to 4 hours 43 minutes.

After that unpropitious introduction, one might well expect to find in the new timetables apologies for the absence of any 'under-4-hours' King's Cross–Edinburgh services in 1991, but four of them are there all right, and everyone is confident that their schedules will be fully 'robust'. They are nevertheless going to be tight, and two drivers are to be used between Newcastle and Edinburgh with these trains, to squeeze the last couple of minutes out of the short lengths of the route cleared for more than 110 mph. Thinking traditionally, one would have expected the 'Flying Scotsman' workings to have been among those selected for these 3-hour 59-minute 'flyers', but to have done this would have missed an opportunity of taking the airlines 'head-on'.

The 'Flying Scotsman' has never been a business train, so the 'flyers' will correspond much more closely to the pre-war 'Coronation'. All four trains will be Pullmans, which will take an increasingly important share in East Coast services, as will be described later. The morning trains will depart at 08.00 from King's Cross and 06.30 from Edinburgh. In the afternoons the corresponding return workings will both leave at 15.00, which is a full hour earlier than the 'Coronation' did in steam days, but there is a good marketing reason for this. Detailed analysis has been carried out to determine the passenger profile of the whole route during each 20-minute period throughout the day, and this shows that the present 15.00 from King's Cross carries far more Edinburgh passengers than the 16.00, which is actually the key evening train for York. On this evidence the case for giving the fast schedule to the earlier train was overwhelming.

All these 'flyers' will call at York and Newcastle only, and the preliminry timings and speeds are as follows:

Section	Distance (miles)	Timings (minutes)		Average speeds (mph)	
		Down	Up	Down	Up
King's Cross–York	188.4	$101\frac{1}{2}$	$105\frac{1}{2}$	111.4	107.1
York–Newcastle	80.2	47	47	102.4	102.4
Newcastle–Edinburgh	124.7	82	$80\frac{1}{2}$	91.2	92.9

Throughout this chapter I am quoting the working times, rather than the public ones, many of the latter being, as usual, slightly more generous. The arrival times at York and Newcastle for the down trains shown above, for example, are likely to be $2\frac{1}{2}$ and 3 minutes later in the public timetable, thus reducing the apparent stopping time from 3 minutes actually booked at each point.

In the light of these figures, the two down 'flyers' will establish a new record average for the East Coast Route, and presumably Britain as well, beating the 1989 booking of 110.5 mph by one of the 'Hybrids' between Peterborough and Stevenage, which does not feature in the preliminary 1991 timetables. Compared with the RPS 'Fastest HST Times' quoted in Table 29, each of these bookings is faster by several minutes, and they are, of course, expected to be achieved every day, rather than being a chance recording. As already described in Chapter 10, the performance of the Class '91s' is extremely impressive, and on the evening following my interview with Laurie Holland, I timed the down 'Yorkshire Pullman' to average 112.6 mph, start-to-stop, from Stevenage at Grantham, without any particular effort, other than the acceleration over the concluding stretch to Stoke Summit.

Having considered the 'flagships' of the future electric services, before looking at the other proposals in more detail we need to take into account the number of trains which will be available in 1991. The on-going utilization of the 31 'InterCity 225' sets will involve 27 or 28 being in service every day, which corresponds to availabilities of 87 and 90 per cent. In addition, the East Coast Route is retaining eight HST sets, of which seven will be rostered for daily operations on certain of the services which operate off the electrified lines. Half of these are 'short-distance' workings, such as the Harrogate or Cleethorpes services, while the others involve the longest through journeys of the lot, to and from Aberdeen and Inverness. The two types of working are neatly balanced, however, and a unit which has covered an up working from Lincolnshire, say, in the morning peak is available to form one of the later long-distance services from London to Scotland. The same type of arrangement applies in reverse to the sets which start their day's work in northern Scotland. The Hull services will initially be worked by HSTs, but, from May 1992, the mid-day King's Cross–Hull working and its return will be covered by an 'InterCity 225' set, with a motive power change taking place at Doncaster in both directions.

At the time when these preliminary schedules were drawn up, only 26 of the 'InterCity 225' sets were expected to have been delivered and commissioned, so some additional HSTs were to be retained. These were even expected to fill in on the Leeds line, as well as working some of the Newcastle services, while many of their workings were to be appreciably accelerated. The 'Highland Chieftain', and the 10.30 and 14.00 services for Aberdeen, are all booked to reach York in no more than 107 minutes, only $3^{1}/_{4}$ minutes more than the corresponding RPS 'Fastest HST Time', at an average of 105.6 mph.

Electric operation of the line from Edinburgh to Glasgow Central via Carstairs and Motherwell is also starting in 1991, and eight East Coast services will work through in each direction. These will not normally call at Carstairs, but most will stop at Motherwell, which forms an important centre for business and leisure passengers. Market research has shown that there are strong business links between the North East and Strathclyde, and the change of trains currently necessary at Edinburgh is seen by potential users as a 'minus' factor in their journey planning. Although the through services to and from King's Cross will be slower than those using the West Coast Route to and from Euston, there will nevertheless be some useful benefits from the former. For instance, the 18.00 from King's Cross to Glasgow will give a much later start from London than is possible from Euston, while in the afternoon the up services by the two routes from Glasgow will alternate, doubling the travel possibilities. In the down direction both the 'flyers' for Edinburgh will continue to Glasgow, but the 06.30 up Pullman from Edinburgh would leave much too early if it were started back in Strathclyde. The up evening 'flyer' will begin its journey from Glasgow at 14.00, and will be followed by two further East Coast workings at 16.00 and 18.00 through to London. There will also be a departure at 20.00, but that will only run as far as York, taking the place of the present Aberdeen–Leeds train.

There are other changes planned for the Aberdeen services, the first southbound HST at 06.55 being diverted to Poole instead of London, which provides an example of one of the new uses being found for the diesel units displaced from the East Coast Route by electrification. The last southbound HST from Aberdeen to London goes back by an hour, but, thanks to the faster running, its arrival at King's Cross will be only three-quarters of an hour later. The 'Aberdonian', like the 'Highland Chieftain', will retain its name, but the title 'Flying Scotsman' may undergo a major metamorphosis. Traditionally applied to the 10.00 from King's Cross, it has, in recent years, been used for the 10.30 departure, running through to Aberdeen. Although a final decision had not been made at the time of writing, one proposal is for *all* East Coast trains that cover the London–Edinburgh stretch in either direction in 4¹/₂ hours or less to be given the name 'Flying Scotsman'. This would be supplemented by the addition of the word 'Pullman', where appropriate, and would thus continue the naming policy used on the London–Leeds services in recent years, there being five down 'Yorkshire Pullman' trains in the 1990 summer timetables.

This conveniently brings us to the subject of Pullman services, which have been steadily expanded as part of InterCity's campaign to secure a larger proportion of the business market. The importance attached to this was indicated

Wine list and dinner menu from the 'Yorkshire Pullman'.

by the fact that the first two rakes of Mark IV stock that Metro-Cammell delivered were both 'large' Pullman sets, with a much higher proportion of first class coaches than the normal sets. This was in line with the general East Coast Pullman policy at the time the contract was placed, the HST sets for the 'Yorkshire Pullman' and the 'Tees-Tyne Pullman' both including extra first class coaches. The latter at one time had a '2+9' formation — and a slightly easier schedule in consequence. In the light of experience, and the growing population of the Pullman concept, three different types of formation will be used on the East Coast Route, all nine-car sets. Normal trains will be made up as follows: six Standard class, the Service vehicle, and two First class. It will be possible to use these as Pullmans if required, since all First class vehicles are capable of being 'dressed' as Pullmans and provided with the corresponding standards of crewing and service. There will then be the 'small' Pullman sets, which will have an additional First class vehicle in place of a Standard class one. The two 'large' Pullmans will continue with the formation, initially used for the 'Yorkshire Pullman', which is four Seconds, three Firsts and two Service vehicles, approximately half the length of the last-mentioned also being provided with First class seating. It may take some time to reach finality with the set formations, as the arrangements are dependent on the delivery of the extra 31 Mark IV coaches, which are not due to be constructed until after the completion of all the full rakes.

The morning business peak is more concentrated than the evening one, and, for this reason, a number of Pullmans will only operate in one direction, in the same way as the 'Birmingham Pullman'. From the North East there will be two 'Tees-Tyne Pullmans', leaving Newcastle at 06.30 and 07.00. The former will call at Darlington and Northallerton, before running non-stop to Stevenage at an average of 105.0 mph. The second service will call at Durham only, and will be marginally faster. Neither of these trains will call at York, which traditionally supplies a number of passengers for the 'Tees-Tyne Pullman'. It therefore gets its own Pullman, departing at 7.40, which runs ahead of the Durham train, but only averages just over 100 mph on its non-stop journey to King's Cross. All three trains are into London before 9.45, significantly earlier than the previous single Pullman, They are followed by the 'Edinburgh Pullman', or, as it may be called, the 'Flying Scotsman Pullman', due to reach London at 10.29. This will also provide a Pullman service for passengers from Newcastle (dep 07.53½) and York (dep 08.43½). This policy will enable the market to be segmented geographically, and give scope for growth, which was not possible with the previous stopping pattern.

Business travel is spread over a much longer period in the evenings, although this is, to some extent, masked by the leisure and commuter peaks, plus the small amount of outward business travel which takes place at the same time. Reference has already been made to the choice of the 15.00 for the down evening 'flyer' for Edinburgh and Glasgow, which will be a Pullman service, and the 'Tees-Tyne Pullman' will still run at its traditional time of 17.30, with an additional stop at Grantham. It will nevertheless still reach York in less than 2 hours from King's Cross.

For the West Yorkshire traffic, the pattern of business trains which has been developed over the last few years will remain virtually unchanged. In the down direction there will be an electric Pullman to Leeds at 15.50 from King's Cross, and this will be followed by the 16.25 HST for Harrogate, which could also become a Pullman if there is sufficient demand. There are then the 17.03 and 17.40 electric Pullmans, with different stopping patterns, the latter being retimed 10 minutes earlier than its traditional slot. Finally comes the 18.10 for Bradford, which will initially have to be diesel-hauled on the last leg of its journey, until the overhead wires have been extended in that direction as part of the West Yorkshire PTA's up-grading of its rail services. There is also to be an 18.15 commuter working from King's Cross to Doncaster, using the refurbished Mark II coaches introduced in the summer of 1990. Although these were initially worked by the Class '91s' (and the solitary Class '89' *Avocet*), the demand for the 140-mph locomotives on the long-distance workings will necessitate a small number of Class '86s' (or maybe Class '90s') being transferred to the East Coast Route.

The marketing of the new 'InterCity 225' services will not be solely on the basis of their shorter journey times, but is seen as being a synergistic effect, also taking into account the attractive external appearance, the improved internal ambience, and the better facilities available for the 'InterCity On-Board Services' (ICOBS). Already market research has shown that passengers rate the cleanliness of the Mark IV toilets as being better than on other trains. The much improved vestibule areas have also proved more attractive to travellers, with the tip-up seats starting to be used before the trains are 60 per cent full.

There is to be no 'IC225' symbol at the top of the appropriate timetable columns, as the existing 'IC' covers all the vital parts of the InterCity brand: first class seatings, refreshment facilities and seat reservations. ICOBS's contribution is thus an important one, especially at the top end of the scale, where the Pullman specification is being up-graded. The Mark IV service vehicles also provide significantly better facilities for formal meals. Modular trolleys enable supplies and food to be loaded far more easily and quickly than is the case with the HSTs, and used crockery and cutlery will be sent off the train before being dealt with, thus enabling the crew to look after the passengers right up to the last moment. With shorter journey times, both these aspects of the new cars make a significant contribution to the quality of the service available.

'Cuisine 2000', the cook-chill system which was introduced a few years ago on the West Coast Route, has been abandoned, partially because of the general concern over hygiene. InterCity has now developed a series of menus which can be cooked on the train, using some previously prepared ingredients such as sauces. The quality is higher and the portion control better — after I had made a passing reference to 'Cuisine 2000' in one of my *Railway Magazine* articles, I received a very critical letter from a reader on that aspect of the system. There is a three-month cycle for the main menus, to provide a change for the frequent traveller, and the crews receive training on new dishes, in the course of which they cook and serve them to each other. More space is available in the kitchen area of the cars, and the equipment is not only more advanced than that provided on the HST 15 years ago, but it can be changed much more quickly. A faulty microwave, for example, can be replaced during the turn-round of the set, if word has been sent forward, whereas on the HSTs such an operation could only be carried out in the depot overnight. Clearly the ICOBS specification has to vary between different types of service, and for the less busy, leisure-orientated train it is still difficult to provide a full meal at a price its passengers would consider reasonable. Over the years various different possibilities have been tried, and the new 'ambient stable meals' may provide the answer. Generally speaking, however, the enhancement of buffet facilities is easier to achieve than the provision of low-cost full meals.

Although I have tried to give readers an outline of the way in which the new Anglo-Scottish railway will operate from 1991, there is no doubt that many further changes will take place during the next few years. Traffic patterns are especially hard to predict in the light of greatly enhanced services, and, in spite of all the market research carried out by BR, there will inevitably be peaks and troughs in the demand for seats which will necessitate further change. What is certain is that InterCity will constantly monitor the situation, and develop the appropriate tactics and strategy to deal with whatever situation might arise in the future. That sector of BR is required to cover its costs and make a return on its assets, which means that it has to attract a lot of passengers. It has to do this while being constantly exposed to all the competitive modes of transport, as well as the passenger's ultimate option of staying put. The electrification of the East Coast Route and the introduction of the 'InterCity 225' trains will undoubtedly provide a splendid opportunity for the introduction of faster, more reliable, and more comfortable journeys in the years to come, as well as being a showpiece for British equipment and rolling-stock.

INDEX

The main stations on the East Coast Route are mentioned too frequently for all of them to be included; page numbers refer only to the more significant mentions.